I0892092

Berlin School Glossary

Berlin School Glossary

An ABC of the New Wave in German Cinema

Edited by
Roger F. Cook, Lutz Koepnick, Kristin Kopp and Brad Prager

intellect Bristol, UK / Chicago, USA

First published in the UK in 2013 by
Intellect, The Mill, Parnall Road, Fishponds, Bristol, BS16 3JG, UK

First published in the USA in 2013 by
Intellect, The University of Chicago Press, 1427 E. 60th Street,
Chicago, IL 60637, USA

A catalogue record for this book is available from the British Library.

Cover designer: Holly Rose
Cover image: Stills from *Gespenster* (2005) © Schramm Film Koerner & Weber.
Copy-editor: MPS Technologies
Production manager: Jelena Stanovnik
Typesetting: Contentra Technologies

Print ISBN: 978-1-84150-576-3
ePDF ISBN: 978-1-78320-061-0
ePub ISBN: 978-1-78320-062-7

Printed and bound by Hobbs, UK

Table of Contents

Acknowledgment

The editors of this book wish to thank the Research Council of the University of Missouri as well as Washington University in St. Louis for their generous support of this project and its publication.

List of Berlin School Films Referred to in the Following Pages

Afternoon (*Nachmittag*, 2007). Directed by Angela Schanelec. Director of Photography: Reinhold Vorschneider. Produced by Nachmittagfilm (Berlin). Premiere: February 13, 2007, Berlin Film Festival. 97 min.

Beats Being Dead (*Etwas Besseres als den Tod*, 2011). Directed by Christian Petzold. Director of Photography: Hans Fromm. Produced by Schramm Film Koerner & Weber (Berlin). Premiere: February 16, 2011, Berlin Film Festival. 88 min.

Be My Star (*Mein Stern*, 2001). Directed by Valeska Grisebach. Director of Photography: Bernhard Keller. Produced by Filmakademie Wien (Vienna) and the Hochschule für Film und Fernsehen »Konrad Wolf« (Potsdam-Babelsberg). Premiere: February 15, 2001, Berlin Film Festival. 63 min.

Bungalow (2002). Directed by Ulrich Köhler. Director of Photography: Patrick Orth. Poduced by Peter Stockhaus Filmproduktion GmbH (Hamburg). Premiere: February 7, 2002, Berlin Film Festival. 85 min.

The City Below (*Unter dir die Stadt*, 2010). Directed by Christoph Hochhäusler. Director of Photography: Bernhard Keller. Produced by Heimatfilm GmbH + Co KG (Cologne). Premiere: June 29, 2010, Munich Film Festival. 109 min.

The Days Between (*In den Tag hinein*, 2001). Directed by Maria Speth. Director of Photography: Reinhold Vorschneider. Produced by November Film GmbH (Berlin). Premiere: January 2001, Max Ophüls Festival, Saarbrücken. 119 min.

Dealer (1999). Directed by Thomas Arslan. Director of Photography: Michael Wiesweg. Produced by Trans-Film GmbH (Berlin). Premiere: February 11, 1999, Berlin Film Festival. 71 min.

En route (*Unterwegs*, 2004). Directed by Jan Krüger. Director of Photography: Bernadette Paaßen. Produced by Schramm Film Koerner & Weber (Berlin). Premiere: February 11, 2004, Berlin Film Festival. 81 min.

Everyone Else (*Alle Anderen*, 2010). Directed by Maren Ade. Director of Photography: Bernhard Keller. Produced by Komplizen Film GmbH (Munich and Berlin). Premiere: February 9, 2009, Berlin Film Festival. 124 min.

Falling (*Fallen*, 2006). Directed by Barbara Albert. Director of Photography: Bernhard Keller. Produced by Coop99 Filmproduktion GmbH (Vienna). Premiere: September 4, 2006, Venice Film Festival. 88 min.

The Forest for the Trees (*Der Wald vor lauter Bäumen*, 2003). Directed by Maren Ade. Director of Photography: Nikolai von Graevenitz. Produced by Komplizen Film GmbH (Munich and Berlin). Premiere: October 23, 2003, Hof International Film Festival. 84 min.

Germany 09: 13 Short Films About the State of the Nation (*Deutschland 09—13 kurze Filme zur Lage der Nation*, 2009). Various directors. Produced by Herbstfilm Produktion GmbH (Berlin). Premiere: February 13, 2009, Berlin Film Festival. 152 min.

Geschwister (*Geschwister—Kardeşler*, 1997). Directed by Thomas Arslan. Director of Photography: Michael Wiesweg. Produced by Zweites Deutsches Fernsehen (ZDF) (Mainz) and Trans-Film GmbH (Berlin). Premiere: October 14, 1997, Mannheim Film Festival. 84 min.

Ghosts (*Gespenster*, 2005). Directed by Christian Petzold. Director of Photography: Hans Fromm. Produced by Schramm Film Koerner & Weber (Berlin). Premiere: February 15, 2005, Berlin Film Festival. 85 min.

Hotel (2004). Directed by Jessica Hausner. Director of Photography: Martin Gschlacht. Produced by Coop99 Filmproduktion GmbH (Vienna) and Essential Filmproduktion GmbH (Berlin). Premiere: May 16, 2004, Cannes Film Festival. 76 min.

I Am Guilty (*Falscher Bekenner*, 2005). Directed by Christoph Hochhäusler. Director of Photography: Bernhard Keller. Produced by Heimatfilm GmbH + Co KG (Cologne). Premiere: May 15, 2005, Cannes Film Festival. 90 min.

In the Shadows (*Im Schatten*, 2010). Directed by Thomas Arslan. Director of Photography: Reinhold Vorschneider. Produced by Schramm Film Koerner & Weber (Berlin). Premiere: February 15, 2010, Berlin Film Festival. 86 min.

I Spent the Summer in Berlin (*Ich bin den Sommer über in Berlin geblieben*, 1994). Directed by Angela Schanelec. Director of Photography: Angelika Levi. Produced by the Deutsche Film- und Fernsehakademie Berlin GmbH (dffb) (Berlin). Premiere: February 20, 1994, Berlin Film Festival. 49 min.

Jerichow (2008). Directed by Christian Petzold. Director of Photography: Hans Fromm. Produced by Schramm Film Koerner & Weber (Berlin). Premiere: August 28, 2008, Venice Film Festival. 92 min.

Longing (*Sehnsucht*, 2006). Directed by Valeska Grisebach. Director of Photography: Bernhard Keller. Produced by Rommel Film e.K. (Berlin). Premiere: February 15, 2006, Berlin Film Festival. 85 min.

Lovely Rita (2001). Directed by Jessica Hausner. Director of Photography: Martin Gschlacht. Produced by Coop99 Filmproduktion GmbH (Vienna). Premiere May 14, 2001, Cannes Film Festival. 80 min.

Lucy (2006). Directed by Henner Winckler. Director of Photography: Christine Anna Maier. Produced by Schramm Film Koerner & Weber (Berlin). Premiere: February 14, 2006, Berlin Film Festival. 93 min.

Madonnas (*Madonnen*, 2007). Directed by Maria Speth. Director of Photography: Reinhold Vorschneider. Produced by Pandora Filmproduktion GmbH (Cologne). Premiere: February 11, 2007, Berlin Film Festival. 125 min.

Marseille (2004). Directed by Angela Schanelec. Director of Photography: Reinhold Vorschneider. Produced by Schramm Film Koerner & Weber (Berlin). Premiere: May 18, 2004, Cannes Film Festival. 94 min.

Orly (2010). Directed by Angela Schanelec. Director of Photography: Reinhold Vorschneider. Produced by Nachmittagfilm (Berlin) and Ringel Filmproduktion (Berlin). Premiere: February 13, 2010, Berlin Film Festival. 83 min.

One Minute of Darkness (*Eine Minute Dunkel*, 2010). Directed by Christoph Hochhäusler. Director of Photography: Reinhold Vorschneider. Produced by Heimatfilm GmbH + Co KG (Cologne). Premiere: February 16, 2011, Berlin Film Festival. 90 min.

Passing Summer (*Mein langsames Leben*, 2001). Directed by Angela Schanelec. Director of Photography: Reinhold Vorschneider. Produced by Schramm Film Koerner & Weber (Berlin). Premiere: February 10, 2001, Berlin Film Festival. 85 min.

Ping Pong (2006). Directed by Matthias Luthardt. Director of Photography: Christian Marohl. Produced by Junifilm GmbH (Berlin). Premiere June 19, 2005, Cannes Film Festival. 89 min.

The Robber (*Der Räuber*, 2010). Directed by Benjamin Heisenberg. Director of Photography: Reinhold Vorschneider. Produced by Nikolaus Geyrhalter Filmproduktion GmbH (VIenna) and Peter Heilrath Filmproduktion e.K. (Munich). Premiere: February 15, 2010, Berlin Film Festival. 98 min.

School Trip (*Klassenfahrt*, 2002). Directed by Henner Winckler. Director of Photography: Janne Busse. Produced by Schramm Film Koerner & Weber (Berlin). Premiere: February 8, 2002, Berlin Film Festival. 86 min.

Sleeper (*Schläfer*, 2005). Directed by Benjamin Heisenberg. Director of Photography: Reinhold Vorschneider. Produced by Coop99 Filmproduktion GmbH (Vienna) and Juicy Film (Munich). Premiere: May 19, 2005, Cannes Film Festival. 100 min.

Sleeping Sickness (*Schlafkrankheit*, 2011). Directed by Ulrich Köhler. Director of Photography: Patrick Orth. Produced by Komplizen Film GmbH (Munich and Berlin), Ö-Film GmbH (Berlin), and Why Not Productions (Paris). Premiere: February 12, 2011, Berlin Film Festival. 91 min.

The State I Am In (*Die Innere Sicherheit,* 2000). Directed by Christian Petzold. Director of Photography: Hans Fromm. Produced by Schramm Film Koerner & Weber (Berlin). Premiere: September 1, 2000, Venice Film Festival. 106 min.

Something to Remember Me By (*Toter Mann*, 2001). Directed by Christian Petzold. Director of Photography: Hans Fromm. Produced by TeamWorx Filmproduktion (Berlin and Munich). Premiere: October 26, 2001, Hof International Film Festival. 88 min.

This Very Moment (*Milchwald*, 2003). Directed by Christoph Hochhäusler. Director of Photography: Ali Olcay Gözkaya. Produced by fieber.film (Munich/Geiselgasteig), Zweites Deutsches Fernsehen (ZDF) (Mainz), Colonia Media Filmproduktions GmbH (Cologne), Schmidtz Katze Filmkollektiv GmbH (Halle), Cine Image (Munich), and the Hochschule für Fernsehen und Film (HFF) (Munich). Premiere: February 11, 2003, Berlin Film Festival. 87 min.

Vacation (*Ferien*, 2007). Directed by Thomas Arslan. Director of Photography: Michael Wiesweg. Produced by Pickpocket Filmproduktion (Berlin). Premiere: February 13, 2007, Berlin Film Festival. 91 min.

Valerie (2006). Directed by Birgit Möller. Director of Photography: Kolja Raschke. Produced by Credofilm GmbH (Berlin). Premiere: July 17, 2006, Munich Film Festival. 84 min.

Windows on Monday (*Montag kommen die Fenster*, 2006). Directed by Ulrich Köhler. Director of Photography: Patrick Orth. Produced by Ö-Filmproduktion Löprich & Schlösser GmbH (Berlin). Premiere: February 10, 2006, Berlin Film Festival. 92 min.

Wolfsburg (2003). Directed by Christian Petzold. Director of Photography: Hans Fromm. Produced by TeamWorx Production for Film and Television GmbH (Berlin). Premiere: February 11, 2003, Berlin Film Festival. 90 min.

Yella (2007). Directed by Christian Petzold. Director of Photography: Hans Fromm. Produced by Schramm Film Koerner & Weber (Berlin). Premiere: February 14, 2007, Berlin Film Festival. 88 min.

The Glossarists

AJF is Anne Jost-Fritz (Washington University in St. Louis)
BP is Brad Prager (University of Missouri)
BW is Brigitta Wagner (Indiana University)
CB is Claudia Breger (Indiana University)
CH is Chris Homewood (University of Leeds)
CS is Carsten Strathausen (University of Missouri)
ER is Eric Rentschler (Harvard University)
GG is Gerd Gemünden (Dartmouth College)
JF is Jaimey Fisher (University of California, Davis)
JH is Jennifer Hosek (Queen's University)
JMK is Jennifer M. Kapczynski (Washington University in St. Louis)
JvM is Johannes von Moltke (University of Michigan)
KK is Kristin Kopp (University of Missouri)
LH is Lisa Haegele (Washington University in St. Louis)
LK is Lutz Koepnick (Vanderbilt University)
MA is Marco Abel (University of Nebraska, Lincoln)
MDR is Michael D. Richardson (Ithaca College)
NMA is Nora M. Alter (Temple University)
PC is Paul Cooke (University of Leeds)
RFC is Roger F. Cook (University of Missouri)
SE is Stefani Engelstein (University of Missouri)
SF is Sean Franzel (University of Missouri)
VK is Valerie Kaussen (University of Missouri)

Introduction: The Berlin School— Under Observation

A woman searching haphazardly for a child she believes was abducted many years earlier, a young conscript who abruptly decides military service is not for him, a woman so covetous of her husband's affections that she abandons her stepchildren in the tall grass of a foreign landscape—why are these and other similarly doleful downcasts the central protagonists, the 'heroes,' of the newest new wave of German-language filmmaking? They are hardly mainstream cinematic protagonists, even where German cinema is concerned. They are neither scheming Nazis, nor outspoken antifascists, nor are they suffering from subjection to the whims of the East German secret police, and nearly none of them can be described as a 'world historical individual' on the verge of making decisions that affect more than only himself or herself. They are, by and large, unattached, undistinguished, and wayward persons in the process of confronting that dearth of sense and meaning associated with everyday life in the Western world. Through such figures a set of contemporary directors has opened a filmic inquiry into Europe's present and future.

The films featuring these and other similar protagonists have come to be identified as the work of the 'Berlin School.' Although it may be misleading to corral under a single label the diverse range of short and feature film projects to which it has been applied, the films studied in the present volume share a number of specific and stylistic commonalities, and these commonalities provide the rationale for examining them here as a body of work. The films' perspectives on contemporary, Western anomie—the films' themes—are connected to their evidently interrelated forms. Many techniques suggest a mode of filmmaking that questions and resists both the plotting and tempo of conventional narrative cinema and, simultaneously, the lifeworld that gave birth to it: the signature long takes, for example; the way sequences sometimes pass from one to the next without signaling, now and again mirroring the logic of a dream; and how the varied films' ambient sounds take on a life of their own, often jarring and occasionally disjointed from the images on screen. Although each of these and other formal hallmarks do not appear uniformly throughout the body of films—and many of the variations among these works are indeed worth dwelling upon—their shared themes and commonalities can hardly be overlooked.

Offering an itinerary of filmic strategies employed by Berlin School directors, Kristin Kopp describes the films' sparse, often uncommunicative dialogue, the de-emphasizing of traditional character development, and the films' tendency toward the appearance of 'nonacting' whereby their actors seem to 'engage in everyday activities from their own milieu as if there were no camera present.'[1] Along these lines, the directors of the films studied throughout the pages of this volume might linger on their protagonists longer than would be necessary to deliver narrative information, or, similarly, they might continue filming an empty space even after all the characters have disappeared from the frame.[2] They are more interested in the forms through which their characters' lives are lived, specifically the form as it is made manifest in the gestures their characters adopt, the means by which they (fail to) communicate, and the environments with which they surround themselves. Many of the films' directors are taking the measure of their world as though they were eyeing it through a scientist's apparatus, inquiring into why their characters live as they do, and taking pains to avoid the appearance of omniscience. They reduce their own role to that of an objective, even disembodied observer, even though their images often evoke a decidedly embodied response from the viewer. Although these films never achieve quite that ultimate degree of narrative minimalism, they frequently experiment with approaching it. Similarly, when it comes to the films' mostly modern German and Austrian surroundings—the milieus of their mostly middle-class subjects—key elements recur. Again and again cars, pools, and hotels are the major components of these characters' worlds in which the slow-paced events can be said to unfold. They comprise the strange terrain of the contemporary West, and they too are subject to unyielding scrutiny.

Owing to the emphasis on milieu, Berlin School films de-emphasize plot as the structure through which meaning is conveyed, and they marginalize the narrative and filmic strategies generally associated with its development. Although many of the films studied in this compendium—in the following *glossary*—have narratives that can be described in straightforward, deceptively simple terms (and a degree of emplotment is perhaps inevitable and is even pursued by those Berlin School directors with an interest in genre films, such as Christian Petzold[3]), most of the films studied here downplay the filmic strategies conventionally employed to aid in a plot's comprehension. As a result, the films foreground environs and habits, atmospheres and objects. The generally Germanic worlds of these films provide a sort of compound text, one wherein they document overlapping worlds in overlapping ways and nearly do the work of intercutting themselves with one another. To this composite text, this book aims to serve as a parallel, and similarly composed response.

The now commonly accepted name *Berliner Schule* (Berlin School) may have first appeared in 2001 in Merten Worthmann's review of Angela Schanelec's film *Passing Summer* in the German newspaper *Die Zeit*.[4] However, the film journalist Rainer Gansera is widely credited with coining the term. A few weeks after Worthmann's use of it, in a review of Thomas Arslan's *A Fine Day* he wrote: 'Increasingly, something like a "Berlin School" has begun to emerge. It includes three directors, Thomas Arslan, Angela Schanelec and Christian Petzold, whose similarities are becoming more evident even as they begin to develop their own particular style.'[5] The three had been students at the German Academy of Film and Television in Berlin (the Deutsche Film- und Fernsehakademie Berlin, or 'dffb') in the late 1980s, and made their first feature films in the mid-1990s. While at the dffb, they had studied under Harun Farocki and Hartmut Bitomsky, teachers and filmmakers noted for their political approach to the visual image. The teachers and students found a certain affinity, and, together with Michael Baute and Ludger Blanke, both noted film critics and publicists, an informal group referring to itself as the 'Politbüro' coalesced around an alternative film-political agenda.[6]

While the commonalities in the work of the original trio of directors arose out of this shared context of influence and personal exchange, a second wave of filmmakers hailing from other cities and film schools began to produce films in the same basic mold. Film reviewers and publicists thus extended the 'Berlin School' label to include this group that became known as its second generation of filmmakers. As the compass of the Berlin School has continued to expand, it has become difficult to determine exactly which directors belong to it. Most frequently and prominently discussed in this context are Christoph Hochhäusler and Benjamin Heisenberg, both graduates of the Academy of Television and Film in Munich; Valeska

Grisebach of the Vienna Film Academy; Ulrich Köhler and Henner Winckler, who both studied at the University of Fine Arts in Hamburg (the HFBK Hamburg); and Maren Ade, a later graduate of the Academy of Television and Film in Munich. Other filmmakers stand in various degrees of proximity to this central grouping, or have made individual films included in discussions of the Berlin School, including most notably Sylke Enders, Elke Hauck, Matthias Luthardt, Maria Speth, and Sören Voigt. The connections and similarities extend as well to Austrian cinema, and to the Vienna film production collective *coop99*, in particular. Its members have collaborated on Berlin School films, including *Sleeper* and *Longing*, particularly as producers and cinematographers, and their work often reflects a shared set of aesthetic and thematic concerns. Given the fluidity of the Berlin School label, we have decided to include the *coop99* films that display the closest affinity to their German counterparts, those of Barbara Albert and Jessica Hausner, in this project.

Even as it has expanded the Berlin School has not had much market success. Their films have, with few exceptions, performed poorly at theaters in Germany. Only *The State I Am In*, Petzold's film about the legacy of German terrorism, and *Everybody Else*, Maren Ade's drama about marital relationships, have attracted more than 100,000 viewers domestically (121,000 and 186,000 theatergoers, respectively). For the most part their films have premiered at film festivals and played only on television, most notably as part of the ZDF Kleines Fernsehspiel series. And German television has provided the lion's share of the modest funding for these low-budget productions. Both the majority of German film critics and in a few cases even well-known filmmakers (for example, Doris Dörrie[7] and Oskar Roehler[8]) have criticized them for alienating viewers with their uncompromising focus on form. A small number of top film critics in the German media have praised the aesthetic artistry of Berlin School films, and in doing so have reaped the scorn of the resurgent German film industry. In a vitriolic attack on these critics, Günter Rohrbach, the president of the German Film Academy and a producer of commercially successful movies, denounced them as 'autistic.' He complained that they heap critical acclaim on these small-budget films that cannot attract an audience while spurning German productions that do well at the box office and have helped to revive German cinema.[9]

Despite their failure at the box office, and mixed critical reception at home, Berlin School films have had relatively good success at film festivals and with film enthusiasts abroad. Most prominently, film critics writing for

Cahiers du cinéma in France and *Sight and Sound* in England have echoed the acclaim they have gained at film festivals (the Berlinale in particular) and from a few leading German film critics. While *Sight and Sound* has probably focused on them more than any other foreign film publication, *Cahiers du cinéma* has gained more attention by suggesting that the emerging Berlin School could be the beginning of a 'nouvelle vague Allemande,' a term that has found resonance in French film criticism.[10]

The French New Wave has indeed provided a fruitful point of reference for the Berlin School directors. It has surfaced in a seminal fashion in the film journal *Revolver*, which has been the key platform for critical discussions of the Berlin School and its role in contemporary cinema. In 1998 Hochhäusler teamed up with three fellow students—Benjamin Heisenberg, Jens Börner, and Sebastian Kutzli—at the Munich film academy to launch the journal. As part of a book collection of select articles from the first eight years of the journal, the group offered a retrospective look at its founding.[11] Frustrated by the lack of intellectual interest at the Munich academy (Hochhäusler called it an 'intellectual wasteland'), they wanted an organ that would play a role in the German film scene comparable to that of *Cahiers du cinéma* in France. But they wanted to focus more on the craft and tradition of filmmaking rather than sponsor a theoretical discourse along the lines of the renowned French journal.[12] When asked if the inclusion of a text by Godard in the first issue of the journal was an attempt to make a programmatic connection with the nouvelle vague and *Cahiers du cinéma*, Hochhäusler and Heisenberg demarcate the new wave in German cinema from its French predecessor. Hochhäusler declares that the films pursued by the new group of filmmakers in Germany are something quite different from what the French New Wave wanted. Heisenberg concurs, explaining that they included Godard in the first issue as part of a discussion of new film approaches, such as Dogma 95 and the use of video, rather than as a representative of the older, prior New Wave.[13]

The fact that 'German New Wave' has not been able to supplant even the problematic 'Berlin School' as the accepted title for this film movement is in this respect fitting. In a more generic sense, however, the term 'New Wave' as we use it in our title is apt. Attempting to describe the kind of filmmaking the *Revolver* group wants to promote, Hochhäusler states that art is always asking the same question, the question about life, even if the approach differs widely according to the historical context. In other words, as cultural responses to the present state of things evolve, artists, and in this case filmmakers, will continually form new waves that challenge the status quo. Steering away from the question of 'realism,' he maintains that the key question for German cinema now, but apparently for international cinema as well, is 'what is realistic today?'[14] He cites the Dardennes Brothers and recent British realism as examples of film movements in other countries that are pursuing this same basic goal while producing films in their own distinct style. It is in this sense that the Berlin School belongs to a 'New Wave' that is international as well.

Why now?

The Berlin School did not appear *ex nihilo*. It emerged to some extent from a long tradition of German avant-garde filmmaking. There are a number of pathways to approach the question of how this particular set of filmmakers came to be seen as part of a film movement. Examining the influence of a filmmaker such as Harun Farocki is but one among many ways to chart the group's initial trajectory. As the entry 'Predecessors' in this volume points out, many of the filmmakers' predecessors have thus far remained unavowed and a story that narrates only the Berlin School's sudden appearance misleads. Young German filmmakers active in the late 1960s, such as Klaus Lemke and Rudolf Thome, were surely influences (the style of Lemke's *Brandstifter* [1969] and Thome's *Rote Sonne* [1969] can certainly be perceived in Berlin School films) as were other dffb-trained filmmakers prominent in the early 1990s.[15] However, Farocki's singular influence is indisputable.[16] A Czech-born German filmmaker, Farocki has been making films for over 45 years, most notably documentaries such as *Images of the World and the Inscription of War* (1989) and *How to Live in the German Federal Republic* (1990). One glance at his postmillennial work, including *I Thought I Was Seeing Convicts* (2000), which consists of images taken at a maximum-security prison in Corcoran, California, bespeaks Farocki's longstanding fascination with surveillance images, and it is no coincidence that he was working on that project when he began his collaboration with Petzold on the screenplay of *Ghosts*. One can draw a similar conclusion looking at Farocki's surveillance-fixated *Eye/Machine I-III* (2001–03), short films that, on the one hand, are an examination of the Foucauldian panoptical gaze, but, perhaps more important, are installation works that constitute a Berlin School-style experiment in locating an idealized zero point of narrative focalization. They are provocations akin to the static camera in Benjamin Heisenberg's *Sleeper* and *The Robber*, each of which explore, at points, the dedifferentiation of narrative film from surveillance footage, or whether a feature-film camera can claim to show anything along the lines of objective truth. Farocki's work asks what it would mean and whether it would be possible for the filmmaker to adopt credibly the pretense that he or she is not subjectively constructing the frame and everything in it.

The theoretical questions introduced in Farocki's work play a role in any narrative history of the Berlin School, but so do the influences of other, earlier European new waves. How different, one might ask, are Michelangelo Antonioni's *L'Avventura* (1960) and *Red Desert* (1964) from Berlin School films made four decades later, including Maren Ade's *Everybody Else* and Petzold's *Yella*? Like *L'Avventura*, Ade's film goes deep into the private lives of a couple on vacation who are coming face-to-face with their alienation from one another. The films even share similar landscapes: the lovers' distance from one another is expressed through the atmosphere of a remote rocky outcropping. Like *Red Desert*, *Yella* explores an unfriendly industrial city and asks whether new Western spaces have themselves become deserts. The languid pace of these films hardly calls any real feeling of romance to mind; the love stories never allow their characters more than a moment's refuge. The important influence of the French New Wave, and of Godard in particular, manifests itself prominently in the preference for open endings. Godard's films adopt what Richard Neupert calls 'open text' strategies, or, borrowing from Françis Vanoye, a form of 'dysnarration' in which the film's narrative openly challenges itself, revealing the arbitrariness of the very concept of narrative.[17] In a study of the French New Wave, Neupert chooses Godard's *Weekend* (1967) as a paradigmatic case. From the Berlin School, one could as easily refer to the examples of Hochhäusler's *I Am Guilty* or Ade's *The Forest for the Trees*.

Not only did the Berlin School *not* come from nowhere, but it can also be understood as a subgroup within a larger postmillennial renaissance in German film. This overall revitalization of German cinema since the end of the last century has been well documented: during the years shortly before and after the fall of the Berlin Wall, especially during the 1990s, the German film industry produced decidedly less internationally renowned and distributed films. Although there are multiple accounts of German film production in the 1990s, Tom Tykwer's *Lola rennt!/Run Lola, Run* (1998) is generally put forward as having been a turning point. Along with Fatih Akın's *Kurz und schmerzlos/Short Sharp Shock* (1998) and the director's most revered film *Gegen die Wand/Head-On* (2004), such popular films defined an internationally distributable mode of German production. They moved beyond the art house niche, and were identified outside Germany as *the* expression of ultramodern and forward-looking

German language cinema. At the other end of the spectrum the so-called German heritage film, which brought the defining moments of the German past—particularly the tumultuous events of the twentieth century—to life, defined the other internationally recognized tendency.[18] Touristic returns to the past in the form of costume dramas depicting the Nazi era (such as *Der Untergang/Downfall* [2004] and *Nirgendwo in Afrika/Nowhere in Africa* [2001]), the decline and fall of East Germany (such as *Das Leben der Anderen/The Lives of Others* [2006]), or the exploits of the Baader-Meinhof terror group (such as *Der Baader Meinhof Komplex/The Baader Meinhof Complex* [2008]) garnered prizes at festivals and even Academy Awards. Arguably, it is in reaction to these two tendencies—the fast-paced editing of Tykwer's *Run Lola, Run* and the traditional storytelling arcs of Germany's historical films—that the Berlin School carves out its own style.[19]

In contrast to historical films that can be labeled political interventions insofar as they take a position—even if it is one that is meant neither divisively nor disruptively—on the causes and consequences of totalitarianism, Berlin School films have a politics predicated on confronting spectators with static images and with sporadically disjunctive sounds. The long takes and discordant audio in their films force spectators to reassess their relationship to events on screen. While the dialogue in Berlin School films can be provocative, navigating the alternations between silence and sounds (of lapping water, rushing traffic, or cawing crows) is often more challenging.[20] In addition, Berlin School films rely on narrative disorganization and irony—again: dysnarration—as well as plot ellipses to confound conventional expectations. Their aesthetics are predicated on negation insofar as their critical potential comes from denying the spectator what it is that they want or expect to see. Although Berlin School films may be engrossing, these films—in their open text constructions and in their employment of silence—rebuff the pleasures of affirmative cinema. They engage in an aesthetics of refusal insofar as they say no to the flashy tropes of action films, romantic comedies, and costume dramas, and they have thus consciously attempted to hold their films pure, or to avoid films' most marketable tendencies, which include sentimentality and pop soundtracks.[21] In this regard, they are loosely similar to Denmark's Dogme films. Although their rules are not clearly articulated, Berlin School filmmakers have likewise stripped away the most readily co-optable artifices. Distinct from their Danish counterparts, their movement has no manifesto. Apart from taking the opinions and perspectives in the journal *Revolver* in the aggregate, Berlin School directors have even avoided the pitfalls of policy making.[22]

What does it mean to say that the Berlin School's politics are predicated on provocative disjunctions of sound and image? That such images are disjunctive and that they do not wrap things up for the viewer is precisely the point. To examine a paradigmatic case, one could look at Angela Schanelec's cinematic frames. Schanelec wants viewers to linger long on her compositions and in this way she issues a challenge: we are meant to scrutinize her frames for that which we do not see—to react to the cinematic equivalent of negative space.[23] The viewer has to ask, 'What is not there?' and furthermore, 'Why do I feel as though she is showing me more nothing than something?' In this sense the images resist being mere hermeneutic conveyors of information. We look for what is missing, and her sparse and slowly-changing frames thus function as overt reminders that *we* are the sites at which the films take place; in other words, the spectator's presence completes the film. The approach offers a deliberate contrast with films that would boast that their action takes place entirely on screen—the idealized mode of 'action' cinema. In Schanelec's *Marseille*, Sophie, the protagonist, literally points her camera at the viewer, making the winking assertion that the image's realization depends on us **[Fig. 1]**. The film's most cited sequence challenges viewers along precisely these lines: shortly before the film's end, looking down a street in the city of Marseille, Schanelec shows us a scene that entails very little movement. The shot—in the temporal and possibly physical space of which a crime or assault transpires—holds us fixed to a single standpoint **[Fig. 2]**. The question of what we are seeing quickly becomes, 'What do I expect to

FIG. 1: *Marseille*.

FIG. 2: *Marseille*.

see, and why has this been withheld from me?' The absence of represented action is surely a metaphor for unrepresentable things—a violent act, even a traumatic one perhaps—but it also stands for that which is generally excluded when we look at a city street. Sophie's camera lens had, until that point, restricted her view of the city of Marseille, and our gaze had been analogously restricted. By not rendering the details of a key incident explicit, Schanelec asserts that looking, not to mention filming and editing, insofar as they are always already restricted, are by definition obstacles to knowledge.

But contending that these films are only about the act of seeing gives their practical political meaning short shrift. Although Berlin School films often resist interpretation and co-optation, which is precisely their strength, their representations inevitably appear in a language and context such that they cannot avoid depicting politically contentious themes.[24] Despite the claim that *Marseille* is really about what has been included and excluded from the cinematic frame, that film also directly addresses the political nature of border crossings and takes up questions of mobility and privilege in the contemporary Fortress Europe. As discussed in the entry 'Borders,' the blues and yellows used throughout Schanelec's film deliberately recall the colors of the European Union, and their use is a means of encoding questions about the privilege and freedom of movement Sophie takes for granted. One could likewise say that Schanelec's later film *Orly* (2010) has a politics of the image, but that it also adopts a politics vis-à-vis modern, capitalist commercial space. *Orly* depicts a number of stories of human interaction: a couple meeting for the first time; a mother and son traveling to the son's father's funeral; a young couple biding time as they wait for their flight. The dialogue and the images draw attention to common human experiences, and they are each moving scenes that recall for the viewer Schanelec's theatrical training. The film provides a sense of the very real and very slow passage of time, and its mainly discrete stories unfold in little bubbles within the shared, public space of an airport. From a formal perspective, the film is about cinematic selectivity. Stories unfold in the middle ground amidst the constant flow of foreground and background activity one would find in an airport. The camera and microphones alternately have to filter out and allow for an enormous amount of unconnected activity. *Orly* seems to be only about this formal filmmaking process, yet at the film's end all of the terminal's flights are suspended owing to a threat to security that may or may not be associated with an abandoned bag mentioned in an earlier sequence. The global political context of the threat—one that is possibly, but not explicitly, terror-related—is barely even tangential to the subtle human dramas that unfold. What is central, however, is the image of the empty, evacuated airport, which recalls the emptiness of Hannover in Petzold's *Yella*. Those films' evacuated spaces and architecture offer a view of a posthuman future. They depict what has been left behind after life has done away with life. What remains are empty shells of human habitation. The content of a letter read in voice-over just before the end of *Orly* becomes a parable with a theological point (God, we are informed, doesn't give interviews), yet this is merely a derivative of the point Schanelec makes when she presents us with the lingering images and the near-silences of the evacuated space—the non-place—of the terminal.[25]

The same dual claim can be made about Hochhäusler's *This Very Moment*, which is, on the one hand, about evacuated landscapes—spaces that seem emptier than the moon—as well as carefully studied, bisected image compositions, and a stepmother's uncanny anxieties, yet, on the other hand, also about the movement of culture and capital across the Polish-German border and the eastward expansion of Western economies in the postcommunist era.[26] These two modes of reading are, of course, not entirely distinct from one another. Films about seeing as such can also be about the culture and politics of Germany after the fall of the Berlin Wall. The maxim that politics *is* vision is trivial and tired; films invariably function on multiple levels. Berlin School films are about seeing and framing, but they are also about Europe, the Euro, and neoliberalism. Thus when one asks: why does the Berlin School appear, and why does it emerge at *this* particular time, the answer has to be partly that it is an abreaction to major (that is, mainstream) tendencies in German film—that is, they are *not* heritage films, nor are they the audience-pleasing films of Tykwer, Akın and Dörrie—but that they also represent an abreaction to Germany itself in the new millennium. Their view of contemporary Western capitalism, of neoliberalism, is that life is overshadowed by ponderousness and pointlessness. The malaise in Hochhäusler's *The City Below*, to choose another example, suggests the opposite of fulfilling, purposeful political action. It does not seek a footing for anticorporate protest in the way that, for example, Hans Weingartner's *Die fetten Jahre sind vorbei/The Edukators* (2004) did. The films look suspiciously upon rational models of civic participation and even on reasonable paradigms of protest; at their best they are disinterested in putting forth images of productive political engagement at either the personal or the collective level.

It may be preferable to suggest that these films' major characteristic is that they are *achronometric*, or that they resist both straightforward narrative time, as well as the ostensibly forward movement of historical time (that is, progress). Films such as *The Edukators* embed themselves in historical developments and suffer from being overwhelmed by a surfeit of history. Their pasts conveniently buoy up the concept of the present they seek to maintain. Hochhäusler's *The City Below* is in this sense deliberately achronometric. On the one hand, it reflects the time of its production: it is concerned with capitalism's present as the Eurozone falls into turmoil. In this regard it centers on the newly pervasive sense of panic, and on the riots and collapse; it reflects a very contemporary anxiety. On the other hand, in both its form and its content, the film aspires to stand outside the march of time. Does the film depict a world of today or tomorrow, and why does Hochhäusler opt for a deliberate temporal disorientation, that is, where are we, in the film's own timeline, when the ruckus at its end begins?

In this way, the film is, in its form and its content, aligned against historical progress. A similar play with timelines is at work in *Yella*.[27] Not only are the film's events predicated on a wrinkle in time (does the bulk of its plot take place in the blink of an eye?), but in a larger sense, it remains unclear whether *Yella* takes place in today's or tomorrow's Germany. Its spaces and architecture hardly make this known. It is about promises made by the West—the promises of unification—which remain unfulfilled, which now resemble an accumulation of yesterday's used-up hopes. A similar tenor can be found in a number of Berlin School films, including, for example, Ulrich Köhler's *Bungalow*, in which an explosion that may or may not have anything to do with terror attacks (in the end it does not) is greeted by the film's bored subjects with something akin to indifference. It can likewise be found in Petzold's *Ghosts*, where Berlin is partly today's Berlin, insofar as it is under construction, but is also tomorrow's postindustrial city, its urban landscape a desert.

The films examined in this volume are less linked by overt political attitudes than by that slowness, that identifiably languid pace, which is exactly that to which their critics object. This slowness—this achronometric pace, which sometimes reverses itself and which, unlike the heritage film, refuses to embed itself in history and be co-opted by ideologies of progress—is an indication that these films cannot imagine forward historical movement. They are reluctant to pursue images of the future, and, in this way, are out of time.

A new (German) cinematic realism?

As the previous section has demonstrated, Berlin School directors eschew the representative practices of mainstream narrative film in favor of less controlling modes of constructing the gaze of the viewer, the sequence of shots, and the action and flow of time in their films. In short, they present the audience with the opportunity of seeing and constructing filmic reality more autonomously, no longer tethered to a prefabricated view of the world that serves the purposes of the commercial film industry. This mode of filmmaking has generated talk of a new or 'neo-neorealism.' At a 2004 forum organized by the editorial staff of *Revolver*, Christoph Hochhäusler and Nicolas Wackerbarth pressed four directors loosely associated with the Berlin School to state whether they saw themselves as part of a 'new realist school' of filmmaking in Germany.[28] Neither they nor their interviewers were ready to offer a definite answer to this question, but everyone seemed ready to accept that the tag 'realist' fit their work in some way. The emergence of an independent cinema that explores areas of everyday life not normally addressed in films is not confined to the German-speaking countries. In a 2008 *New York Times* article A. O. Scott identifies a 'resurgent realism' in cinema worldwide and describes the films that belong to it in this way: 'they are movies about the harshness and strangeness and beauty of life as experienced in everyday circumstances by ordinary people. Their stories are small and their methods modest, but they nonetheless have an uncanny ability to enlarge your perception of the world.'[29] The films that Scott sees as part of this global 'neo-neorealism,' as he calls it, include those of the Dardenne brothers in Belgium, a wave of independent American films, and new work from Iran, Romania, Korea, and other countries. Although Scott does not mention them, we would also put in this group the Berlin School and the young German and Austrian filmmakers associated with it.

The term 'realism' crops up in discussions of the Berlin School in a way that suggests it could also be considered a local variant of the recent global trend cited by Scott. Film critics and scholars have employed it frequently when attempting to describe the aesthetic approach that links Berlin School films. The filmmakers themselves have been more cautious in applying it to their work. Still, they are in agreement with film critics on one key aspect that binds them together and aligns them with the filmmakers mentioned by Scott. This is their opposition to the growing global dominance of a Hollywood cinema that thrives by feeding the audience illusory forms of reality. In a coauthored article five German critics identify resistance to mainstream cinema's overbearing control of the audience as the root of the Berlin School's realist aesthetic. Its filmmakers, they write, resolutely avoid manipulating either reality or the viewer, and everything else follows from this basic principle. At the *Revolver* forum on realism Hochhäusler asked the directors directly: 'What is the cinema to which you are opposed? ... To what extent is your cinema a cinema of resistance?' When Henner Winckler responds that he sees the Berlin School as part of a larger European movement, he also describes what they all oppose in a manner that resonates with Scott's claim that the global new realism rejects the 'tyranny of fantasy' imposed by Hollywood. Winckler states that what arose in Germany (as well as in Denmark, Austria, Belgium, France, and other places) was in reaction to the artificiality of the global cinema of the 1980s and early 1990s.[30]

As Berlin School filmmakers have struggled to get a handle on how, or whether, their style of filmmaking relates to realism, they have encountered a question that inevitably surfaces in such discussions, at least since André Bazin developed his theories of cinema based on the ability of film as medium to capture reality: is the realism of the Berlin School primarily a matter of reducing or eliminating the aesthetic intervention of the filmmaker? In a provocative line of questioning Hochhäusler challenged the four filmmakers to explain how what they are doing is more than simply letting the objective eye of the camera do its work. He elicited from them an agitated denial of his insinuations. Sylke Enders adamantly rebuffed the idea: 'Once again—for me "realistic" does not mean "the absence of aesthetic form (*Gestaltung*)."'[31] And Sören Voigt insisted that realism, as he understands it, requires *more* aesthetic intervention in filmmaking than conventional cinematic narrative ('Realismus heißt *mehr* gestalten').[32]

Speaking at a 2009 Nordrhein-Westfalen symposium on the aesthetics of avant-garde filmmaking in the digital age, Valeska Grisebach tackles this issue by focusing her address on two seemingly divergent topics: realism and auteur film. Echoing the position of Enders and Voigt, she argues that even when, or perhaps particularly when, the goal is to make films that establish a connection to reality the auteur vision of the filmmaker must play a strong guiding role. In direct contravention to this, the commercial film industry exploits the notion that the camera can capture raw reality without aesthetic intervention. As part of its single-minded focus on profit, *Produzentenkino*, as Grisebach calls the dominant mode of cinema, dictates the anonymity of the filmmaker and promotes movies that are devoid of individual critical perspectives. *Autorenkino*, a film practice that avidly foregrounds the individual standpoint of the filmmaker, arose, Grisebach explains, in defiance of this industry standard. Still, she does not believe that the filmmaker who is intent on generating a new 'regard for reality'[33] should assume a radical auteur position. Rather, one must negotiate a balance between these two positions as they are staked out across the cultural terrain of contemporary cinema.

Berlin School filmmakers display a kinship to the French New Wave filmmakers in this regard. In Grisebach's account, the realist aesthetic of the Berlin School seems to fall somewhere between a post-World War II neorealism that largely conceals the aesthetic artifice of its 'objective' camera and the auteurism of the French New Wave, which openly displayed its stylistic innovations. Referencing these movements from the 1950s and 1960s can of course provide only an approximate taxonomy for a film practice that has sprung up as part of a contemporary resistance to Hollywood's global dominance. Petzold's films can serve as a signature example of how Berlin School filmmakers have positioned themselves between the countervailing forces of *Autoren*-versus *Produzentenkino* in recent German cinema. Petzold has said he works with and within the remainders of genres.[34] His approach recalls that of Rainer Werner Fassbinder, a director of the New German Cinema who also took up classical Hollywood genres, and in particular, melodrama, and reworked them in an alternative fashion. There are, however, significant differences in the way Petzold, and other Berlin School filmmakers, work with genre and Fassbinder's more manifest auteur style. In the case of the latter, the overly stylized performances of the actors, the unnatural displays of emotional intensity, and the provocative caricature of narrative conventions are elements of Brechtian defamiliarization that disrupt identification and disclose the inner workings of cinematic representation. Berlin School directors, in contrast, try to eliminate the distance between the audience and the image, drawing the viewer physically into the film world through affective responses rather than openly deconstructing the performative, representational aspect of a filmic text. Petzold maneuvers within the existing framework of what Jacques Rancière has called 'the contract between the director and the audience.'[35] Unwilling to simply abandon the film public as it is currently constructed by mainstream film, he seeks out points of overlap and common understanding on which one can build an alternative cinema. As seen in his so-called trilogy of ghost films, Petzold works with the remnants of realist representation, in the graveyard of genre as it were, to disrupt the trance-like, habituated responses to formulaic stories and engage the viewer more actively in the sensible force of the image.

Thus, Petzold, and the Berlin School as a whole, situates the viewer more as an active coproducer of an alternative filmic reality than as a critical observer of deconstructed generic conventions. Here there is perhaps a fine line between their mode of coping with the dominance of Hollywood genres and that of Fassbinder, or of New German Cinema more broadly. It is more a matter of degree, the extent to which one takes up genre conventions and plays with them consciously in an auteur mode. Berlin School filmmakers do not try to conceal the artifice involved in their stance toward reality, but they also do not overtly foreground their aesthetic techniques. Rather than confronting dominant film conventions head-on, they resist them passively while teasing out a new relation to the image. Hochhäusler puts this aspect at the heart of his theoretical statements about the challenges facing an alternative cinema. He proclaims that in a counter-cinema 'the frame is a gaze, not an image,' one that opens up the eye of the viewer to new possibilities rather than restricting it to the formulaic textual controls of a dominant film industry.[36] What is at stake in the Berlin School critique of post-unification heritage films is however more than just the cinematic (re-) construction of the German past. The cinematic mode of representation in these films is itself anathema to the Berlin School. The consensual contract with the viewer that undergirds them derives from the classical era of Hollywood cinema. It promises the viewer that in the film there will be things that need to be done and that the hero will indeed do them. In *Sophie Scholl—Die letzten Tage/Sophie Scholl: The Last Days* (2005), *Das Wunder von Bern/The Miracle of Bern* (2003), and *The Lives of Others*, to name only a few obvious examples, there are clear-cut struggles to engage in, and the protagonists act dynamically and heroically in the face of evil or hardship. Over the same period the Berlin School directors have offered a steady diet of phlegmatic protagonists who neither have anything to do, nor are they in search of anything to do.

The disengagement of the protagonists in Berlin School films is directed not only, and perhaps not even primarily, at the social and political culture in contemporary Germany. Even as the Berlin School directs attention to political questions surrounding such issues as border crossings, terrorist threats, or the vacuity of life in *post-histoire* capitalist society, it is first and foremost about cinematic practices. It rejects films that lay out a clear path of action for their heroes. Predicated on an inflated faith in representational realism, they presume to produce an authentic, intact version of reality, whether past or present. As Grisebach argues in her critique of *Produzentenkino*, this mode of representation removes all trace of an individual point of view of the filmmaker(s) in order to sustain the illusion that film reproduces reality as it is. In contrast, the realism of the Berlin School emanates from what she calls a proper *Standort*, that is, from an individual point of view that is part of a social, cultural, and political context the filmmaker shares with the audience.

Building on this idea, Grisebach asserts that a filmmaker does not work in isolation, but rather within a 'concrete filmic discourse,' and thus needs 'a partner, an audience, a public.'[37] Or as Hochhäusler declares in point-blank fashion, 'a new cinema is not possible without a new public.'[38] And there seems to be a consensus that individual films or the work of an individual director cannot do this alone. Barbara Albert maintains that 'there needs to be a multitude of films working toward the filmic construction of more complex realities.'[39] Even as they recognize that their success hinges on the formation of a collective public, the Berlin School filmmakers harbor no illusions about the enormous, if not insurmountable obstacles facing them. When prompted by the suggestion that the emergence of the Berlin School might herald a new age in German cinema, Petzold was quick to temper expectations: 'Indeed, German cinema has become much more interesting of late. It has become really a very rich cinema—but cinema as such does not exist anymore. There are films, but there is no public for them. We have to face this without illusions; and you can't change it either.'[40] And yet, as pessimistic as this declaration is, it seems to suggest that film still plays a meaningful role in the new media landscape. Petzold does, after all, continue to make films for a public of some kind.

Grisebach expresses a guarded hope that the newest wave in German cinema might grow and reach a critical mass of diverse filmmakers and viewers. She declares that if this does happen, it will require an international public representing different cultural perspectives and formal approaches. The manifold character of this realism, its inclusion of different individual *Standorte* both within and across cultures, is an essential part of what would constitute it as a counter-cinema. What would bind both the filmmakers and their audience(s) together is their opposition to a representational realism that has become the lingua franca of global (Hollywood) cinema and to its inherent claim that its standard form of cinematic narrative presents an authentic view of the real world.

The demise of cinema Petzold references might also be seen as providing an opening for an alternative cinema that takes shape in the vacuum created by the rise of the ubiquitous small screens of new media. This new 'cinema' will not be restricted to the public venues of movie theaters. It will need to partner with other media, including, above all, with the medium that first began to threaten cinema's standing atop the pyramid of modern visual culture: television. The funding, distribution, and success of the Berlin School—or lack thereof as representatives of the German film industry like to proclaim—already depends largely on German (and Austrian) television. And while the staging area for film (the big screen)—as well as the medium itself—has changed dramatically, cinema holds the hope, if not the promise, pinned to it in its formative years of producing a collective vision shared by its filmmakers and its public. When Hochhäusler proclaims that 'cinema can only survive in its audience,'[41] this also implies that if it can, it will do so in ways that the cultural productions of the new media do not, at least not as a collective social product. Such a cinema is also something different from the films churned out by the contemporary Hollywood industry for global consumption. In contrast to the kind of alternative cinema that might produce an autonomous, diverse public, the global cultural industry offers a monolithic representation of the world that eclipses individual participation in the rendering of reality—on the part of either the filmmaker or the viewer. As such, it entertains the audience but does not survive in it.

Perspectival approaches: A 'glossary'

Taking recourse to the work of the French postwar film critic André Bazin, Dudley Andrews has recently described cinematic realism not as the art of simply trying to capture profilmic events most faithfully, but rather of inviting viewers to engage in an aesthetic of discovery: 'What is on screen is not reality but its precipate, its tracing, its remains, which, like the mummy, may allow us to conjure the presence of something fuller, the phantom of that paradoxically more solid reality that hovers spectrally around, behind, or before the screen.'[42] Realism, in Andrews's perspective, asks viewers to accommodate their perception to the organization of visibility in the world, rather than—like the arsenal of digital new media—rework this world so as to produce convenient, pleasurable, or opportune conditions for perception. Realism is dedicated to the world beyond the screen in all its material, moral, social, and existential complexity, whereas the virtual worlds of new media displace our curiosity about this world and its working with alternate universes and purely manufactured modalities of seeing.

The films of the Berlin School, one might argue, largely follow this program of realism, often perhaps somewhat naively returning us to a world not yet populated by ubiquitous ambient screens and electronic mediations. These films' organization of sights and sounds is committed to an aesthetic of discovery. Rather than aiming directly at the viewer's neurological makeup, Berlin School films depict a world on screen whose voids, folds, absences, and mere indications make the viewer wonder about what is beyond the choreography of cinematic visibility. Similar claims can be made about the organization of narrative time, of temporality and duration, in those films. As indicated above, their narratives rarely follow dramatic arcs or teleological patters; they privilege portrait over plot, observation over development, ellipses over continuities. Berlin School directors often approach their characters in a distanced, objective manner, void of omniscient gestures and more reminiscent of late nineteenth-century literary naturalism. Faced with a profound lack of information, the viewer is compelled to carefully scrutinize the behaviors of characters to understand their current attitudes and motivations, yet in the end many of these films refuse tidy resolutions and leave us with more questions than answers. Berlin School films, in this way, instead of reworking the viewer's attention within tightly organized temporal structures, encourage the spectator to view the diegetic world at their own pace and to explore echoes between the often far from climactic temporality of lives on and off the cinematic screen. Life, in the world of the Berlin School, is at once too big and too small, too slow and too messy, too dull and too intricate, in order to be pressed into the iron regime of dominant cinema's narrative time. Rather than model the world on screen along the temporal conventions of commercial filmmaking, Berlin School films hope to disentangle the different aspects of cinematic time, asking the viewer to accommodate their experience of the film to the organization of temporality in the everyday world, including this world's often-conflicting temporalities, its ambiguities of memory and hope, its structures of loss, standstill, rupture, and displacement.

The organization of this book is inspired by the Berlin School's realist experiments with cinematic temporality and narrative structure. Because Berlin School filmmaking privileges process over project, openness over closure, this volume moves away from conventional approaches focusing on self-contained works and singular authors. No one individual film can possibly contain what Berlin School cinema is all about; each film associated with Berlin School filmmaking operates like a relay station playing through certain possibilities and passing them on for other and different iterations. Though recent German cinema has no doubt witnessed a certain return of the auratic figure of the auteur, and even though German film studies, in particular in its Anglo-American constellations, has often gladly embraced the re-emergence of auteurist stances as a relegitimation of its own critical practice, the charge of this book is to depart from the legacy of auteur studies, their focus on singular authors and their expressive signatures. Similar to the way in which Berlin School films refuse narrative continuity and self-contained integration, the organizational structure of *Berlin School Glossary* considers the films of the Berlin School as sites of ongoing and open transaction that cut across a still developing body of work. What is gathered in the pages that follow does not pretend to offer the reader a conclusive catalogue of formal elements and thematic commonplaces, of authorial signatures and identifiable instances of self-expression. Rather, what is at stake is to represent Berlin School filmmaking as a network of non-causal connections, echoes, and influences. In this network, individual films exist as nothing other than unstable nodes of cultural and cinematic transfer whose multidirectional vectors cannot be forced into the unity of one coherent, let alone teleological, narrative.

First found in Middle English, the term 'glossary' describes an alphabetic list of terms that addresses a certain subject matter. Glossarists are those who organize individual glosses into such glossaries, a gloss being defined as the act of explicating, interpreting, or paraphrasing a particular issue. Glossaries should not be seen as encyclopedic in intent and nature, for they do not aspire to provide inclusive knowledge and seamless understanding. Their function, instead, is to offer commentary, that is, perspectival approaches to something that defies a certain sense of unity and uniformity. Accordingly, the aim of this book's twenty-three glossarists is less to offer analytical interventions and intricate close readings of individual products, as it is to identify and comment on the recurring themes and formal strategies of most recent German cinema; it is to exhibit the complexity of Berlin School filmmaking by exploring certain links, associations, and interconnections between its projects. Our ambition therefore is also far from wanting to gloss over the aesthetic or political unconscious of the films in question, or from endowing the auteurs and individual films of this newest German cinema with mind-numbing cultural shine. On the contrary, in assembling our glosses according to the simultaneously systematic and completely arbitrary order of the alphabet, our intention is to break up illusions of shimmering coherence so as to reveal underlying and unnoticed correspondences. Much like the narrative structures of many Berlin School films themselves, the alphabetical logic here serves the purpose of rendering more systematic what seeks to confound systematicity while simultaneously insisting on the unsystematic nature of what we may want to call the real in the first place. As the following glosses cut into, intercut, and recut the body of Berlin School films, their objective is to foreground a multiplicity of logics that drive this by no means homogeneous movement and in so doing to enable a better understanding of what these films share with each other across the boundaries of their individual narratives.

As it pursues what we might call indeed a (neo)realist aesthetic of discovery, the Berlin School raises important questions about the relation of contemporary filmmaking to various avant-garde and neo-avant-garde movements of the postwar era. As importantly, however, it also urges us to think about the way in which filmmakers, film critics, and film scholars not only participate in ongoing conversations about the cinematic canon, but in these conversations constantly redefine what belongs, and what should not belong, to the canon in the first place. The films of the Berlin School are predominantly small and minor films. They rely on minimalist means and defy the grand narratives and sensory spectacles of mainstream cinema. As was to be expected, the rhetorical smallness and formal rigor of much of

Berlin School filmmaking has quickly transformed their interventions into German film studies' newest good objects: legitimate examples of German cinema worthy enough to be added to the canon of film art and therefore, for instance, shown in art-houses' series or taught in college seminars. Though many of our glosses are written with considerable sympathy for the Berlin School's experiments with sound and sight, it is the nature of the gloss to display a certain irreverence and indifference toward questions of canonization as well. As it freely cuts through and across recent German art cinema, *Berlin School Glossary* aspires to manifest some of this kind of critical irreverence. The primary task of the following glosses is to reveal and discover, not to enshrine heroic gestures and claim this cinema's timeless qualities. In fact, for the contributors to this project to trace important tendencies of recent German filmmaking most appropriately means to suspend the usual work of canon-making and canon-unmaking. Rather than promote recent German filmmakers and cinematic works as members of a new canon, then, the glosses of this book understand the smallness and inconclusiveness of Berlin School filmmaking as good reasons to change our very thinking about the function of canonicity amid our increasingly postcinematic condition.

RFC, LK & BP

Notes

1 See Kristin Kopp, 'Christoph Hochhäusler's *This Very Moment*: The Berlin School and the Politics of Spatial Aesthetics in the German-Polish Borderlands,' *The Collapse of the Conventional: German Film and its Politics at the Turn of the Twenty-First Century*, eds Jaimey Fisher and Brad Prager (Detroit: Wayne State UP, 2010), 285–308. The passages referred to here are on pp. 289–91.

2 Marco Abel remarks, 'Relentlessly focusing their camera on seemingly unremarkable events, these films exhibit a tendency to "stare," thus effecting an alteration of that which they stare at from *within* the act of seeing (and listening) itself.' See 'Intensifying Life: The Cinema of the "Berlin School"' *Cineaste* 33.4 (2008), http://www.cineaste.com/articles/the-berlin-school.htm.

3 On Petzold's relationship to genre films, see his remarks in 'The Cinema of Identification Gets on my Nerves: An Interview with Christian Petzold,' interview with Marco Abel, *Cineaste* 33.3 (2008), http://www.cineaste.com/articles/an-interview-with-christian-petzold.htm. See also, Jaimey Fisher, 'German *Autoren* Dialogue with Hollywood? Refunctioning the Horror Genre in Christian Petzold's *Yella* (2007),' *New Directions in*

German Cinema, eds Paul Cooke and Chris Homewood (London: I. B. Tauris, 2011), 186–203.

4 Merten Worthmann, 'Mit Vorsicht genießen,' *Die Zeit*, September 27, 2001, http://www.zeit.de/2001/40/200140_langs._leben.xml/komplettansicht.

5 Rainer Gansera, 'Glücks-Pickpocket. Thomas Arslans traumhafter Film "Der schöne Tag,"' *Süddeutsche Zeitung*, November 3 and 4, 2001. See also Rüdiger Suchsland, 'Langsames Leben, schöne Tage. Annäherungen an die "Berliner Schule,"' *Film-Dienst* 13 (June 2005): 6–9.

6 Hanns-Georg Rodek, 'Der politische Beobachter: Mit der Kamera die Gesellschaft unter die Lupe nehmen: Der Berliner Filmemacher Christian Petzold,' *Berliner Morgenpost*, September 24, 2003.

7 Quoted in Marco Abel, 'Intensifying Life.'

8 Rüdiger Suchsland, '"Man macht sich was vor, und das ist auch gut so…": Oskar Roehler unplugged,' *Artechock*, October 24, 2004, http://www.artechock.de/film/text/interview/r/roehler_2004.htm.

9 Günter Rohrbach, 'Das Schmollen der Autisten,' *Der Spiegel*, January 22, 2007, 156–57.

10 See Elisabeth Lequeret, 'Allemagne: La Génération de l'Espace,' *Cahiers du cinéma* 587 (2004): 47–51.

11 'Revolver Selbst-Gespräch,' *Revolver: Kino muss gefährlich sein*, ed. Marcus Seibert (Frankfurt a.M.: Verlag der Autoren, 2006), 9–30.

12 Along with directors in the most recent wave of independent German cinema, those interviewed in the journal include members of an older generation of German filmmakers (Alexander Kluge, Werner Herzog, Harun Farocki), as well as foreign directors of note (Wong Kar-Wai, Abbas Kiarostami, Lars von Trier).

13 'Revolver Selbst-Gespräch,' 13–14.

14 'Revolver Selbst-Gespräch,' 13.

15 In 'Predecessors' Eric Rentschler mentions the filmmakers Michael Klier, director of *Der Riese* (1984) and *Ostkreuz* (1991), and Michael Freerix, director of *Chronik des Regens* (1990), among others.

16 For more on Farocki as a precedent and influence, see Marie Krämer, 'Harun Farocki: Lehrer und Mentor der Neuen Berliner Schule,' *Augenblick* 47 (2011): 36–51.

17 On open text form, see Richard Neupert, *The End: Narration and Closure in the Cinema* (Detroit: Wayne State UP, 1995), esp. 137. For the term 'dysnarration,' see Francis Vanoye's *Récit écrit—récit filmique* (Paris: Éd. CEDIC, 1985), esp. 208. See also the entry 'Endings' in this volume.

18 On the term, see Lutz Koepnick, 'Reframing the Past: Heritage Cinema and Holocaust in the 1990s,' *New German Critique* 87 (2002): 47–82.

19 In Marco Abel's assessment, one of the very first English language accounts of the Berlin School, he provides a parallel historical account, citing films such as *Downfall*, *The Lives of Others*, and *Goodbye Lenin!* Abel concludes, 'the politics of the image which [those films] perpetuate is remarkably conservative.' See 'Intensifying Life.'

20 On this, see the entries 'Ambient Sound' and 'Silence' in the present volume.

21 For example, Matthew D. Miller (in 'Facts of Migration, Demands on Identity: Christian Petzold's *Yella* and *Jerichow* in Comparison,' *The German Quarterly* 85.1 [2012]: 55–76) notes that popular 'unification films' including *Goodbye Lenin!* and *The Lives of Others*, have provided 'ultimately triumphant treatments of unification.' By contrast, he writes, 'Petzold's *Yella* and *Jerichow* subtly expose divisions in a Germany only officially united.' Those two films, Miller asserts, 'study, rather than suture, lingering wounds' (58).

22 One example of a policy-like manifesto is Ulrich Köhler's essay 'Why I Don't Make "Political" Films,' which reads as a treatise. It is a refusal to make a film that can be co-opted, not only by historical ideology, that is, by narratives of progress, narratives that render the past over and done with, but by history itself. He complains about high-profile historical films, and makes his point without pulling any punches: 'The governmental funding agency likes movies that "wrap up" political education in narratives—citizens should not strain themselves too hard. And on the wrapping you find, for example, a touching love story between a Turkish girl and a skinhead. Filmmaking as wrapping paper: This is the aesthetic program of social democratized cultural policy' (11). Here, however, he does not claim to be speaking for anyone but himself. See Ulrich Köhler, 'Why I Don't Make "Political" Films,' trans. Bettina Steinbrugge, *Cinema Scope* 38 (2009): 10–13. Originally published in German as, 'Warum ich keine "politischen" Filme mache,' http://newfilmkritik.de/archiv/2007-04/warum-ich-keine-„politischen"-filme-mache/.

23 In 2001 Merten Worthmann, who already refers to a 'Berlin School,' observed this tendency early on in Schanelec's work. Worthmann writes: 'Was man nicht sieht, aber spürt, sind die Auslassungen. Ein Schnitt trennt Wochen, manchmal Monate. Die Augenblicke der größten Aufregung werden ausgespart. Man bekommt nur ihren Vorschein zu sehen oder ihre Nachwirkungen.' See Merten Worthmann, 'Mit Vorsicht genießen.'

24 In a critical assessment of the Berlin School, Andrew Tracy takes note of a number of Berlin School films' explicit illustrations of social and political issues, including 'the matter-of-fact episodes within a low-security prison for mothers and children in Maria Speth's *Madonnas*' and 'the impasting of immigrant angst over the trite genre mechanics of Christian Petzold's highly overrated *Jerichow*.' See Andrew Tracy, 'States of Longing: Films from the Berlin School,' March 2, 2009, http://mubi.com/notebook/posts/states-of-longing-films-from-the-berlin-school.

25 Schanelec is asked specifically about Marc Augé's concept of the 'non-place' (*Nicht-Ort*) in 'Warten ist geschenkte Zeit,' interview with Susanne Kippenberger about *Orly*, *tagespiegel.de* November 7, 2010, http://www.tagesspiegel.de/weltspiegel/reise/warten-ist-geschenkte-zeit/1975462.html.

26 See Kristin Kopp, 'Christoph Hochhäusler's *This Very Moment*: The Berlin School and the Politics of Spatial Aesthetics in the German-Polish Borderlands,' esp. 298–302.

27 On *Yella*'s relation to historical time in Germany after the fall of the Berlin Wall, see Brad Prager, 'Passing Time Since the *Wende*: Recent German

Film on Unification,' *German Politics & Society*, 28.1 (2010): 95–110. See also Miller, esp. 61–68.

28 '*Revolver* Live: Neue realistische Schule?' *Revolver: Kino muss gefährlich sein*, ed. Marcus Seibert (Frankfurt a.M.: Verlag der Autoren, 2006), 342–63.

29 A. O. Scott, 'Neo-neo-realism,' *New York Times Magazine*, March 17, 2009, http://www.nytimes.com/2009/03/22/magazine/22neorealism-t.html.

30 'Neue realistische Schule?' 354.

31 'Neue realistische Schule?' 356.

32 'Neue realistische Schule?' 356.

33 Marco Abel, '"A sharpening of our regard": Realism, Affect and the Redistribution of the Sensible in Valeska Grisebach's *Longing* (2006),' *New Directions in German Cinema*, ed. Paul Cooke and Chris Homewood (London: I.B. Tauris, 2011), 204–07.

34 Abel, 'Cinema of Identification.'

35 Jacques Rancière, *Film Fables* (Oxford: Berg, 2006), 75.

36 Hochhäusler, 'Right to Reply.'

37 Grisebach, 'Von hier aus,' 86.

38 'Neue realistische Schule?' 359.

39 'coop99: Film-Produktion,' in *Revolver: Kino muss gefährlich sein*, ed. Marcus Seibert (Frankfurt a.M.: Verlag der Autoren, 2006), 191.

40 Abel, 'Cinema of Identification.'

41 Hochhäusler, 'Right to Reply.'

42 Dudley Andrews, *What Cinema is!* (Chichester, UK: Wiley-Blackwell, 2010), 41.

Ambient Sound

At one point in *Passing Summer*, the protagonist's lover, Thomas, having just returned from Paris, meets with his business partner at a café. They talk about an interview Thomas conducted with an elderly, well-known artist or perhaps photographer. In keeping with Schanelec's usual practice of not providing supplementary information about the characters or events in her films, the viewer knows nothing about why Thomas went to Paris, except for what is revealed in this short exchange with his partner, who only appears in this one scene and is only identified as a business partner in the closing credits. Thomas plays for him an 18-second excerpt from the recording he made of the interview to illustrate what he had said to him as they were walking to the café—namely, that the interview had produced nothing. The only speech on the recording is of the interviewee, saying in French: 'There's nothing to say. I can't tell you anything. There's nothing to say. Nothing.' However, in the background there is a constant chorus of what sounds like a large group of birds. When he stops the tape, his partner asks, 'What's with the birds?' Thomas, who seemingly had not given them much thought, explains that they were in the trees outside the apartment window even though he could not actually see a single bird.

There is no other mention in the film of the interview or its role in Thomas's work. This scene has no connection to any other part of the film, with one exception. The last shot of the film is a 20-second stationary view of a single vertical row of apartment windows with trees in full foliage filling the right half of the screen. On the soundtrack we hear the same chirping of birds as on the tape along with the ambient sound of street traffic. As occurs often in Berlin School films, the sound from the final scene continues as the credits roll over a blank screen. Only through the audio link back to the earlier scene can the viewer apprehend the significance of the final shot in the film—that is, it shows the apartment building in Paris where the interview took place **[Fig. 3]**.

See ENDINGS

But what is the significance, we might be inclined to ask? Except for the simple fact that Thomas is in it, the episode at the café plays no role in

FIG. 3: *Passing Summer.*

the plot's already thinly woven web of characters and events. Moreover, as we hear on the tape, the interview provided Thomas and his colleague nothing for their project, of which we also know nothing. The remainder of the scene after the exchange about the birds concerns even more trivial matters that have nothing to do with the rest of the film. After the colleague asks Thomas about a bottle of syrup he had asked him to buy in Paris, the scene closes with a quick exchange about the rain in Berlin while he was away.

The complete lack of connection to any storyline notwithstanding, this scene is not merely an exercise in antinarrative aesthetics for its own sake. The point of including these banalities is precisely to highlight the *nonsignificance* of the dialogue and events with respect to the narrative and to direct attention instead to the film's alternative sound design. Employing the tape recording as a soundtrack-within-a-soundtrack, Schanelec emphatically foregrounds the role of ambient sound in her filmmaking. The return of the chorus of birds at the end of *Passing Summer* is also indicative of an alternative sound design typical of the Berlin School. Rather than follow the mainstream practice that relegates audio to a supporting role for visually constructed film narrative, Berlin School filmmakers give more autonomy to sound and direct the viewer to audio and visual signals that lie outside the normal regime of cinematic attention.

Once freed from its service to narrative, sound is able to assume a whole array of thematic and affective functions while in the guise of purely ambient noise. In *Windows on Monday*, for example, sounds related to the remodeling of the house reinforce both Nina and Frieder's affective state of mind associated with the project. Rather than addressing their foundering marriage directly, Frieder attempts to regenerate his relationship with Nina through their shared work on the renovation. Apathetic about her marriage and child, Nina becomes irritated by his obsession with the remodeling. Early in the movie, we see her hanging out upstairs in the bathroom to avoid being a part of it. After Frieder comes to get her, we watch the two of them scraping wallpaper off the entrance walls. Within a few minutes she has had enough and leaves, telling him that she is going to pick up their daughter. Frustrated by her departure, he moves over to where she had been working and continues to scrape and rip wallpaper off the walls **[Fig. 4]**. In the virtual absence of other sounds during this scene, the scraping stands out dramatically. It not only symbolizes the tension between Nina and Frieder, it also conveys it physically to the viewer.

See RENOVATION

Later, on the Monday referenced in the title, and after Nina and Frieder's relationship has further disintegrated, a construction crew is working feverishly to install the couple's new windows. As the manager explains that they could not get the particular wooden frames he wanted, Frieder walks around mum, clearly unappeased by the attempts to satisfy him with an alternative. During their conversation, the workers are drilling, hammering, and clawing at an industrious pace to remove the old windows, even though there is no agreement yet on the replacements. The racket caused by the renovation overshadows the other incidental noise on

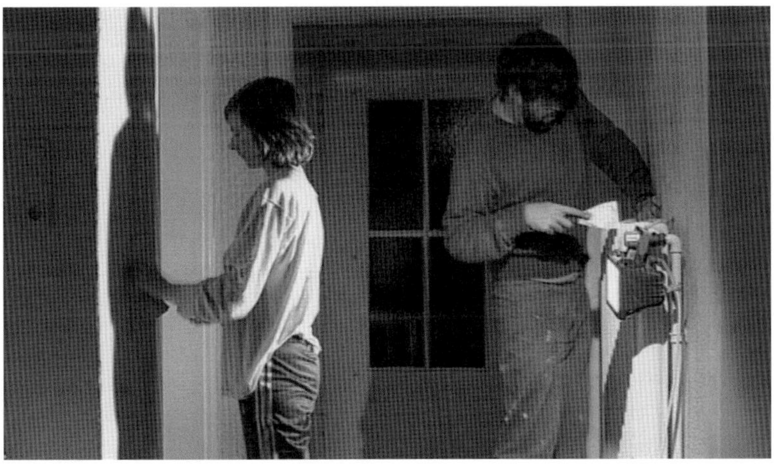

FIG. 4: *Windows on Monday.*

the soundtrack. The sounds of renovation again act physically to generate in the viewer Frieder's affective state of mind, which, in this case, stems not so much from the thwarted plan for the windows as from the project's confirmed failure to regenerate their marriage now that the windows have arrived.

Some ambient sounds appear so frequently in Berlin School films that they serve as recurring motifs. The chirping of birds or the rustling of tree leaves (in *Passing Summer*, *This Very Moment*, *Longing* and *Vacation*) and splashing or lapping water (in *Bungalow*, *Marseille*, *Hotel* and *Vacation*) are prominent examples. The ambient sound encountered most often is that of street and highway traffic. As a common part of our modern lifestyle, noise from motor vehicles is prevalent in many feature films, often contributing to the intensity of action or dialogue. In the work of Berlin School directors, this noise adheres more to a naturalistic sound perspective and is, at the same time, tied more integrally to the central, if not explicitly articulated, themes in their films. In *Bungalow*, the rumbling of truck engines punctuates the otherwise relatively tranquil environs of a nondescript provincial region somewhere in Germany. From the military convoy in the long opening shot, to the trucks on the two-lane highway visible from the bungalow's patio, to the tractor-trailer that pulls up in the film's final scene and then pulls away apparently with Paul in the cab, the reverberating sound of powerful vehicles signal that the protagonist's return to the mid-size town where he grew up cannot lead to contentment.

In *I Am Guilty*, Armin takes occasional walks along the autobahn to the restroom at a rest stop not far from his house. These escapes from his protected but stifling home environment are accompanied by the ambient noise of the traffic roaring past. The blaring sound from the intermittent scenes along the autobahn imparts to the viewer a sense of Armin's tenuous hold on respectable society as strongly as any narrative events or dialogue. In the course of the film, he begins inexplicably to slip into a quasi-criminal path outside the normal world of family, friends and socially acceptable employment. The tension surrounding his eerie withdrawal builds in concert with the cumulative noise from the autobahn, eventually erupting into the piercing and squealing electric music that accompanies his surreal fantasy of having sex in his own bedroom with the leader of a biker gang from the rest stop.

As the Berlin School filmmakers' experience working with ambient sound has evolved, its integration into the alternative narrative style of their films has also become more intricate. The incorporation of ambient sound into the thematic structure of the story reaches perhaps its peak in *Yella*. There, Petzold employs both ambient sounds that are used frequently in Berlin School films, such as chirping birds, rustling leaves, lapping and splashing water, as well as more dramatic sounds to convey the complex subjective world of his protagonist. The natural sounds common to Berlin School films mark and sustain Yella's imagined vision of the course her life might take in the West. For example, as long as the sound of birds is audible, Yella remains completely caught up in the long subjective vision that begins just before Ben drives off the bridge into the Elbe River. When the chirping suddenly stops, the silence arouses an eerie feeling in her, and the fantasy starts to lose its hold. It is restored and sustained when the silence is pierced by a cawing crow, followed by lapping water or the wind rustling the leaves on a tree—sounds she heard at the beginning of her fantasy.

See WIND

At the same time, whenever the sound of water, rustling leaves or the cawing of a crow returns during her vision, it portends her death on the shores of the Elbe. After the second, actual and fatal crash, Yella's body is pulled out of the river and laid in the same position on the same spot on the shore that she had assumed when she dragged herself out of the river in the earlier scene. Now we first hear from off-screen a crinkling noise and then see its source, an aluminum foil blanket that is being laid over her lifeless body. As the blanket comes to rest and the sound fades, the film cuts to its final image, a shot of leaves rustling in the tree above her **[Fig. 5]**. This is the same image and same accompanying audio that we saw and heard after the first crash. There, it was a subjective shot showing the first thing that Yella saw and heard when she awakened. Now, as she lies dead on the shore, this image is linked back to Yella not by her looking up at the tree, but rather by an eerie similarity between the crinkling of the aluminum foil blanket and the sound of the rustling leaves. The association produced by these two final sounds in the film confirms that the sight and

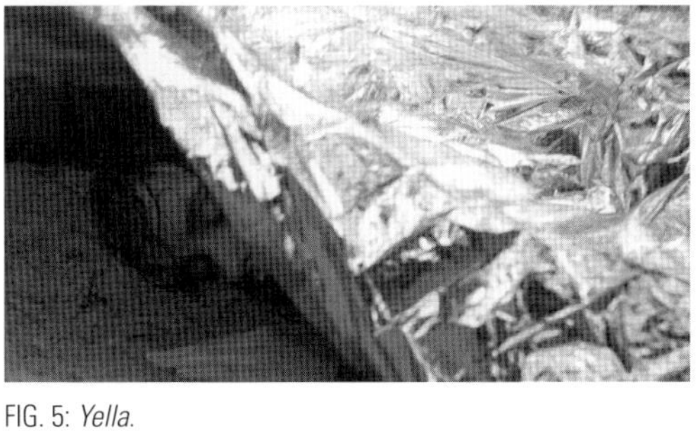

FIG. 5: *Yella*.

sound of rustling leaves that had initiated her imagined account of her life in the West and appeared at crucial junctures during her fantasy were a premonition of her impending death.

In *Yella* Petzold takes this set of sounds that had become almost a trademark of Berlin School films and deploys them to mark the caesurae between the virtual and the real in Yella's experiences with venture capital. The film's most compelling piece of sound design contributes to the same thematic point by expanding the viewer's sensory engagement with the image. Yella's shift to—and then back from—her vision is triggered by the vibrations of Ben's car bouncing along the cobblestone road leading up to the bridge. As we watch the exchange between Ben and Yella intensify in the first version of the scene, the car and the film image begin to shake. The camera cuts to a shot through the windshield **[Fig. 6]**, in which we see and hear the front of the car bouncing along the cobblestone road.

See CARS

The shaking continues for approximately 30 seconds, until Ben turns the steering wheel hard to the left and Yella tries in vain to stop him. The switch back to this point in the film, after almost 70 minutes of uninterrupted subjective scenes, occurs when Yella is in the back seat of the taxi, head turned to the side, distraught over the outcome of her attempt to make a business killing and forge a life together with Philipp. The reverberating sound of Ben's car on the cobblestone road begins while Yella is still in the taxi. Serving as a sound bridge, it jars her out of her fantasy as the film cuts back to a shot of her sitting in the passenger seat of Ben's car, head turned to the side in the same manner **[Fig. 7]**.

FIG. 6: *Yella*.

FIG. 7: *Yella.*

This time, as the shot switches to the front of the car and the cobblestone road, and then back to the interior, Yella sits passively as Ben swerves and crashes the car through the railing and into the Elbe. The sound and vibration of the car literally shake the viewer out of the subjective world of Yella's vision, which, until then, had likely not been perceived as such. Shaken along with Yella out of a trance-like vision, the viewer also experiences with her the resigned realization that the world of finance capitalism cannot provide her the life about which she fantasizes.

Another moment of sonar penetration had already prefigured her sound-induced premonition of the eventual failure and resignation. When Ben appears at her house, unsolicited, just as she is leaving, and asks, 'Can I give you a ride to the airport? Just to the airport?,' there is a sonic boom overhead. Yella turns her head toward it, and the camera pans quickly across the sky following the roar of the fighter jet, without catching sight of it. When the camera returns to Yella, her face reveals that she already senses and is resigned to her fate without knowing it **[Fig. 8]**. Here Petzold deploys the nature of aural perception to signal that the story we are about to see is a belated vision of this awareness. Because sound travels through space as vibrating waves, the identification of its source usually lags behind the perception, coming only after the sound has penetrated the ear or, in the case of a loud blast, the whole surface of the body.[1] Sound thus poses the question for sight to answer: 'Where is it coming from?' The sonic boom penetrates Yella in a dynamic fashion, divesting her of the hope she clings to futilely of a successful life supported by the high-stakes world of finance. She only becomes cognizant of its effect after the whole scenario of her career in finance capitalism has played out in the few seconds before Ben drives the car off the bridge. The ambient sound of the sonic boom, which is then echoed in the sound and vibration of the car traveling over

FIG. 8: *Yella.*

the cobblestones, penetrates the body of both Yella and the viewer and prefigures the belated audiovisual account of the whole story.

RFC

Note

1 Vivian Sobchack, 'When the Ear Dreams: Dolby Digital and the Imagination of Sound,' *Film Quarterly* 58.4 (Summer 2005): 2–15; here, 10–11.

The Anti-Hauptstadt

Family country houses, road trips, suburbs, forests, France, vacation islands. With few exceptions, the films of the new wave in German and Austrian cinema betray a decided ambivalence toward iconic urban space and often take place in more vaguely defined national terrain or in transnational border zones. One might consider, for example, spaces of transit in Ulrich Köhler's *Bungalow*, Maria Speth's *Madonnas*, and Christian Petzold's films *The State I Am In* and *Yella*; or the house and forest cabin in Köhler's *Windows on Monday*; the rural village in Valeska Grisebach's *Longing*; and the vacation homes in Thomas Arslan's *Vacation* or Maren Ade's *Everyone Else*. Certainly, this mixture of mobility and stasis beyond—but also occasionally within—Berlin reflects spaces of action made possible through globalization, through the changing contours of Europe, through Germany's East–West integration, and through geographic and economic relationships between characters' places of origin (their *Herkunft*) and current lifestyles, whether urban, rural, or suburban. But the preoccupation of these films with what can be termed the *Anti-Hauptstadt*, an avoidance both of Berlin and of clearly visible markers of place, is not only thematic; it is reinforced in numerous formal choices available to the filmmakers. A case in point is the work of Angela Schanelec, whose films *Passing Summer* and *Afternoon*, both stories of quotidian malaise, convey the region of Berlin-Brandenburg as an all but anonymous backdrop for slow-paced lives and narrative stagnation.

See BORDERS

Schanelec's low-key approach to Berlin runs counter to the urban discourse of the time. The late 1990s and early 2000s saw a film boom in the revamped, unified capital, and the renewed commercial ambitions of the post-unification national film industry paralleled those of city marketers and the federal government to construct an appropriate and attractive city image for the next millennium. More than a capital or Europe's largest construction site, Berlin was something of an urban laboratory as politicians, planners, architects, artists, historians, business leaders, and inhabitants alike wrangled over the city's past and future. In 1994 the funding organization called the Filmboard Berlin-Brandenburg (subsumed by Medienboard Berlin-Brandenburg in 2004) was established in order to increase film development and production in the region. Chiefly an economic enterprise—one that placed the capital in competition with other film regions like North-Rhine Westphalia, Bavaria, Schleswig-Holstein, and the 'new' states of the former East—the Filmboard's initiatives, coupled with the German Federal Film Board's (FFA) presence in the city, implicitly (and sometimes explicitly) encouraged filmmakers to make clear, unmistakable reference to Berlin in their films. One need only recall the latest incarnation of this trend, The German Federal Film Fund (DFFF), inaugurated in 2007, in part to entice prestigious, large-budget English-language coproductions to Germany. Early beneficiaries such as *Speed Racer* (Andy and Lana Wachowski, 2008), *The Reader* (Stephen Daldry, 2008), *Valkyrie* (Bryan Singer, 2008), *The International* (Tom Tykwer, 2009), *Inglorious Basterds* (Quentin Tarantino, 2009), *Unknown* (Jaume Collet-Serra, 2011), and *Hanna* (Joe Wright, 2011) unite international star power with extensive location and studio shooting in Berlin-Brandenburg. It is not unusual in these films and their domestic equivalents (Dorris Dörrie's *Kirschblüten—Hanami/Cherry Blossoms* [2008] comes to mind) for viewers to come across unmistakable German landmarks. Their inclusion is highly encouraged by the DFFF's evaluation policies.

Mainstream cinema's more unequivocal commitment to recognizable locations makes Schanelec's refusal to engage with commercially coded urban space all the more conspicuous. Though dependent on the same regional and federal production coffers (albeit for much smaller budgets) as these other films, Schanelec repeatedly resists and challenges conventions of geographic specificity. Employing a formal and stylistic register that favors states over actions, long takes over rapid cutting, and the everyday over grand events, Schanelec's *Anti-Hauptstadt* films shift Berlin's millennial cultural centrality to the peripheries of perception.

Passing Summer opens without an establishing shot. The protagonist Valerie (Ursina Lardi) is framed in close-up, looking down, in shallow space, the background reduced to unfocused patches of white and green as the occasional cyclist or pedestrian passes the café window behind her. When her friend Sophie arrives, the women sit in two-shot, the background still blurred [**Fig. 9**]. Their discussion of Sophie's upcoming visit to Rome and the nationality ('Polish or Russian') of Sophie's father's cleaning lady as well as a mention of Germany contrast the shot's own lack of orienting information. The city outside is simply the 'here' to which they refer in conversation, a nebulous backdrop to the interpersonal relationships and

FIG. 9: *Passing Summer.*

elliptical incidents of the 'slow life' alluded to in the film's German title, *Mein langsames Leben.*

Filmed predominantly indoors and on sidewalks, *Passing Summer* offers few shots of deep, urban space and even fewer landmarks. Even when a train station—Bahnhof Friedrichstrasse—is visible in long shot, Schanelec's framing deemphasizes the location. What is important in her approach to place might be called a cinematographic attitude, in this case, the camera's behavior toward the rare landmark's presence. Whereas countless Berlin films of the past 15 years signal location through the unambiguous, privileged framing of the Brandenburg Gate, the famous Television Tower at Alexanderplatz, the Victory Column, Potsdamer Platz, or prominently displayed and recognizable signage, Schanelec reduces the markers of Berlin's uniqueness to an aesthetics of urban banality. As aspiring photographer Johanna accosts professional photographer Thomas, the love interest of Valerie, who rents a room from his sister, whose child is cared for by Johanna's friend, the station is only vaguely discernable in the blurred background behind his head. A subsequent close-up of Johanna's face all but obscures the visual information (parked and moving cars, out of focus) behind her **[Fig. 10]**. Though the word 'Friedrichstrasse' is legible in a subsequent long shot of the station, the camera position (directly in the street) serves more to embed Johanna's departure into a multifaceted urban street scene, amid cars, motorcyclists, pedestrians, and objects, than to call attention to the station itself. As the shot's nonfictional register absorbs the fictional character

FIG. 10: *Passing Summer.*

into this belated establishing paradigm, it is not 'Friedrichstrasse' in any of its historical connotations that matters, but only the street (the *Strasse*) itself. The sign is only one of several elements in the shot to connote 'city.' Johanna's placement in the static urban view that ends this scene might have more to do with the type of encounter she has just had. 'You are the brother of the woman whose kid Maria takes care of, aren't you?' she had asked Thomas, hoping he could evaluate her professional potential. Schanelec's city is a place where personal connections can instantly materialize from and dissolve into the anonymous elements of the street.

In the more aesthetically austere *Afternoon*, Berlin is kept at a distance both narratively and visually. A loose adaptation of Chekhov's *Chayka/The Seagull* (1895), the film is set at a lake house at the city's periphery. Shot in and around Potsdam, the dacha drama about the depressed young writer Konstantin (Jirka Zett) and the creative and interpersonal frustration of languid summer days engages with the terrain of the formerly East German state of Brandenburg, far less familiar to audiences socialized in the West than iconic views of West and East Berlin. Critical to the cultural, economic, and spatial integration of the unified capital within the greater region, this German state encircling what was once West Berlin has gradually regained its pre-Cold War status as the city's organic outskirts and countryside, a place of recreation and real estate investment for Berliners of means. No longer a border between the political ideologies of the two German states, this partner in Berlin's regional film funding has been annexed narratively in numerous city–country dichotomies (along with Mecklenburg-Vorpommern and Saxony-Anhalt), used to furnish a variety of fictional film landscapes, and increasingly extolled in the pages of Berlin magazines *Zitty* and *Tip*. By relegating Berlin to a geographical reference point, a diegetic 'over there,' Schanelec both acknowledges the capital and declines to picture it.

Once again the notion of a cinematographic attitude toward place is instructive. Though *Afternoon*'s setting legitimizes Brandenburg as a space of narrative action, Schanelec reinforces Berlin's symbolic distance through the politics of her frame. When Konstantin and his estranged (girl)friend Agnes visit the city one evening, they are filmed in medium shot and two-shot. The shop lights are a blur behind Konstantin. Another camera position looks down on the back of Agnes's head, the side of Konstantin's midsection and the sidewalk between them as he declares that it is 'disgusting' to drink good wine from a plastic cup and as she recounts her friend's desire to see a photograph of him. Location is secondary to their mutual alienation. Agnes sips her wine (perhaps defiantly) from her plastic cup as Konstantin, of whom she had no photograph to show her friend, remains just out of reach. Even when the camera pans to follow his exit from the frame and her motion after him, the façades of the shops, now in focus in a wider shot, reveal neither a specific Berlin landmark nor a definitive Berlin location. Instead, the characters' tense communication is transposed to an auditory and temporal perception of urban space as a constant layer of amplified ambient street sound accompanies the long takes of this drawn-out scene.

See FRAMINGS

See AMBIENT SOUND

The mundane and modest Berlins of *Passing Summer* and *Afternoon*, cities of unspectacular urban views and meandering lives, contrast starkly with commercial cinema's pointed showcasing of Berlin landmarks, classical plot structures, and high production values. Whereas aspiring coproduction blockbusters like *The International*, *Unknown*, and *Hanna* effectively reassert the German capital's geopolitical centrality in the age of the European Union with all the excitement of global intrigue and all the clarity of a tourism board, Schanelec's city defamiliarizes Berlin's political topography, introduces its interstitial spaces, and infuses its common places with a potential for new, highly personalized meaning. Even leaving and returning to Berlin are hardly worth the reassuring signposts of urban establishing shots. Simple cuts mark unexpected transitions between city and countryside or Berlin and Paris in *Passing Summer* and between Marseille and Berlin in *Marseille*. In Schanelec's *Orly*, a series of vignettes set in the eponymous Parisian airport, Berlin figures merely as the unseen destination of a young German couple. Allied both with Christian Petzold's spectral, mobile entry into Berlin in *Ghosts* and with the low-key Berliner youth milieu of Valeska Grisebach's *Be My Star*, Henner Winckler's *Lucy* and even Thomas Arslan's more specifically Kreuzberg-inflected *Geschwister*, Schanelec's approach to

See URBAN MINIATURES

Berlin shares with other Berlin School productions an appreciation for restrained geographical referentiality.

See FAMILIAR PLACES

The *Anti-Hauptstadt* is at once hyperlocal and transnational in its assault on Berlin's hackneyed topographies. Reflecting an antimetropolitan Berlin as well as a regionally extended one, an absent and distant Berlin as well as one immediately and transnationally accessible via the next cut, Schanelec's art house reinterpretation of the nation's new-old capital over and against commercial cinema's continued, uncritical alignment with the goals of Germany's federal and regional funding politics suggests just one way that the film aesthetics of the new wave in German and Austrian production becomes a film politics.

BW

Bad Sex

In Christoph Hochäusler's *This Very Moment*, Sylvia, after abandoning her stepchildren Lea and Konstantin on a country road in Poland, returns home where she awaits the arrival of her husband Josef. Saying nothing of what has transpired, she responds to his inquiry about the children with an aggressive kiss and a request: 'I want to sleep with you.' The film quickly cuts away to a shot of the two of them mid-climax, lying nearly motionless on a bed under an unpainted ceiling, their bodies—he is stark naked, she is fully clothed—half hidden by a camera angle that suggests the perspective of a voyeur who has stopped short of entering the room upon discovering the two in an intimate moment **[Fig. 11]**. But the scene is as unerotic as it is squirm-inducing; partly because of the circumstances of which the viewer is aware (and Josef is not) and partly because of how the couple is positioned in the static, medium shot of the bedroom. Occupying very little of the frame, they lie crosswise on a bed that appears wedged under a low, sloping ceiling, with Sylvia's head hanging down at an awkward angle.

FIG. 11: *This Very Moment*.

Neither the uncomfortable looking position of their bodies nor their grimacing expressions suggests any sort of pleasure or sexual satisfaction.

Most of the films by Berlin School directors avoid convoluted plots and fantastic situations and traffic in the everyday, often banal moments that compose the characters' lives. Even those films that culminate in shocking events—*Lovely Rita*, whose sullen protagonist wordlessly murders her parents; *Yella*, which concludes with the revelation that Yella's escape from the car driven by her ex-husband into the Elbe was mere fantasy; or *This Very Moment*, whose final shot is of the two children disappearing down a lonely road, seemingly lost forever—primarily employ a realist style that lingers over moments usually eschewed in a conventional narrative cinema that foregrounds action and favors short, rapid cuts. Instead, characters are defined not by what they do in extraordinary situations, but by what they do in ordinary ones.

One of these ordinary situations is sexual intercourse, scenes of which can be found in nearly all of the Berlin School films. In keeping with the films' commitment to realism, these scenes are shot in a decidedly non-Hollywood style—instead of soft focus shots, montages of hands moving across writhing, glossy bodies, and smooth jazz soundtracks, these scenes are single, fixed camera scenes, with medium shots and a distinct lack of music, either diegetic or nondiegetic. However, the absence of the usual devices to evoke sensuality goes beyond realism. The lack of eroticism present is not just a question of editing or a moment of verité, but rather due to the fact that these are instances of unfulfilling, unsatisfying, and in some cases, unfinished sexual activity—in short, of bad sex.

What, exactly, constitutes bad sex in these films—or as a concept in general? Certainly, it can be a highly subjective definition, one dependent on a variety of factors: the gender of the participant, the circumstances of arousal and completion (or lack thereof), unequal levels of attraction, or emotional engagement. Given that these films tend to focus on individual protagonists, this last point is particularly relevant here: it is often precisely the fact that one partner seems to be enjoying the moment, oblivious to the dissatisfaction of the other, which heightens the displeasure of the protagonist. We can also approach the question from the perspective of representation—how do the films portray these encounters? To what extent do they offer an eroticized vision of intercourse? This may be the most salient point—that we as viewers are the ultimate arbiters of good and bad, that the uncomfortable or even comic feelings that these scenes engender in the viewers is what defines their nature. But bad sex is here best understood not merely as sex that does not appear pleasurable to those engaged in it, or as sex that, however seemingly pleasurable it is, is poorly (or unerotically) represented, but rather as the convergence of these two perceptions: one or both of the participants is having a distinctly unpleasurable experience, as is the viewer, forced to sit through the intercourse. It is not so much an instance of identification, as one of a sympathetic experience of palpable discomfort.

Where do these encounters take place? For the most part, they do not take place in spaces that reflect real intimacy or sense of home or belonging. Most often, they take place away from home—in hotels or rented rooms, vacation houses or resorts. On the one hand, this can be seen as an attempt to reeroticize a sexual relationship that has gone stale, by relocating away from the trappings of mundane existence that have led to alienation, and by introducing an element of novelty, danger, or deviance. Sex in motels—the province of adulterers and prostitutes—is dirty, illicit, taboo-breaking. Partners can shed their identities and their inhibitions. But in these films, this displacement only serves to heighten the emotional disconnect. The motels and hotels that we see bear no resemblance to sites of romantic or even tawdry rendezvous—they are cold, barren, spaces, devoid of decoration and seemingly vacant; the protagonists in films such as *Hotel*, *Windows on Monday*, and *Yella* are often the only figures who haunt their hallways and rooms. See HOTELS

At the end of *Windows on Monday*, Nina and Frieder have reunited to attend Nico's funeral. Stopping outside the cemetery gates, Frieder tells Nina of the ironic circumstances of Nico's demise—he fell off his bike and into a ditch, bleeding to death as a result of having taken a blood thinner for another health condition. Their exchange of subtle smiles seems to indicate a shared realization of the arbitrariness of life and a renewed erotic charge brought on by a desire to affirm their own lives through sex. But rather than rekindling an extinguished marital passion via potentially exhibitionistic intercourse, this merely leads to an unsuccessful attempt at fellatio in the back of the family's VW van **[Fig. 12]**. After a few awkward minutes of groping, the film abruptly ends. Even when these moments do take place in a home (as in *This Very Moment*), it is a home that has been stripped of any sense of homeliness. The plastic sheeting that covers the furniture, windows, even the bed, creates a sense of distance from one's own ostensibly intimate space. Bad sex is not merely a question of the emotional alienation of the protagonists, but of their physical alienation as well. See RENOVATION

FIG. 12: *Windows on Monday.*

Bad sex is but the bodily manifestation of the social alienation that plagues the characters that populate Berlin School cinema. Unable to engage in the world, or with others effectively, they resort to sex as a sort of prelinguistic communication, as a means of escape from the constraints of language. But just as the epistemic subject is itself objectively constituted by the society to which it belongs and without which the subject could not exist, so too can individuals not extract themselves from a societal formation whose essential relations are ones that demand abnegation. The price paid by society for the overcoming of nature is the intensification and displacement of domination within the individual, who must deny his inner nature in order to achieve domination over extrahuman nature and other human beings. Subjects become objects, and the reification of relations between individuals, a process described by Adorno as transforming human qualities into 'lubricating oil for the smooth running of the machinery,' makes meaningful interpersonal relationships impossible.[1]

See LANGUAGE

See INTERIORITY

Misery loves company. There is a persistent refusal to allow other characters to have satisfying moments of sexual intercourse. After being taken in by the Pole Kuba, Lea and Konstantin awaken alone in a hotel room. Lea wanders the hotel in search of their ostensible savior. He is easy to find—as Lea walks past an open window she spies him in a dingy room thrusting workmanlike atop a woman whose features are hardly discernable and whose presence is never fully explained **[Fig. 13]**. Momentarily stunned, she quickly recovers and glares at him until he waves her away.

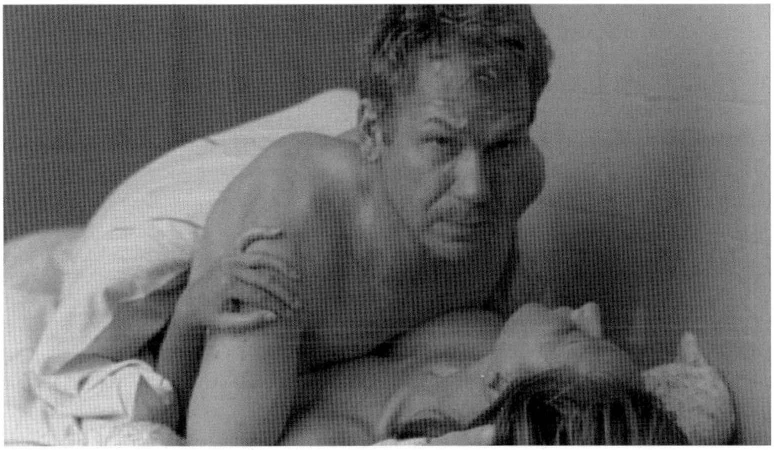

FIG. 13: *This Very Moment.*

In *Bungalow*, it is Paul's brother Max and his girlfriend Lene who are thwarted as they attempt to have a liaison outside by the pool at the family vacation home. Assuming that they are alone, the naked couple is discovered by Paul's girlfriend Kerstin and is forced to quickly dress. Kerstin's shock quickly turns to anger when Paul reveals that he knew they were there and allowed Kerstin to go outside so as to disrupt them. Unable to find satisfaction himself in sexual activity, Paul demands that others be denied this experience as well.

While, in the majority of instances, characters are fundamentally incapable of having good sex, the fact that depictions of instances of good sex are entirely absent from these films is not an indication that it is completely impossible, but rather a reflection of a quasi-Adornian moment in the aesthetics of the Berlin School. For Adorno, true art eschews beauty as the evocation of a false sense of reconciliation; a reconciliation impossible in a world in which relations between individuals have become reified and domination has been internalized. Beauty here can be understood as the portrayal of good sex. Thus, even when characters are able to engage in satisfying sexual relations, the films pointedly refuse to represent this moment. The false reconciliation, the suspension of alienation that a depiction of good sex would provide, cannot be tolerated, as it would represent a break with the philosophy of realism in the films.

The sexual activities of the metalworker and volunteer fireman Markus in *Longing* illustrate this point perfectly. Unsettled after happening upon a double suicide attempt, Markus leaves his wife (and childhood

FIG. 14: *Longing.*

sweetheart) for a training weekend. When praised by a colleague for how he handled the grisly scene, Markus can do nothing but sit silently and drink heavily. As the evening wears on, shots of the boisterous group of firefighters are intercut with shots in which Markus is increasingly isolated, culminating in a long shot in which Markus dances by himself, eyes closed and seemingly oblivious to his surroundings, to the Robbie Williams song 'Feel.' The nearly two-minute long static shot ends abruptly, mid-song, and Markus wakes up alone in the bed of Rose, a waitress from the restaurant. Her smile as she greets him in the kitchen indicates the passionate night they shared, though she pointedly refuses to say exactly what happened when he presses her on the issue later that evening. Nor do we see them having intercourse in a second love scene, which cuts quickly from their impassioned kisses signaling foreplay to the pair, lying next to each other, not touching **[Fig. 14]**. Upon returning home, his wife can sense his distraction. Complaining of a growing distance between them, she plaintively asks him, not once but twice: 'Sleep with me.' The ensuing scene is long and uncomfortable: it depicts not two lovers familiar with each others bodies and physically in sync, but rather a pair of strangers: Ella, his wife, desperately reaching out for Markus, hungrily kissing and groping him as if it were their last night together, and Markus, constantly turning his face away from hers and trying to restrain her and keep their physical contact to a minimum **[Fig. 15]**.

Other films follow this pattern. *Bungalow* has no shortage of scenes of Paul's desperate attempts at meaningful sexual activity, including a

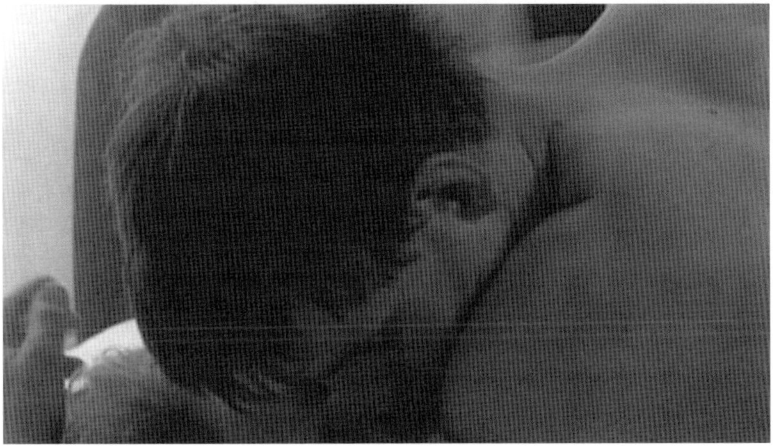

FIG. 15: *Longing.*

prolonged scene in which he somewhat listlessly masturbates. When Lene finally agrees to share a bed with him, either out of pity or out of her own need for validation following her failure to secure a desired film role in a German science fiction film, they take a hotel room above a restaurant. What begins as a rare erotically charged moment—Lene mentioning that she is too hot under the covers, Paul wordlessly indicating that she should disrobe, caressing her bare breasts **[Fig. 16]**—cuts abruptly to the two of them sitting in bed, naked, briefly chatting before dressing and heading

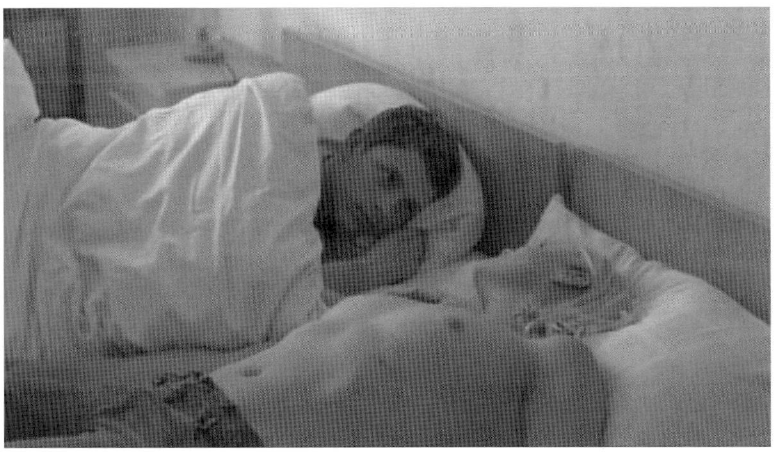

FIG. 16: *Bungalow.*

downstairs to meet up with Max. As with *Longing*, that the pair actually had intercourse is never directly affirmed.

Haunted by visions of her abusive ex-husband Ben, come to take her back to the East, Yella frantically runs to the hotel room of Philipp, whose role as venture capitalist mentor has gradually evolved into partner and lover. Their emotional embrace in the doorway of his room is abruptly replaced by a shot of a naked Yella waking up to Phillipp bringing her breakfast in bed. In the case of *Yella*, there is a double movement at work: not only is good sex not depicted, but it presumably did not even take place, at least not in reality. The film's revelation that Yella has only imagined her escape from Ben in the moments before they both plunge off a bridge and drown in the Elbe relegates her experiences with Phillip to the realm of pure fantasy. This consignment of satisfactory sexual experiences to the realm of the imagination finds its clearest expression in *I Am Guilty*, where Armin's potentially nonconsensual homosexual encounters with a biker gang are never confirmed as anything more than the imagination of the protagonist, the 'false confessor' (the 'falscher Bekenner' of the film's German title), whose memories cannot be trusted.

It is fair to ask why Berlin School directors do not employ abstinence—a lack of sexual activity—to signify the alienation that plagues the characters in these films. To be sure, the participation of these characters in sexual activity is often half-hearted or only reluctantly done in response to the demands of their partners. But why would people who are unable to connect emotionally with their partners, friends, and family actively seek out intimate physical relations that seem only to exacerbate their sense of alienation? And why would they do so with such frequency? Many of the instances of bad sex occur immediately following scenes or moments that call attention to the characters' emotional isolation, giving the impression that the impulse to have inevitably unsatisfying sex is a masochistic one.

Perhaps the repeated attempts at sexual relations should be seen more positively, as a last ditch attempt to reconnect with the human impulses which persist, even in repressed form, in the films' characters. These films, for all of their bleakness, retain a moment of optimism. Like most concepts, bad sex contains within itself its opposite—it is judged to be bad against an idealized vision of what intercourse can be. *Omne animal post coitum tristet*: 'After sexual intercourse every animal is sad.' Why sad? Because 'good' sex contains a moment of communion that, however fleetingly, provides those engaged in it with a moment of physical and emotional euphoria brought on by a sense of reconnection and a suspension of all other concerns.

The willingness to engage in moments of bad sex is an indication that the characters, for all of their problems, still long for a closeness that is denied them. It is the reason that Nina is willing to lie naked on her hotel bed and suffer the advances of the louche tennis pro David Ionesco; why Irene in *Hotel*, even as she inexorably follows the trajectory of her predecessor into oblivion, shares a bed with the unremarkable Erik; why Rita in *Lovely Rita* attempts to seduce a boy too young for her and sleeps with a bus driver too old for her. Adorno concludes *Minima Moralia* with a statement on philosophy that can be brought to bear here. He writes that, in the face of despair, the only reasonable philosophy is one that contemplates all things from the standpoint of redemption, however impossible that may be.[2] Despite the often bleak depictions that characterize Berlin School films, the refusal to portray reconciliation via depictions of good sex, they, too, contain a utopian impulse, an impulse that can be seen in the persistence of their characters with regard to sexual happiness. For these lost souls, the only possible standpoint for sexual intercourse is the assumption that it will be physically, and emotionally successful, that it will, in fact, allow its participants to overcome their alienation and find redemption, if only for a moment, in a renewed community with others, however impossible that may be.

MDR

Notes

1 Theodor W. Adorno, 'The Position of the Narrator in the Contemporary Novel,' *Notes to Literature. Volume 1*, trans. Shierry Weber Nicholsen (New York: Columbia UP, 1991), 30–36; here 32.

2 Theodor W. Adorno, *Minima Moralia: Reflections on a Damaged Life*, trans. Edmund Jephcott (London: Verso, 2005 [orig 1951]), 247.

Beginnings

> Chaque commencement d'un film est aussi pour le spectateur un *apprentissage* des règles du jeu, du mode d'emploi spécifique à ce film.
>
> (Every beginning of a film is, for the viewer, also an *apprenticeship* in the rules of the game, in the instructions specific to that film.)[1]

Four title cards provide the basic credits in a simple white, sans serif font on a black background: producer and distributor, coproducers, the names of five actors, 'a film by Angela Schanelec—MARSEILLE.' Together, they provide 20 seconds of silence, a threshold for the spectator to transition from everyday life to the film, from the loud lure of trailers and commercials in the movie theater or from the activity in the house around the DVD player to the diegesis. From outside the story world to inside.

The first shot appears on the screen: a close-up of a driver steering a car through city streets, filmed in a three-quarter profile from the back. We see the silhouette of her head against the bright sunlight on the façades outside; the rear view mirror dimly reflects her eyes **[Fig. 17]**. The cut

FIG. 17: *Marseille.*

from the credits to the moving image is simultaneous with the switch from silence to sounds: the shifting gears of the engine, the first words, spoken, 'C'est où?' ('Where is it?') asks a passenger off-screen. The driver responds with a question; 'Tu connais le coin?' ('Do you know the neighborhood?') and the passenger responds 'no.' Neither do we, as spectators. So we go along, realizing that we've joined a conversation and a developing relationship *in medias res*. The driver suggests there might be a map in the glove compartment and we hear the passenger rummage around for one, but apparently she gives up, 'no,' she says. When the driver pulls up after a while to purchase a map from a newspaper stand on a street corner, the camera pans with her but remains in the car. Only when she has taken her seat again and handed the passenger the map does the camera pan in the other direction to reveal the passenger, also in three-quarter profile from the back: Sophie, the protagonist of the film. Two minutes into *Marseille*, after holding on Sophie for a few seconds, the first shot concludes with a cut, after which we find the two women in the apartment.

See CARS

How do the films of the Berlin School invite and accompany the spectator over the threshold that constitutes the beginning of a film? There are of course as many answers to this question as there are films of the Berlin School. But several choices that Schanelec makes in *Marseille* resemble those made at the beginnings of other films from this group—choices about sound and image, about atmosphere and mood, about storytelling.

Like *Marseille*, a number of films begin with noticeably tight framings: close-ups that hide as much as they reveal (the back of a head rather than a face, a character's intense gaze without a countershot to reveal the object of that gaze); or close-ups on faces of unknown actors whose physiognomies are unfamiliar. These faces are so many maps that we must learn to read over the course of the film: the close-up of Lennie Burmeister as Paul, dozing off on the troop transport that he will desert in *Bungalow*; the tight framing of Julia Hummer as Jeanne in the opening shots of *The State I Am In*. These are framings that refuse the convention of the establishing shot, the comprehensive overview of a locale that allows us to situate the ensuing action.

See FRAMINGS

Conversely, when Berlin School filmmakers appear to obey this convention on the level of shot scale, they empty out the image of action, or reduce movement to a crawl, as in the extreme long shot that opens Christoph Hochhäusler's *This Very Moment*: alongside the undulating rural road that cuts diagonally across the frame, dotted by telegraph poles, two children move toward the foreground [**Fig. 18**]. Given the enormous depth

FIG. 18: *This Very Moment.*

of the image, their progress seems unbearably slow, a duration underlined by the length of the first take that lasts, like *Marseille*'s, for about two full minutes. Hochhäusler's subsequent film, *I Am Guilty*, similarly opens with a long shot but again frustrates the spectator's desire to see, comprehend, and become involved in an unfolding action: while we hear cars rushing past (traffic courses through the sounds and images of these films at every turn), the virtually black nighttime image looks almost abstract. Only gradually do we recognize the slightly curved silver line traversing the upper third of the frame as a highway guardrail, and only belatedly do we make out the movement across this line as a shadow cast by an approaching pedestrian. After over a minute, he has approached the foreground of the shot and emerges, barely recognizable, in the faint glow of a car's taillights.

See LONG TAKES

The opening of any time-based piece of art is crucial: once the spectator has crossed the threshold from everyday to aesthetic perception, the first sounds of a musical composition, the first steps of a ballet, the first images of a film set a mood. They attune the viewer/listener to the particular atmosphere of the piece, soliciting and directing her attention in particular ways for the subsequent unfolding of the aesthetic experience. In their often understated beginnings, the films of the Berlin School betray an intense awareness of this power to 'prime' the spectator. Initializing and orchestrating the various registers of the film experience, they use the first images not so much for the exposition of narrative information but to create rhythms of perception, generating an 'experiential space of the film's sensual qualities prior to the inception of the action.'[2] Rarely urgent, the mood of these films initially is often quite laconic, using a reduced arsenal of cinematic means to draw the viewer in: sparse, white-on-black credits, long takes, minimal dialogue, location sounds, and no film music unless it is sourced in the image. These choices are deliberate, intended to activate the spectator, to heighten attention and awareness precisely by refusing to anchor the beginning in the sort of 'inciting incident' that screenwriting manuals would mandate.[3] Instead, it is the spectator who is incited—to observe, to listen, to take an interest in details of gesture and inflection that contemporary mainstream film will always subordinate and instrumentalize for narrative purposes (when it doesn't render these details invisible in the first place behind the cinematographic flourishes and editing fireworks that it apparently considers necessary for grabbing the spectator).

But then again, these films do not share the narrative assumptions of mainstream cinema. They operate in a distinct 'mode of narration.'[4] *Marseille*, Angela Schanelec tells us, originated in a story about a character who is mugged. An early version of the film began with this 'inciting incident.' But in the course of writing, Schanelec deliberately moved away from this conception, moving the mugging to the end of the film—and deciding, moreover, to show only its aftermath, not the event itself. In an interview about the film with the editors of *Revolver*, Schanelec explains the decision by setting her procedure apart from a 'classical' approach to narration where,

> in the beginning, something happens for which one need not know the characters yet, because this something is so big that one will inevitably take an interest. Someone is mugged, everything is stolen, what does he do now? To write in this way would have meant that there is a very clearly formulated goal that simply must be reached.[5]

'Classical,' goal-oriented narration mandates a clear sense of beginning and ending, tethering one to the other in a mutually reinforcing conceptual loop: 'The ending is the first thing you must know before you begin writing,' requires the mainstream screenwriting handbook.[6] With the exception of recent forays into genre filmmaking by directors such as Petzold, Hochhäusler, or Arslan, the beginnings of Berlin School films refuse to be tethered to narration in this sense. Instead, they stake their claims in other areas of the film experience—in the relation with profilmic reality, in the observational mood or tone described above, in the fuzzy zone between documentation and fiction. As Schanelec puts it, 'What is important to me is that I manage to interest myself or the spectator in a person without some powerful event.'[7]

Unthinkable that a film of the Berlin School should follow classical protocol and turn endings into echoes of their beginnings, tying up all the loose ends. (*Yella*, with its dramaturgical claim that you just may be able to step out of the same river twice, would provide an intriguing exception to prove this rule). They are neither circular and closed nor flat or static—which is to say: neither do they return to, nor do they fail to develop away from, their starting points. To be sure, at first glance very little seems to 'happen' in a Schanelec film, if by 'happen' we mean significant narrative events. But characteristically, the accumulated microactions and *temps morts* of any given film's duration regularly do add up to compelling narratives that arrive somewhere different from where they departed and remain open when the film ends, like it began, *in medias res*.

See ENDINGS

JvM

Notes

1 Jean Louis Comolli and François Géré, 'Deux fictions de la haine (2)' in *Cahiers du Cinéma* 288 (1978): 4–15; here 12.

2 Britta Hartmann, *Aller Anfang: Zur Initialphase des Spielfilms* (Marburg: Schüren, 2009), 263.

3 Syd Field, *Screenplay: The Foundations of Screenwriting* (New York: Random House, 2005), 97.

4 See David Bordwell, *Narration in the Fiction Film* (Madison, WI: University of Wisconsin P, 1985) 154, 234 and *passim*.

5 See *Revolver: Kino muss gefährlich sein*, ed. Marcus Seibert (Frankfurt a.M.: Verlag der Autoren, 2006), 405.

6 Field, *Screenplay*, 91.

7 Schanelec's phrasing: 'ohne dass etwas Gewaltiges passiert.' See *Revolver: Kino muss gefährlich sein*, 405.

Borders

In Angela Schanelec's *Marseille* and Christian Petzold's *Yella*, boundaries are vaguely defined and barely visible, yet they are also influential and ultimately implacable. Elliptical plots and abstract poetics seem to alleviate the gravity of the films' borders. Schanelec's Sophie appears to wander freely. Petzold's Yella appears to move directly westward and upward. Yet the actions of these protagonists are deeply influenced by what turn out to be border routes. Their turns and returns express circularities typical of late capitalism, an often-tortured circuitousness that dislodges modern time's supposed linearity. Articulated in broader terms, the contemporary borders depicted in *Marseille* and *Yella* give the lie to dominant narratives that proclaim unhindered mobility for both labor and capital.

Particularities of aesthetic and plot representation reveal the significance of borders in *Marseille*. If these filmic elements remain unread, Sophie's aims and actions during her visits to the French city and her daily life in Berlin may seem capricious. As a young German photographer, Sophie seems financially secure and able to participate in university-educated circles in Berlin. Among such a European demographic, travel for travel's sake may be the norm. The narrative sketches Sophie's movements without articulating them clearly. By representing her visit in oblique and disjointed ways, *Marseille* makes audiences work to catch glimpses of deeper dramas such as the supra-individual aims of the protagonist and the challenges facing many locals. Assuming that Sophie's actions are driven entirely by caprice, we may simply observe her actions passively, rather than wondering: Why does she visit precisely this city, borrow a car from the local mechanic Pierre rather than rent one, shoot with celluloid rather than digital? If instead *Marseille*'s more striking representational strategies guide our readings, we may detect in Sophie's actions a political subtext about travel and migration within the 26 European countries known as the Schengen Zone.

Several aesthetic devices point to the significance of official borders in the film. Color is one; the yellows and blues relate the narrative to the 'national' colors of the European Union. In many scenes, blue predominates. In those with earthy background palettes, the conspicuous swatches of saturated colors are yellow or blue: a yellow house wall as Sophie runs for the bus; the puffy yellow and blue jacket of a swarthy man behind her as she sits alone with her thoughts. The aerial panning shot of the highway upon which Sophie travels in Pierre's red car features blue shipping containers and a yellow overpass that resonates with a yellow building in the upper right. *Marseille*'s particular yellow and blue tones highlight the significance of internal and external European borders.

Upon examining the film's color scheme, Sophie's seemingly disparate actions become legible as explorations and documentations of how travel and migration function in the Schengen border city. Freshly arrived, Sophie takes a bus to the end of the line. Dismounting in a working-class suburb, she walks further toward an unspecified location, carrying a bulky item. Dark-skinned boys roughhouse, as did those in the urban mall where she recently made the purchase **[Fig. 19]**. If these scenes are read in terms of their borders, the film is highlighting Sophie's travel in and around a blue-collar migrant community in a *banlieue* (suburb). In another example, guards brusquely stop her from photographing an undefined subject from the second floor of the outdoor mall. Sophie's slow movements as she sets up her shot imply that her urban subject is immobile; it may be private or public, and could perhaps even be security. Questioned later at the police station, the photographer pauses before responding that her subjects are Marseille's streets. Sophie's hesitation and the fact that her work

FIG. 19: *Marseille.*

encompasses more than just the city's streets suggest that she prefers not to share information about all of her occupations with the police.

Read in terms of their borders, the visits that Sophie does *not* make and the sites that she does *not* photograph are as significant as those she does. As a photographer, she seems uninterested in classic tourism. She does not explore the famous Old Port that is both immortalized in numerous artistic representations and that constitutes the stunning bay view from her temporary apartment. Pierre's friend, who champions the town, initially accuses the German visitor of fetishizing and then of ignoring the popular landmark that is now a tourist attraction. Sophie's claim that she passed near it suggests that she may have instead visited Marseille's newer industrial port, France's and southern Europe's most significant harbor. Situated on the Schengen Zone perimeter dividing European Union from non-European Union, it is an important destination for migrants from North Africa crossing into Europe. A visit to this contemporary nexus of capital and labor flows would underscore Sophie's interest in migration as an exploration of the Old Port would not.

Attention to color opens the film to certain ways of seeing; so too, focus on unusual camerawork furthers a cohesive reading of Sophie's actions by suggesting their political motivations. In a scene in her spartan apartment—one that is particularly striking for its slow pacing, long takes, close-ups, and diegetic sound—Sophie methodically tapes her photos up around a large map of Marseille and its environs **[Fig. 20]**. The camera lingers in medium close-up on these images. Although the precise subjects

FIG. 20: *Marseille.*

remain somewhat mysterious, it is clear that they depict borders. For instance, one photograph features a wall topped with barbed wire with a lonely figure off to the right. The amplified sounds of rustling photographic paper remind viewers that Sophie works in celluloid, a medium that, in the digital age, is comparatively difficult to retouch. This scene in particular suggests that the images she produces are aimed to represent Schengen as a zone of fixed limits and boundaries.

Sophie's documentary project, which seems to thematize the challenges of migratory movement, is both reflected in and enabled by her own mobility within the Schengen zone. The film opens with the Berlin resident already navigating Marseille's streets in the automobile of the woman with whom she has swapped lodgings [**see Fig. 17—BEGINNINGS**]. Her French compatriot proceeds to buy Sophie the aforementioned map before acquainting the new arrival with her apartment. Unlike less privileged city inhabitants, the German visitor immediately has what seems to be unlimited access to her new environment. With the well-located, comfortable, and affordable flat as a base, Sophie engages intensely and safely in activities ranging from solitary nightly wanderings to border excursions. Her reentry into Germany from France is as easy as her arrival. A smooth graphic match on her profile, frame right in a Marseille nightclub, bridges to her profile frame right in a similarly illuminated Berlin street. The first markers of the locational shift are the German words of a fast-food worker returning a personal item that Sophie had forgotten before heading to Marseille; it is as if she had never been away. These two elisions of cross-border travel are cases in point; mobility seldom requires effort where this privileged EU citizen traveler is concerned.

See THE CUT

Her freedom of movement notwithstanding, Sophie's supra-individual objectives are not met through linear, but through circuitous, repetitious movement. Her initial attempts to enter into Marseille's migrant cultural life appear thwarted. She hurries through the night streets, crossing the frame from left to right, only to arrive at a locked cinema. She then runs to catch a departing bus, in which she sits uncommunicatively next to migrants. A lengthy profile shot with a shallow depth of focus accentuates her isolation. In both of these scenes, the yellow-blue color motif highlights the border between insiders and outsiders [**Fig. 21**]. In contrast, Sophie's repetitive trajectories allow her not only to borrow an automobile, but also to cross cultural borders. When Sophie begins to return to sites that Pierre frequents, she enters into communication not only with him, but also with members of a working-class, Magreb-influenced subculture. When we see her in a nightclub, visiting with local acquaintances, her French is

Figure 21: *Marseille.*

fluent and she dances to Arabic pop in fluid imitation of Pierre. Through its deployment of color and filmic techniques, then, Schanelec underscores how Sophie's privileged mobility facilitates her international access. She can circle around and back to different communities as she wishes, but members of those communities cannot even move in linear ways, owing to the rules regulating labor flows.

The ambivalence of this logic of movement and access is highlighted when the previously unassailable Sophie is robbed or assaulted upon her return to Marseille. She travels on the night train between Berlin and Marseille and descends down the Marseille station stairs in the early morning. A jump cut from this extreme distance shot outdoors to a close-up in a police station elides depiction of the crime and in this manner potentially implicates Sophie in the transgression. A blue-yellow color scheme associates the police station with official borders. The close-up frames a mid-body profile of a blue-clad policewoman holding a yellow dress that is then exchanged for a blue jumpsuit [**Fig. 22**]. A medium-long shot through a doorway captures the now yellow-clad Sophie seated at an enormous desk. When she is questioned by a police officer who remains off-screen, the guardedness of her response suddenly suggests that she may have even more to hide.

See FRAMINGS

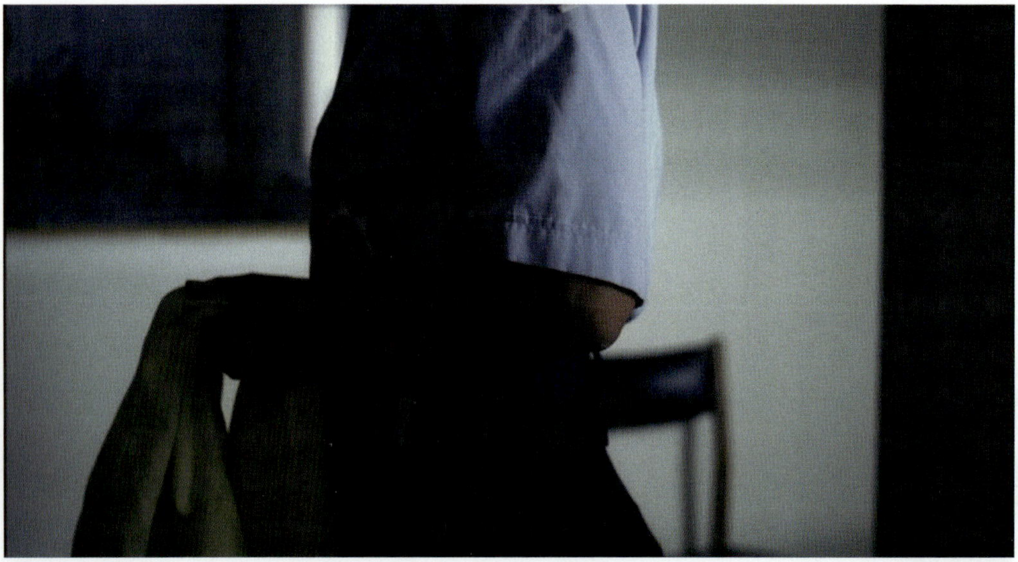

Figure 22: *Marseille.*

However, Sophie ultimately does not lose the privileged mobility that EU insider-status enables. The implication of guilt is short-lived. As Sophie begins to bypass the translator and answer directly in French, she relaxes into tears. She describes an attack in which her heavy bag was stolen and her clothes forcibly exchanged for the blue workman's jumpsuit. Perhaps its motivation was the desperation of undocumented migrant life or anger directed toward Sophie's politically motivated photography. In any case, the police are quick to treat her as a victim and an insider. Upon Sophie's release, the camera tracks her as she walks in the state-provided yellow dress down a boulevard and enters the German embassy [**Fig. 23**].

Marseille does not demand that we read for borders and movement, but if we attend to aesthetic cues such as the blue-yellow color scheme, the unusual camera work and the thematization of documentary photography at the edges of Fortress Europe, a plotline concerning them emerges. The travails of the protagonist Yella in the eponymous feature likewise center on problematic border crossings. Yella's trajectory in this third film of Petzold's 'Ghost Trilogy' seems all about linear movement westward and up the socioeconomic ladder; its narrative of economic and social progress collapses, however, under neoliberal market conditions. As in *Marseille*, borders are marked by exceptional filming and color. Eerie

Figure 23: *Marseille.*

visual and aural effects—the call and flight of ravens, the fall and tinkle of water, apparitions—link the protagonist to her death. *Yella*'s denouement reveals that the protagonist had been dying all along, drowning in the Oder River at the border between the former East and West Germanys. Petzold has commented on Yella's red blouse, so striking in its contrast to the somber palettes of the film's main locations, such as the small Eastern town of Wittenberge or the suburban corporate parks of Hanover's Expo 2000 grounds [**Fig. 24**]. In a sense, Yella embodies the sex appeal of venture capital, whose seduction is all silky surface without a material base. She lives from a suitcase in a hotel room and takes her daily wages in cash. She spends her time in the monocultural urban periphery where production of profit is the only value. Neither the trajectory of capitalism she embodies nor her own trajectory within capitalism promise longevity, let alone sustainable development.

Yella's own sexuality is also driven by her own economic survival and, here too, actions that may at first seem linear are repetitive and circular. Yella embraces Philipp to escape her estranged husband, Ben; when her new partner arrives on any scene, the former one disappears. Philipp is also Ben's slightly more enlightened replacement. Through this new lover, Yella is returned not only to Ben, but also to her father. This connection is established on their first

Figure 24: *Yella.*

postcoital morning, when Philipp peels an orange for her in precisely the same manner as her father had the morning that his daughter left Wittenberge [**Fig. 25**]. Moreover, as in her relationship with Ben, Yella's desire is largely shaped by Philipp's business plans and their success.

In revealing its apparent linearities as circularities, *Yella* shows the destructiveness of interpersonal relationships reified within unfettered capitalism. Yella's shot at 'success' in Hanover means leaving her failed (business) relationship behind. Ben responds to this perceived value imbalance by violently leveling the playing field, turning them both off of the bridge to their deaths. When Yella's single-minded, 'successful' power-brokering turns to blackmail, she drives the experienced CEO of a speculative business venture, Dr. Gunthen, to suicide. Helping Dr. Gunthen's wife with the body, Philipp straightens suddenly and looks directly at Yella as if interpreting Gunthen's suicide to be their impending failure. She backs into the woods, symbolically breaking their bond that had been fueled by the hope of subsequent gains. The next image of Yella in a taxi match-cuts to her once again in Ben's car, as she was in the beginning.

Yella's subsequent suicidal reperformance of Ben's murderous turn into the river may not express remorse as much as recognition of the impossibility

Figure 25: *Yella.*

of 'success' within the system. The denouement reinterprets the opening. The first scene of Yella's drowning shows the destructiveness of market values exemplified by Ben; in the replay, it is embodied by Yella. Having dreamed capitalist success to its culmination in a nightmare, Yella gives up the myth of upward and westward progress. Not attempting to straighten the wheel this time around, she willingly perishes in the river that divides the new Eastern German states from their Western counterparts just as surely as it had divided East from West before 1989. In post-unification Germany, this persistent border is just one of the many economic and geographic chasms that prove impassable for those subject to market logics.

See INTERIORITY

These two films disclose invisible borders that enforce exclusion and expose linear progress in neoliberalism as myth. Reading for these borders illuminates subtexts that anchor the more overt, individual narratives in broader socioeconomic contexts. In *Marseille*, Sophie is obviously a tourist whose visit from the northern capital Berlin to the southern metropolis Marseille expresses an elective affinity between these gritty European centers. The bond is underscored by the relationship that develops so easily between Sophie and Pierre. In *Yella*, geographic, economic, and libidinal borders are visible and appear passable. Yet, once she has entered the high-stakes world of venture capitalism, the protagonist moves in a soulless no-man's-land and eventually destroys Gunthen's oasis-like home there. The borders between Eastern and Western, between the have-nots and the haves, prove impassable. *Marseille* thematizes borders between European nations that are largely trivial for their citizens and borders around these countries that are largely impassable for noncitizens. *Yella* shows how intranationally existing borders hinder a nation's insiders and outsiders alike. Both films insist that variously concretized socioeconomic lines inexorably shape mobility and access both outside and inside Europe.

JH

Boredom

> interchangeable, depressing and boring, and driving people away from cinemas.
>
> —Oskar Roehler, describing Berlin School films[1]

> The whole time I was both excited and bored … always waiting for something.
>
> —Nina Weniger as Sophie in *Passing Summer*

'Boring' is a frequently used adjective in discussions of the Berlin School. In his much quoted 2008 interview, for example, Oskar Roehler uses the term as part of a comprehensive attack on the work of this group of directors. The fact that these films are ostensibly so tedious, however, is particularly worrying because they would also appear to be destroying the very fabric of German film culture by putting people off going to the cinema, their destructive potential ultimately troubling the very survival of the medium. Here Roehler can be understood as participating in a long running debate on the state of German national film culture, traceable in a variety of forms almost to the start of the medium's history, from the *Kinodebatte* ('Cinema Debate') of the 1910s through a whole host of manifestos (from Oberhausen in 1962 to Ludwigshafen in 2005) up to the producer Günter Rohrbach's 2007 attack on the state of film criticism in the German press. What sort of films should the nation support? Should the industry focus its energies on the spectacular potential of film as entertainment, looking to promote projects that can attract mass audiences and that can challenge, to whatever limited degree, the economic dominance of Hollywood? Or, should the industry nurture a more critical tradition that can probe the boundaries of film as a visual medium, a tradition that has long been the nation's international 'calling card' but which many mainstream consumers of film culture at home find either inaccessible or just plain dull? Throughout the discussion of the place of the Berlin School in contemporary German film culture the concept of boredom takes on a quasi-political dimension, being used as a proxy for a wider debate on the nature of German national film and in particular the type of film this state should fund from the public purse. Ironically, however, the politics of boredom, a subtext in so much of the Berlin School's reception, is in fact a key creative force in its production. These films, often described as, at best, slow paced, at worst turgid, often use the concept of boredom as a form of potential energy that actually drives not only the stories they seek to explore but also their aesthetic strategies and ultimately their politics.

The most obvious way in which a sense of boredom infuses the work of the Berlin School is on the level of plot. Again and again, many of the filmmakers under discussion highlight a malaise that appears to surround post-unification bourgeois society. In particular they often focus on the children of the 68ers—now the core of the ruling elite of this society—who, having lived their lives in the comfortable affluence their parents have always provided, are left with a profound sense of crisis as they struggle to find a role for themselves in society independent of this older generation. This is the world to be found in Ulrich Köhler's study of a young national service conscript who goes AWOL at his parents' holiday home, *Bungalow*, Christoph Hochhäusler's *I Am Guilty*, the story of a young man who resorts to falsely claiming responsibility for violent crimes as a way of escaping the tedium of the life mapped out for him by his parents, or the worldview of Maren Ade's young couple walking a tightrope between integration into the professional world of adult life and their need to find individual self-expression in *Everyone Else*. Throughout these films, boredom manifests itself as part of the bourgeois human condition, a contemporary interpretation of a tradition in Western art and philosophy that can be traced from Baudelaire and Schopenhauer to Heidegger, Sartre, and Fromm. In this particular manifestation, the fundamental affluence of the likes of Ade's protagonists leaves them with too much time for introspection, too much time to think about the nature and limitations of their relationships. Thus, the couple we meet in *Everyone Else*, for example, can simply wallow in an ultimately destructive and narcissistic space of mutual dependence. They have nothing better to do.

See DISENGAGEMENT

At times, the characters of these films seem to evoke the 'slacker' ethos made famous in the work of US independent filmmakers such as Richard Linklater and other representatives of the Western society's lost Generation X. The middle-class drifters of Linklater's 1991 film *Slacker*, as well as the walking and talking would-be lovers of his *Before Sunrise* (1995) and *Before Sunset* (2004) make a virtue of their directionless lives, transcending the apparently boring banality of their bourgeois existence in the elective affinities they find in the temporary communities created through the intellectual banter of their conversations. Such interaction allows them to reconfigure and find new value in their previous education and experience, redefining the geography of the spaces they inhabit as one of possibility rather than alienation. In many Berlin School films, however, we find the inverse of Linklater's world. The directionless protagonists that inhabit Maria Speth's *The Days Between*, Jan Krüger's *En route*, or Köhler's *Windows on Monday*, journey through their filmic worlds largely in silence, unable to communicate, and finding little or no solace in the community of others.

And yet the boredom that defines their experience also generates the desire that provides their lives with the only hope of finding direction. This is made explicit toward the end of Angela Schanelec's *Passing Summer*, a film particularly reminiscent of Linklater, but one that highlights some of the fundamental differences between the worldviews in their oeuvres. The film follows a number of interconnected characters over the course of a summer in Berlin as they negotiate the challenges of everyday life, from the difficulty of organizing child care to the existential crisis provoked by having to contemplate the mortality of one's parents. In a stripped down style that echoes through much of the Berlin School, the camera appears intent upon the documentary-like observation of life. However, the realism of the film is troubled by the stylized nature of the characters' conversations which would seem to transfigure the ostensibly realist mode of the camerawork into a deliberately aestheticized performance of reality. At the same time, this stylization also highlights the essential boredom that is at the heart of these characters' experience. The film is partially book-ended by an encounter with Sophie, a 20-something law student whom we first meet in conversation with a friend in a café, contemplating a six-month work placement in Rome, her tired musings punctuated by her grumbling at the arrogance of the waiter. This sequence is then reprised toward the end of the film. She returns to the café where she now ruminates on the experience of living in Rome with a stranger who shares her table [**Fig. 26**]. This was an ultimately unsatisfying period it would seem. She was bored and excited in equal measure, constantly waiting in vain for something to happen. And now she has returned to Berlin where the waiters continue to treat her with distain and where the quasi-philosophical aspirations of her conversation are finally revealed to be so much phatic noise, unable to rise above the level of cliché and only momentarily able to dispel her obvious boredom as she waits for a friend to join her, a friend we never see.

FIG. 26: *Passing Summer.*

Not just her experience of Rome, but Sophie's entire life is defined by the interplay of boredom and expectation. This, in turn, becomes the dynamic that defines the very experience of watching the film itself, once again an approach to filmmaking common to much of the Berlin School. It is, for example, the defining dynamic in the way Valeska Grisebach, Thomas Arslan, Benjamin Heisenberg, and in particular Christian Petzold engage with the tradition of genre filmmaking. 'I make films in the cemetery of genre cinema,' Petzold claims, 'from the remainders that are still there for the taking.'[2] This might involve adopting tropes from the vampire movie to reflect the status of West German urban terrorism as unresolved, 'undead' history within post-unification society in *The State I Am In*,[3] reworking Herk Harvey's horror film *Carnival of Souls* (1962) in *Yella*, a film that presents the grotesquely ephemeral mechanics of white-collar corporate capitalism[4], or reinterpreting James M. Cain's *The Postman Always Rings Twice* (1934) in *Jerichow*, adapted for cinema on numerous occasions, notable examples including *Ossessione* (1943) by Luchino Visconti and Tay Garnett's classic film noir *The Postman Always Rings Twice* (1946). The film adopts many of the key elements of Cain's novel, as well as aspects of its filmic adaptations. However, in Petzold's retelling, the story is stripped to its generic bones, challenging expectations of a film noir in order to reveal the social reality that lies beneath. In the process, Thomas and Laura, played by Benno Fürmann and Nina Hoss, become what Michael Sicinski calls 'place holders' for their respective functions in the noir narrative, without convincingly delivering the expectations such roles normally bring.[5]

See GHOSTS

Consequently, instead of being introduced as a destructively beautiful femme fatale who immediately entrances her future lover—epitomized by the introduction of Lana Turner in Garnett's film in a shot that slowly tracks up her body, fixing her as the knowingly desired object of the young man's gaze—Laura in Petzold's film is generally oblivious to Thomas's initial glances. The famous shot of Turner's toned legs contrasts starkly with the image of Hoss wiping the sweat from her armpits as Laura loads her husband's van with supplies for his snack bars. Here the film evokes the tired rendition of the genre's expectations one finds in Fassbinder's early gangster-noir cycle (*Liebe—kälter als der Tod/Love is Colder than Death*, 1969; *Götter der Pest/Gods of the Plague*, 1970; *Der amerikanischer Soldat/The American Soldier*, 1970), in which the characters simply go through the motions of their generic function. Both Petzold's and Fassbinder's slow pace of storytelling allows for prolonged periods of hollow time created through their characters' inaction. In Petzold's films, however, the characters are somehow less knowing, or perhaps simply more accepting, of their specific function within the narrative than in Fassbinder's. They have no choice but to give way to their reality of tedium and the lack of action in their lives, for all the potential of action and excitement offered by the genre's narrative expectations.

In the tired representation of inaction and the manner in which they seem to focus on hollow time, these films can also reveal a political potential. Central to this is their often self-conscious exploitation of affect. Indeed, the work of some Berlin School filmmakers might best be described as a crucible of affect, dwelling on, and thus foregrounding, the moment before, for example, the flicker of an impulse across a character's face can be resolved into emotional expression and ultimately action, thereby forcing the spectator to engage both emotionally and intellectually with the film in order to fill in the gap and provide this resolution themselves. This is particularly evident in the work of Schanelec. One sees this in the open-ended shots of her character's faces: in the prolonged blank gaze of Sophie at her off-screen conversation partner in *Passing Summer* discussed above, in the close-up of her namesake, played by Maren Eggert, in *Marseille* peering intensely along a street as she looks for a subject to photograph, or in the final close-up of her face which cuts away before she is entirely overwhelmed by her tears **[Fig. 27]**. In all these cases emotions slowly begin to erupt on to the women's faces. However, the film cuts before such emotions become completely clear, before they can be resolved into an 'event,' freezing them at a moment of profound inaction, when they might appear to be at their most 'boring,' but when their affective potential is at

FIG. 27: *Marseille*.

See THE CUT

its most extreme. This in turn points toward an underlying political project within Schanelec's films that challenges the limitations perceived by many of her female protagonists within the world they inhabit.

Remaining with *Marseille*, this can be seen most obviously in a photo-shoot sequence during which a series of women have their picture taken by the photographer Ivan, played by Devid Striesow. Each woman sits uncomfortably in the frame, staring at Ivan who takes their picture off-screen, at times trying to strike up conversation with the women, at times giving them instructions about how to fix their hair or how to hold their hands. The women subtly challenge Ivan's authority, refusing to speak to him or insisting that they remove their hair band for their picture. In so doing, the women gently rebel against the constraints imposed upon them by Ivan's gaze and the frame of his pictures, which define them specifically as factory workers **[Fig. 28]**.

See STRIESOW, DEVID

Consequently, unlike Ivan's implied still camera, Schanelec's moving camera captures their implicit rebellion and gestures to what else these women are, finally coming to rest on an image of a woman sitting behind the man, having a break from work. She slowly lifts her eyes, staring up at Ivan off-screen, Schanelec's camera refusing to constrain her gaze as she stares at the photographer, perhaps in trepidation, perhaps in irritation at his disturbing presence in the predominantly female space of the factory, perhaps she is just bored. It is never clear. However, her slowly changing gaze claims both the space and, crucially, the time that it inhabits, drawing in and implicating the spectator through its underlying ambiguity. Instead of fitting within Ivan's time and space, the shot of the woman's face

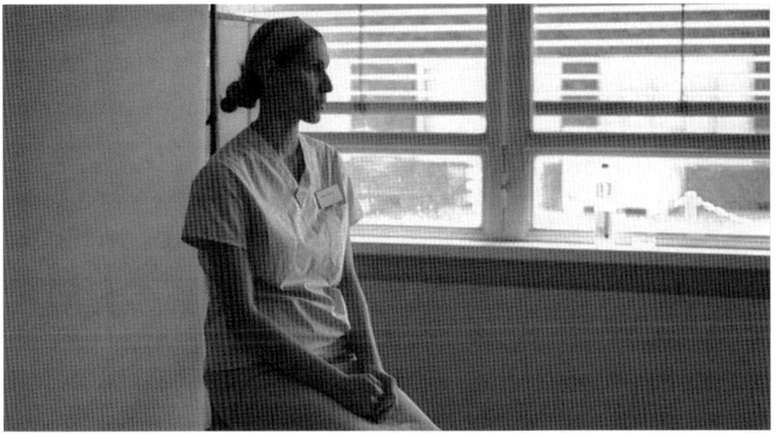

FIG. 28: *Marseille*.

reterritorializes both to make them its own. In the process, a shot that ostensibly focuses on a moment of passive inaction, a moment of tedium in this woman's life, captures the potential of resistance and thus change within the female subjects of the factory in general, elided in the controlled stillness of Ivan's photographs.

See FRAMINGS

An engagement with boredom is a key driver throughout films by Schanelec, Petzold, and other Berlin School directors. While they have often been dismissed as boring due to their rejection of mainstream narrative tropes, presenting the gaps between events rather than the events themselves, the self-conscious use of boredom at times provides them with a form of narrative energy, as the spectator is drawn into and forced to reflect upon the emotional world of the characters through their prolonged and deliberate exploitation of affect. Such films are never likely to have a mass mainstream audience. They do, however, speak to a growing tendency in international filmmaking. Beyond Linklater and Fassbinder, other names often cited in connection with the Berlin School are Robert Bresson, Michelangelo Antonioni, Michael Haneke, and the Dardenne brothers. To these could be added Abbas Kiarostami, Apichatpong Weerasethakul, Carlos Reygadas, and Béla Tarr. Consequently, rather than signaling the end of film as a medium, as Roehler would have it, such work, described variously as 'slow cinema' or 'the school of indirection and inconsequence,' points to the potential cinematic energy that can be realized through the visual contemplation of boredom as both film form and content.[6]

See ECLECTIC AFFINITIES

PC

Notes

1 See 'Grüße vom Nordpol,' *Parallelfilm: Notizbuch Christoph Hochhäusler*, February 17, 2008, http://parallelfilm.blogspot.co.uk/2008_02_01_archive.html.

2 See Marco Abel, 'The Cinema of Identification Gets on my Nerves: An Interview with Christian Petzold,' *Cineaste* 33.4 (2008), http://www.cineaste.com/articles/the-cinema-of-identification-gets-on-my-nerves-an-interview-with-christian-petzold.

3 On this see Chris Homewood, 'The Return of "Undead" History: The West German Terrorist as Vampire and the Problem of "Normalizing" the Past in Margarethe von Trotta's *Die bleierne Zeit* (1981) and Christian Petzold's *Die innere Sicherheit* (2001),' *German Culture, Politics, and Literature into the Twenty-First Century: Beyond Normalization*, eds Stuart Taberner and Paul Cooke (Rochester: Camden House, 2006), 121–35.

4 See Marco Abel, 'Imaging Germany: The (Political) Cinema of Christian Petzold,' *The Collapse of the Conventional German Film and Its Politics at the Turn of the Twenty-First Century*, eds Jaimey Fisher and Brad Prager (Detroit: Wayne State University Press), 258–84; here 266–69; and, Jaimey Fisher, 'German Autoren Dialogue with Hollywood? Refunctioning the Horror Genre in Christian Petzold's *Yella* (2007),' *New Directions in German Cinema*, eds Paul Cooke and Chris Homewood (London: I.B. Tauris, 2011), 182–99.

5 Michael Sicinski, 'Once the wall has tumbled: Christian Petzold's *Jerichow*,' *Cinema Scope* 38 (2009): 6–9; here 8.

6 See Jonathan Romney, 'In Search of Lost Time,' *Sight & Sound* 20.2 (February 2010): 43–4; and Nick James, 'New Crowned Despair,' *Sight & Sound* 18.2 (February 2008): 5.

Cars . . .

. . . have played a crucial role in the development of both narrative cinema and modern capitalism's vision of social mobility. Long before Alfred Hitchcock celebrated the car chase as one of the essential ingredients of twentieth-century filmmaking, automobiles had already helped mobilize the camera, unfetter its perspective from the stasis of the tripod, and bring accelerated motion to the art of motion pictures. In classical Hollywood cinema, cars warranted joyful mobility amid social stagnation as much as they offered shelter, intimacy, and romance in the midst of inhospitable landscapes and gritty metropolitan environments. Similar to how industrial capitalism could not be thought without the manufacturing of ever-new car products at a mass level, so did classical Hollywood filmmaking regularly picture cars as symbolic stand ins for the kind of values and ideologies energizing the capitalist economy: unbridled individualism, goal-oriented entrepreneurship, ceaseless mobility, future-oriented speed. While direct associations of car travel, narrative teleology, and capitalist agility may have become problematic, postclassical cinema has not ceased to assign special privileges to the screen image of the automobile. Cars continue to do and allegorize what both narrative cinema and capitalist mobility are all about, namely not simply to set images and commodities in motion, but, in so doing, to capture the viewer's attention, activate affect, stir our desire for consumption, and cause us to inject the visible with the pathos of mobilized space and spatialized time. Critical filmmakers, on the other hand, routinely turn to the figure of the car in order to develop alternative pleasures, question the ideological association of movement, speed, and capitalism, and probe the framing power of the cinematic dream screen. Even cinematic iconoclasts can rarely resist the temptation to invite viewers to car rides whenever they want to show off their break with cinematic conventions, Jean-Luc Godard here being perhaps the most famous precedent when displaying the disruptive power of jump cuts while having his protagonists drive through hectic Paris traffic (in *À bout de souffle/Breathless* [1960]) or when tracking the mise-en-scène of a gigantic car crash so as to capture the violent underbelly of bourgeois life (in *Week End* [1967]).

The films of the Berlin School are certainly not known for fast-action footage, nervous editing maneuvers, or strategies of hyper self-reflexivity jarring viewers out of their seats. On the contrary, what seems to unify the disparate films of the latest wave of German cinema is their unobtrusive camera work, a pondering aesthetic of long takes rigorously exploring what often turns out to be the absence of rigor, of forward movement and transformative energy in the lives of these films' antiheroes. Images of brooding walkers, of pensive and hesitant pedestrians, their uncertain moves mimicked by the motion of a handheld camera, might at first suit the itineraries of the Berlin School's films much better than an automobile's speed and forward drive. And yet, it does not take much to notice that cars—their iconographic presence, their interior spaces, their movements across diverse urban and rural landscapes—play an important role in many Berlin School films, and that automobiles here once again invite viewers to reflect on the relays between physical motion and narrative development, speed and capitalist circulation, individual mobility and the work of cinematic projection and identification. In line with both mainstream and avant-garde expectations, cars here may often index dormant desires for unfettered movement and individual transformation, for breaking out of the mold of given spaces and social positions, for questioning conventional regimes of representation. In stark contrast to former uses of cars on screen, however, Berlin School automobilism has little patience for successful narratives of progress and change, of individual autonomy and forward movement. Berlin School drivers, instead, use their cars as if automakers had finally equipped their products with reliable autopilot systems. Far from offering spaces of transformative motion and indeterminism, the vehicles of the Berlin School films define automobility as the order of a world in which capital reigns triumphant, yet our anticipation of the future no longer has the power to relieve the burdens of the present and the past. Cars here appear to drive their drivers rather than being driven by goal-oriented motorists. While cars move in circles or transgress nameless and seemingly identical landscapes, drivers steer effortlessly, with blank stares and little attention to what lies ahead of their windshields. Speed is no longer felt as a dynamic displacing the body from given locations and expectations. It simply replays the future in the image of the past. No one is going anywhere in spite of all the movements by which cars crisscross faceless peripheries or frantic urban centers. Motion and standstill fold into each other, similar to the way in which freeze-frames halt cinematic temporality and create something uncanny in between the filmic and the photographic within the

See LONG TAKES

cinematic medium itself. In the Berlin School films' bleak account of the present, to consider a car's interior as a space of meaningful intimacy or even romance appears preposterous: automobility not only erases former boundaries between the public and the private, it is symptomatic of an age which knows emotions solely as functions and effects of advanced media industries and the marketplace's strategic rationality. Largely void of what energized the drivers of both mainstream narrative and many avant-garde films of the past, Berlin School automotorists will not even experience a crash as something that might hurl them into an unexpected direction or discontinuous future. See VIOLENCE

Consider, first, what can be understood as the signature shot of Christian Petzold's 'Ghost-trilogy,' namely those extended close-ups of car drivers shown either from the vehicle's rear or its passenger seat, the camera absolutely static, its subject gazing forward, traffic and landscape passing by, left and right, while no meaningful acts of communication really add much to our understanding of these protagonists' thoughts, visions, memories, or anxieties. Frequently used in particular in *Ghosts*, Petzold's See LANGUAGE prolonged back- and side-seat shots no doubt challenge dominant cinematic expectations as the camera avoids privileging anyone's gaze, frustrates any spectatorial desire for visual reciprocity, and, in so doing, sidesteps how narrative cinema tends to create empathy and identification by organizing its material along a teleological trajectory. The opening minutes of *Ghosts* offer us such a shot for the first time as we witness a yet unidentified man (Pierre) maneuvering his BMW through Berlin's inner city traffic **[Fig. 29]**.

FIG. 29: *Ghosts.*

We hear classical music in the background whose enveloping qualities will shortly be interrupted by the female voice of the car's GPS system reminding Pierre to make a left turn at the next possible opportunity. Later we will learn that Pierre is on his way to pick up his wife, Françoise, from a mental institution, once more temporarily hospitalized because she harassed a female teenager in desperate search for her abducted baby girl, once more haunted by a past whose ghostly presence Françoise is unable to master. But in these opening minutes of the film, the spectator knows none of this. Our eyes rest on Pierre's profile and the blurry shapes of other cars—parked in the middle of the road—as seen through the driver's side window **[Fig. 30]**. No longer seeing the road in front of us, it is difficult not to experience a certain disorientation and claustrophobia in spite of the car's fluid motion, this sense of spatial abstraction only amplified by the GPS's disembodied voice, whose directions are, of course, of no use for eyes not afforded the privilege of a forward perspective. While quite close to the car's driver and allowing him to chauffeur us into the film, we have no idea what to look for, what to read into his face, what to do with our proximity to Pierre and how to map out his path through contemporary Berlin streets. Nothing would therefore be more mistaken than to see close-ups such as this one, scenes of spatial proximity, as allegories of or invitations to spectatorial feelings of intimacy or unproblematic empathy. The world, even at close physical range, can be full of strangeness; it is an uncanny place, hard and perhaps impossible to inhabit and navigate, seemingly in full motion and yet strangely arrested, abundant with existing

See GHOSTS

FIG. 30: *Ghosts.*

avenues and yet in need of our technological superegos to make us find and move along even our most basic pathways.

Consider, second, the opening sequence of Christoph Hochhäusler's *This Very Moment*, in which we meet siblings Lea and Konstantin as they walk along a thoroughly empty highway toward the camera, an ominous soundtrack infusing the image with foreboding horror. 'Come on, now,' Lea commands her brother authoritatively when he stops to tie his laces. When Lea nears the frame of the image, we discern a silver car approaching both kids from behind, coming to a full stop at precisely the moment when Lea has exited the visual field **[Fig. 31]**. As it turns out, the vehicle is steered by the children's stepmother whose belated arrival is greeted with less than enthusiasm, particularly by Lea. Once everybody is in the car, the camera lingers first on Lea's ostensibly annoyed facial expressions, then on Konstantin fiddling with his watch, before finally cutting to a central rear-seat view straight through the windshield, with Sylvia in the driver's position visible on the left, and Lea's punishing voice audible from off-screen: 'I thought you'd pick us up from school.' The ensuing ride through unwelcoming Eastern German and Polish countrysides will turn into a trip refuting any expectation and transforming the interior of the car into a site of torment and agony. Lea challenges Sylvia to the brink of psychic disintegration, questions her role as a guardian, even mocks and physically provokes her. So much so that Sylvia, finally losing her patience, ejects her two passengers in the middle of nowhere. Though an unmistakable sign of bourgeois comfort and mobility, Sylvia's car here emerges as a vehicle

See SIBLINGS

FIG. 31: *This Very Moment*.

of generational reversal, revenge and—in fact—pure evil: an oppressive container exposing the individual to the unrestrained menace of children who punish their parents for the very things they considered their greatest accomplishments, namely social and geographical mobility, parental companionship rather than authority, tolerance and openness instead of conservative close-mindedness. While Sylvia's car might traverse landscapes with abundant signs of reconstruction and modernization, automobilism here facilitates a troubling turnover of temporal relations, a denial of futurity, of forward motion, triggered by the very generation whose age is conventionally associated with society's path into the future. Cars here penalize rather than enable people's quest or need for mobility and progress. Modern culture's latest version of a medieval torture chamber, they define the posttraditional family as one of violent contempt and irreconcilable expectations. Nothing could be more naïve than to think that, in this world, steering a car's wheel would endow you with a certain sense of control or even freedom. Automobilism, instead, defines the present as a permanent state of exception: hell on earth, forever repeating repressions of the past in monstrous forms and altered shapes.

Consider, third, the final sequence of Ulrich Köhler's *Windows on Monday*, a film tracking the strained relationship between Nina and her husband Frieder as they are trying to renovate their home, yet fail to maintain healthy mutual bonds and—without really knowing why—drive each other into ever more pronounced isolation. In the film's final few minutes, we follow the estranged couple in their VW van to a funeral of a neighbor's child, attended by nearly the entire village. However, instead of participating in the ceremony, Nina and Frieder drive by the cemetery and, in a hapless attempt at reconciliation, try to make love in the rear of the van while funeral music is initially playing far in the background **[see Fig. 12—BAD SEX].** The landscape outside is dreary. In the distance, framed by the van's dirty rear window, we see cars passing along a rural freeway—signs of motion and liveliness that do not extend to what will ensue within the car. For not much to the viewer's surprise, lust quickly turns into frustration, with both protagonists simulating what it might mean to desire each other rather than following the dictates of their bodies, and Frieder in fact quite visibly unable to
See BAD SEX
uphold his erection. The final shot shows the faces of both protagonists, their bodies exasperated without having reached any climax, their gazes unable to meet, their lives and aspirations as dead as the landscape outside, fatal stillness having crushed any hope for true meaning and change. Far from liberating both protagonists from their pasts and presents, the van here takes on the

function of a grave, a site of speechless despair and ineptness. Romance and intimacy are not of this world, not even as a promise. The realm of privacy is a black hole, yet no form of mobility will ever lead you anywhere anymore. Emotions are a thing of the past; like cars, they no longer hold any promise to carry us beyond ourselves, to transgress the dreary orders of the day, to suspend the dull repetition of the always same.

See BOREDOM

As these three examples indicate, Berlin School films no longer seek to triangulate the presence of cars with teleological forms of narrative and capitalist visions of social mobility, not simply in order to play out one against the other, but to suspend the ideological ground to which all three are deeply indebted: goal-oriented individualism, progressive temporality, and emotive subjectivity as a funnel of individual meaning and pleasurable consumption. Cars here neither channel transformative energies and progressive stories of change, nor do they endow their users with what it might take to author one's own life, to capitalize on their instrumental rationality or to find some sense of fulfillment in situations of emotional reciprocity. In the bleak world of the Berlin School, cars instead iterate and, in so doing, reveal the hidden truth of boundless capitalism and narrative cinema, namely their secret or not-so-secret denial of contingency, of indetermination, of surprise, and of the incommensurable. Not even the event of a car crash, amid this world, succeeds in cracking open the vessels of frozen time and derailing the dull automatisms of the day. On the contrary, as staged perhaps most dramatically in Petzold's *Yella* **[Fig. 32]**, Berlin School crashes draw the viewer into fatal narrative traps, mise en

FIG. 32: *Yella*.

abymes of representation and storytelling in whose contexts any weak hope for escaping today's devaluation of lived experience becomes unattainable. Car crashes here confirm and reinforce, rather than disrupt, what guides the lives of most Berlin School protagonists: the logic of the loop. That everything could be different as it might seem, and yet that, in the end, nothing will ever really make any difference at all—this is one of the most devastating insights we might glean from the Berlin School's vision of the present as an age of agitated, albeit meaningless, automobility.

LK

The Cut

Editing decisions can determine a film's style on two levels, corresponding to two meanings of the French term *découpage* (literally: cutting up, splicing): on the one hand, this concept refers to the global level of the film—the shooting script (if one was used), or at any rate the film's overall organization, the arrangement of its various segments, whether these are defined in terms of narrative, theme, or other aesthetic criteria. On the other hand, the term describes the shot breakdown of an individual scene or action: the act of planning and constructing specific sequences out of spatial and temporal fragments.[1] The degree zero of *découpage* in this latter sense would consist of the *plan séquence*, the long take that constitutes the unity of a sequence without editing. Although some such shots do occur in the films of the Berlin School, contributing to the overall impression of slowness, the use of editing to compose a given sequence is far more common in these (and other) films. See LONG TAKES

The German term for this procedure is *Auflösung* (literally: dissolution), a notion that ties the constructive, compositional act of editing to a prior decomposition. Piecing together the logic of a scene through editing, then, is essentially a question of *recomposing* it from fragments. Classical cinema treats this process analytically, which is to say: it analyzes the fragments with a view toward an overall goal (which is usually defined in Aristotelian terms of narrative coherence, the unity of time and space), and then synthesizes them into a unified sequence. Obeying the norms of continuity editing, this approach builds a continuous, recognizable sense of space from a calculated arrangement of long, establishing shots and progressively closer shots punctuated by occasional 're-establishing' shots that provide guidance to the viewer.

By and large, the Berlin School films adopt this approach to *Auflösung*, or scene construction: with the exception of some experimental shorts (Schanelec's and Hochhäusler's contributions to *Germany 09: 13 Short Films About the State of the Nation*, for example), few of these films are avant-garde works of art that advocate a radical break from convention.

But they do offer significant modifications that, in the case of Angela Schanelec for instance, gesture toward the undoing—or *Auflösung*—of *Auflösung*, that is, the dissolution of *découpage*. This is not only a question of the long takes which, given the average feature length of these films, inevitably also means fewer cuts (Schanelec's feature length films tend to have no more than 70–100 shots); it is also a question of how to *arrange* the flow of images within the scene and from one scene to the next.

In a studied—some would say: mannered—departure from classical editing, Schanelec does not repeat shots from the same camera set-up. (Indeed, some of her immediate 'colleagues' in the Berlin School find it 'curious that Angela refuses' to play by conventions such as shot/reverse shot.[2]) To the degree that her films offer 'establishing shots,' she does not come back to these to re-establish a space for the viewer, nor does she interpret the action through different shot scales—long, medium, or close-up—from the same camera position. The Hollywood mode of production shoots for 'coverage,' repeating takes from various angles and positions to provide the editor with options. Schanelec and her team, by contrast, limit the editor's options during shooting: they tend to maintain the same camera position for repeated takes and never overlap the end of one shot with the beginning of another in a way that would provide the editor with a choice of where to make the cut. There is, as the editors of *Revolver* suggest in an interview with Schanelec and her cinematographer Reinhold Vorschneider, no safety net.[3]

This is not to say that there is no shot breakdown in individual scenes; but in films like Schanelec's *Passing Summer*, that breakdown is resolutely linear, unfolding in a planar geometry. In one shot, we may see a couple speaking on a balcony in the background with the camera positioned inside an apartment, and in the next, we will see them in close-up from the side, the camera taking up a position on the balcony at a precise right angle to its original axis **[Fig. 33]**. But this constitutes the only cut in the scene: neither will any of the conversation be rendered in the classical cinematic idiom of shot/reverse shot, nor will the camera resume its position inside the apartment when the characters leave the balcony and go out for dinner. As the action continues off-screen (a space that carries equal weight, in Schanelec's films, as the space contained within the frame), the camera will linger, immobile, as if to underscore the absence of the cut.

Such decisions about camera placement, framing, and *découpage* at the level of individual scenes affect the overall flow of films like *Passing*

FIG. 33: *Passing Summer.*

Summer, whose German title, *Mein langsames Leben*—literally, 'my slow life'—could be taken as programmatic for the Berlin School. In Schanelec's films, this slowness derives from a manifest interest in still photography (thematized explicitly in films like *Marseille* and *Orly*), which has led critics to compare the experience of watching her films to that of leafing through a photo album or contemplating pictures at an exhibition. But what these comparisons discount is the temporal dimension of film: its power, as a time-based medium, to structure the flow of time and direct the viewing experience. This is why Schanelec refuses the notion, suggested by critics, that her films consist of 'tableaux,'[4] for this might imply a failure to relate the images to one another—whether as a linear sequence, as the film inevitably does in its very unwinding, or as some more complex temporal structure in the spectator's aesthetic experience. See SEEING AND SAYING

By the same token, we should not confuse the 'discovery of slowness' that has been attributed to Schanelec and Arslan in particular, with an absence of temporal structuring. Rather, that impression is clearly the result of careful editing choices which include not only 'lengthening' devices such as the long take or the static camera, that is, decisions to delay the cut to a following scene; they also include the deliberate use of ellipses, the creation of 'dramaturgical black holes,' as one critic put it[5]: after watching an action unfold in one scene, perhaps even lingering on the scene after the action has concluded, the viewer can suddenly be transported, by way of a straight cut, to the next locale and across an intervening time span of minutes, days, or even months (which of these it is can often only be determined retroactively by the viewer). In other words: while the *Auflösung* of individual scenes can accentuate slowness and make it palpable as an aesthetic experience, the *découpage* of the film as a whole, the joining of scenes and sequences, can suddenly accelerate the narrative in completely unexpected ways. Together, these strategies make up what Noël Burch has described as the 'dialectical notion inherent in the term *découpage*.'[6]

JvM

Notes

1 See Noel Burch, *Theory of Film Practice*, trans. Helen R. Lane (New York: Praeger, 1973), 3–4.
2 See *Revolver: Kino muss gefährlich sein*, ed. Marcus Seibert (Frankfurt a.M.: Verlag der Autoren, 2006), 24.
3 '[K]eine Sicherheiten in der Auflösung.' See *Revolver*, 411.
4 See *Revolver*, 413.
5 See Birgit Glombitza, 'Dem Leben abgeschaut,' *Die Zeit* 40, September 23, 2004, http://www.zeit.de/2004/40/Angela_Schanelec.
6 See Burch, *Theory of Film Practice*, 4.

Disengagement

Several Berlin School films feature protagonists who are haplessly struggling to carve out a place for themselves in a contemporary Germany that provides material abundance but fails to produce an environment favorable for cultural and psychological well-being. The central figures in *Marseille*, *I Am Guilty*, and *Bungalow* are at stages of their lives when they should be establishing their independence and embarking on a career. However, they are all drifting with no sense of direction and seem to have little interest in searching for any. Irene in *Hotel* and Melanie in *The Forest for the Trees* have each assumed a first position in what they expect to be a career path, only to find themselves isolated among cold, uncaring fellow workers and stuck in lives devoid of meaningful emotional relationships. Both films end with mysterious, supernatural events that suggest that their protagonists have come to accept the emptiness around them, but that offer no indication of what might become of their lives. They prefer rather to remain disengaged from the social order they inhabit and the life paths it offers.

This unwillingness of the protagonists to construct solidly grounded lives for themselves affords one of the Berlin School's few affinities with New German Cinema. In particular, it calls to mind the title character of Rainer Werner Fassbinder's *Die Ehe der Maria Braun/The Marriage of Maria Braun* (1979). After her husband is sentenced to prison for the murder of an American serviceman, Maria works obsessively during Germany's reconstruction to build a future life for Hermann and herself upon his release. The decision to defer her 'marriage' while she works to secure a house and financial base for it represents allegorically the Federal Republic's path to recovery after World War II. Her cold, mechanical pursuit of financial success as the basis for future fulfillment and happiness mirrors the way West Germans engrossed themselves in the rebuilding of their economy as a way of avoiding emotional entanglement with the past. In *This Very Moment*, the allegorical function of the house and marriage with respect to German unification echoes that of Maria Braun's marriage.

See PREDECESSORS

In this case, Sylvia's (the East's) integration into the new family (the unified Federal Republic) has already occurred, but the long-awaited happiness has proven to be illusory. The new wife from the East cannot assume her expected role as mother of the stepchildren who were born and bred in an alien sociocultural world.

Yella also deals with the inability of Eastern Germans to assimilate to the Western-dominated way of life in unified Germany in a way that recalls *The Marriage of Maria Braun*. The dramatic core of the film story turns out to be Yella's imagined vision of what her life in the West would be were she to take the job in Hanover and succeed in the high-stakes world of finance capitalism. At the critical juncture where she must decide whether or not to pursue happiness via a career in finance, an entire scenario of where that path might lead plays out in her mind. Her vision of the corruption and destruction that could ensue if she were to become financially successful causes her to accept her fate at the hands of her maniacal former East German partner and husband/lover, rather than cross the Elbe River (the former border between East and West Germany) and take the job in the
See BORDERS
Western business world. In a similar vein, Maria Braun becomes a successful businesswoman and secures the material foundation she had worked for, only to have all of it to go up in smoke when Hermann returns.

In their allegorical reference to the East–West divide that remains in the unified Federal Republic, *This Very Moment* and *Yella* present a more tightly, thematically constructed narrative than one typically finds from Berlin School filmmakers. Their films tend to avoid allusions to national history or identity in particular. Perhaps the true Berlin School equivalent to the explosion that ends Maria Braun's marriage occurs in *Bungalow*. Shortly after arriving at his family's bungalow-style house while AWOL from the German military, Paul walks into his father's home office and causally looks around at the architectural drawings posted around the room. He then strolls over to the drafting board, quickly surveys the drawing of a postmodern-style public building, lifts the rule from the board, repositions it over the sketch and draws a straight line through the middle of it **[Fig. 34]**. With this one stroke, he registers his rejection of the idea that modern architecture and the construction industry can design and build an environment that will lead to meaningful human existence. This one isolated gesture serves well as the signature mark of the Berlin School's resistance to the belief that the technological and organizational expertise that comes with economic growth is the key to building a better world and a richer life in the Federal Republic.

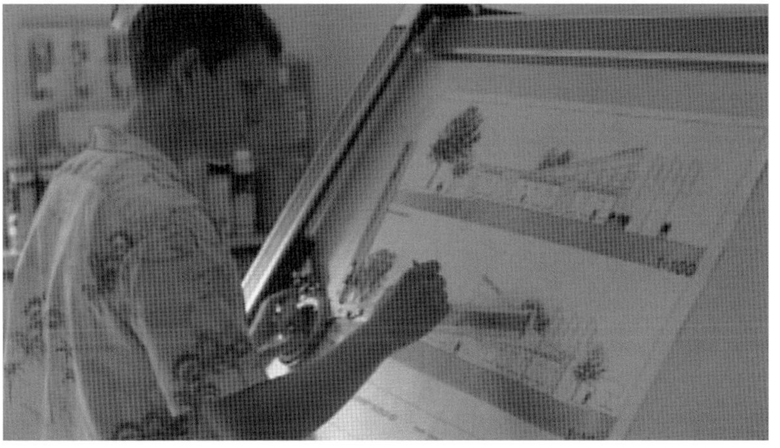

FIG. 34: *Bungalow.*

The protagonists of the Berlin School wander through contemporary Germany as if it offered a limited set of predetermined choices, all of which lead nowhere. Unmoved by the neoliberal belief that Western capitalist democracies have fulfilled their promise, they simply do not take part in the new Germany, much as Nina had refused to join Frieder in renovating their family house in *Windows on Monday*. Rather than an active resistance to a political or economic system, their refusal is the contemporary German variant of Herman Melville's mid-nineteenth-century American office worker Bartleby, who explained his lack of participation with the simple 'I would prefer not to.'[1] If Paul's stroke through the design on the drawing board of the new Germany marks these protagonists' strident rejection of the options it offers, then the ending of *The Forest for the Trees* displays the kind of alternative they find in the passive resistance practiced by Melville's Bartelby. A closer look at the film's final sequence will serve to bring this choice into focus and also suggest how it relates to the cinematic strategies of the Berlin School.

See RENOVATION

Thwarted at every turn in her attempt to adjust to her new life, Melanie falls into despair and takes her car for an aimless drive through the countryside. The camera situates the viewer in the passenger seat, observing Melanie who breaks down crying as trees pass by in a blur. After she slowly collects herself, she takes her hands from the steering wheel and lays them in her lap while the car continues moving at the same speed. Within a few seconds the viewer begins to expect a violent

See CARS

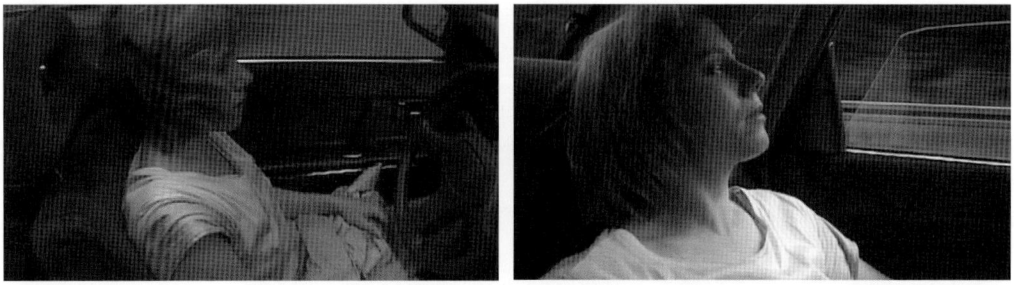

FIG. 35: *The Forest for the Trees.*

See VIOLENCE

and fatal crash. The car, however, remains under control and on the same course as the scene goes on in this manner for almost two more minutes. Melanie unfastens her seat belt, calmly takes off her jacket and begins to observe the trees streaming past. She then climbs into the backseat and looks out the window, clearly more relaxed and engaged in the present than she had been throughout the entire film **[Fig. 35]**. The liberation Melanie experiences in this final scene releases her from the futile struggle she has been waging to forge a new life in an incompatible environment. As she finds a sense of ease in the back seat of the car, she is simply asserting that she would prefer not to assume the role in society that has been laid out for her. The imaginary option of letting the car continue of its own accord signals that she is ready to become the next in the line of Berlin School protagonists who are content to drift aimlessly, avoiding the choices offered by the new Germany.

This is however not merely, or even primarily, a change in course made by the protagonist in a film story. The film itself takes a sharp turn away from the representationalism of mainstream narrative toward a cinematic form more in keeping with the Berlin School. The film's director, Maren Ade, has said that she wanted to break from the realism of the film and was in fact surprised that many viewers at first interpreted the scene as a suicide attempt. However, for the viewer who has accompanied Melanie throughout the movie and probably felt empathy for her growing dejection, this would be a likely response. Only when the gradual shift to something akin to magical realism takes hold does the concern for Melanie give way, permitting a new mode of participation. If the first response is an anxious feeling that she is trying to kill herself, then, as the car continues under its own agency, a primary or physical engagement with the image takes precedence over a secondary identification with the characters or plot. The

See INTERIORITY

narrative overcoding of the scene according to story and character recedes, and the viewer experiences more freely the kinesthetic effects of this strange ride. The absence of control over the moving vehicle accentuates this physical response, first with respect to the fate of the film character, but then, more acutely, with respect to the viewer's own body.

This shift in narrative perspective at the end of the film brings Ade more closely in alignment with Berlin School directors who practice a Bartelby-like noncompliance in the realm of cinema. The affect stirred in the final scene is associated with Melanie's urge to escape her stifling situation at her new job in a strange city. It also touches an underlying disposition that has built up against the confines of the narrative construct that has conveyed her discontent. The final scene produces bodily participation in the onscreen movement in a way that breaks from the patterns prefigured by representational realism. This mode of departing from narrative cinema mirrors the way Berlin School films stage their protagonists' disengagement from life in the Federal Republic. Just as the filmmakers do not enlist the disaffection and alienation of their characters to mount a political or social attack on the forces shaping their lives, they also do not express their resistance to mainstream filmmaking in a blatantly contrastive style. Like their protagonists, they register their resistance by noncompliance in the world within which they move and work. Their films ignore the industry standard of a mainstream cinema that has created the expectation of dramatic life stories and now thrives on the demand for them. Just as their protagonists drift apathetically through an industrious modern world that demands constant and intense participation, their films stand as strange nonparticipants in the midst of a film industry that produces elaborately constructed narratives at a feverish pace.

RFC

Note

1 Marco Abel, 'Intensifying Life: The Cinema of the Berlin School,' *Cineaste* 33.4 (Fall 2008), http://www.cineaste.com/articles/the-berlin-school.htm.

Dorfdiskos

Discotheques arguably encapsulate certain basic features of the filmic medium itself. Two cases in point: discos have tremendous narrative potential, frequently serving as primal theaters for dramas of individual self-expression and personal connection or conflict; and as with cinema auteurs, nightclubs often make names for themselves through innovative sound and light design. The suggestion that the disco shares a likeness with cinema bears itself out in Berlin School films, which are often taken with the setting of the dance floor. But though these films explore the disco as a relative of the cinematic stage or set—as a dark room that relies on displays of light and sound, one that displays bodies and their movements for all to see—the Berlin School repeatedly lingers with local *Dorfdiskos* that are altogether behind the times. Setting action in unhip provincial nightclubs helps these films denaturalize the disco as a place of conventional dramatic intensity or flashy performance, instead depicting characters who find themselves (either wittingly or not) in underwhelming, uncomfortable environs. Out-of-the-way *Dorfdiskos* become stages for alternative forms of bodily movement, awkward miscommunication, and complex or conflicted emotions.

In general, Berlin School directors deploy few of the set pieces of commercial television, video, and film, deliberately defining themselves in opposition to mainstream global media industries.[1] In the case of nightlife scenes, these films do not depict beautiful people in ecstatic states of conspicuous consumption familiar from music videos and advertisements, nor do they present the viewer with tightly choreographed ensemble dance pieces or melodramatic images of bodies in close proximity. It is much more common for these films to treat provincial discos as places to which grown-up characters return with nostalgia, mourning, or discomfort. This recollective stance is suggested by repeated references to the 1980s that call to mind the era's outdated music and tacky dance moves. It is not accidental that the 1980s are a repeated point of reference, for many Berlin School directors came of age in this era. Part of the awkwardness of the *Dorfdisko* is its visual and auditory (i.e., musical) anachronism; for the Berlin School this anachronism is productive because it encourages a different kind of viewer attention that is attuned both to unusual or undramatic interpersonal relationships and to the strangeness of out-of-the-way locales.

Angela Schanelec's *Passing Summer* engages with these issues in perhaps the most compelling and sophisticated manner. The film's main character Valerie has left Berlin to visit her dying father in southern Germany. After attending to her father's affairs during the day, she, her brother, and a female acquaintance go to a quiet local disco. Valerie asks her brother to dance with her and he demurs, noting that no one is dancing. But she finds one person on the dance floor, occasioning all three to look; rather than showing the dancer him or herself, the camera simply shows the three watching **[Fig. 36]**. Gazing at this solitary figure leads to a personal moment between the siblings, as the brother mentions his memory of Valerie dancing in her youth like Jennifer Beals from the 1983 hit film *Flashdance*. After Valerie's mildly embarrassed assurance that she no longer takes up the entire floor with the 1980s-era abandon, the film then segueways into a long take of the two dancing together. The camera views the dance floor from the perspective of the friend at the bar, a line of sight that the previous shot of all three figures implied. We watch Valerie and her brother and their considerably different dancing styles: Valerie is all arms, while her brother, played by Devid Striesow, is more of a shoulder

See SIBLINGS

See LONG TAKES

See STRIESOW, DEVID

Fig.36: *Passing Summer*.

Fig.37: *Passing Summer.*

gyrator. This dance scene obliquely suggests an atmosphere of mourning, as brother and sister seem to bond by dancing together to guitar-driven rock music.

But along with suggesting that dance serves as an outlet for expressing personal loss, this scene encourages reflection on the activity of viewing itself. We watch these figures as they watch a dancer, and then we take in their own dancing. The fact that the camera remains static as Valerie and her brother twist in and out of the frame draws our attention to the frame as much as to the characters' actions themselves **[Fig. 37]**. We are aware of the existence of the broader *Dorfdisko* but we also know that parts of it are cut off by the camera frame. The camera returns later to the female friend at the bar, focalizing the camera's gaze through her line of sight and, by extension, through another person watching the dance floor located in the blurry background behind the dancing siblings. Both of these onlookers stand in for the unmoving camera, which seems to be situated in the *Dorfdisko* but not on the dance floor itself. This parallels an earlier scene in the film where a young girl asks her babysitter to entertain her by dancing to the Schubert song 'Der Erlkönig' (1815). Protesting that this nineteenth-century *Lied* is not really danceable, the babysitter nonetheless accedes to the girl's request, but we only see the child as she watches **[see Fig. 60—FRAMINGS]**. As in the *Dorfdisko*, the camera is more interested in the act of viewing than in the curious task of translating Schubert into a twenty-first-century dance idiom.

Barbara Albert's *Falling* takes up the *Dorfdisko* setting in a more conventional manner, telling the story of five 30-something girlfriends

Fig. 38: *Falling.*

who return to their hometown in the Austrian countryside and spend a wild night of partying, reminiscing, and reconnecting (the film was shot in the town of Horn, about 100 kilometers northwest of Vienna). These women attended secondary school together and grew apart in intervening years, and their reunion is occasioned by the funeral of a favorite teacher. Similarly to *Passing Summer*, *Falling* explores emotions of loss, mourning, and reminiscing through scenes of dancing. The film follows the group as they visit important places from their past; at one point, they crash the wedding reception of one of the women's ex-boyfriends. Held in a garish outdoor tent, this reception is not without tacky group dances, including a rowing dance done to the 1970 *Schlager*-music hit 'Er hat ein knallrotes Gummiboot' ('He has a candy-red rubber boat') **[Fig. 38].**

The group then decides to go to an old teenage haunt, the club 'das Brooklyn,' wedding party in tow. With ever more alcohol, the group's carnivalesque abandon reaches new levels, layering ecstatic highs and embarrassing physical and emotional lows. At one point Ursula Strauss's character Alex even performs a pseudo-striptease that she quickly regrets, partnering with the bride in removing her shirt and bra to the beat of electronic house music, as the wedding party and other patrons of 'Das Brooklyn' goad them on. But along with serving as a stage for drunken chaos, the *Dorfdisko* also enables sober reflection, as Birgit Minichmayr's character Brigitte dances alone and mourns the deceased teacher with whom she had had an ongoing relationship, accompanied by pensive guitar and piano-driven music **[Fig. 39]**. In both cases, the camera is positioned closer to

Fig. 39: *Falling.*

the dancers than in *Passing Summer*, more on the dance floor amidst the dancers than at a static position of remove; this situates the viewer closer (both literally and figuratively) to the characters and to their tumultuous emotional states. The scenes in this *Dorfdisko* move between a full dance floor and a relatively empty one, between collective chaos and individual reflection, between passé house music and more contemplative pop songs. Dance—whether at the wedding reception, 'das Brooklyn,' a campfire, or in front of a truck stop Burger King—serves as a central metaphor of the film, signifying release, letting go, 'falling' (to quote the title), an experience, that is to say, that lets these figures momentarily break free from the constraints of the everyday and come to terms with their pasts.

While *Falling* and *Passing Summer* use provincial nightclubs to explore relationships between both siblings and friends, other Berlin School films treat the *Dorfdisko* as a theater of anxious sexual desire. In Jessica Hausner's *Hotel*, the main character Irene goes to a local disco in the unspecified Austrian vacation town where she works. The young people there—likely a mixture of locals and workers from nearby resorts—dance to house music amidst forest kitsch such as hunting trophies, animal skins, and wagon wheels **[Fig. 40]**. As in *Passing Summer*, this disco scene employs long takes and a relatively static camera. The camera is positioned in the middle of the dance floor, as dancers move in and out of the frame. Coordinated with a switch in music (from house music to a guitar-heavy pop song), the camera turns from watching Irene's friend/rival—also played by Birgit Minichmayr—to Irene and a young man with whom she exchanges tentative

Fig. 40: *Hotel.*

glances. Clearly focusing on Irene and her apprehensive romantic forays, the camera nonetheless seems taken in as much with the strangeness of the setting as with character actions. A later scene returns to this unnamed *Dorfdisko*, and shows the same young man as he fights with other young men who are physically moving in on Irene, who takes on attributes of the hunted animal. The lack of specification of where exactly in Austria the events are taking place lends an atmosphere of mystery and abstraction to the mountain setting in general, and to the disco location in particular. The eeriness pervading the entire film is intensified by the *Dorfdisko*; intermittently illuminated by the flashing lights, its animal skin covered walls stand out as a haunting, yet elusive backdrop to the film's uncanny account of Irene's sex life.[2]

See LANDSCAPE

See BAD SEX

Ulrich Koehler's *Bungalow* also tells its story of the fits and starts of a young libido through scenes in a *Dorfdisko*. The main character Paul returns to his parents' home after deserting from his military service, and he lounges around, aimlessly passing summer days in the small town of Marbach/Lahn in Hesse (the town where Koehler himself grew up). The arrival of Paul's brother and his Danish girlfriend to the bungalow does little to shake Paul out of his disaffection, though he clearly becomes attracted to the Danish woman, either in imitation of or in quasi-oedipal rebellion against his brother as a father figure. A slow night takes them to the local disco in town, the 'Anyway' (an actual establishment in a nearby town). This *Dorfdisko*—likely even more empty than usual due to the summer holidays—becomes yet another venue for Paul's wandering late-teen libido, as he unsuccessfully tries to catch the attention of his brother's girlfriend before finding his own ex-girlfriend from school days playing pinball with a former classmate **[Fig. 41]**. Boredom and the malaise of returning to the town where one grew up are basic affects running throughout *Bungalow*, and the scenes in the 'Anyway' only serve to heighten this. In contrast to *Hotel*, this *Dorfdisko* is not an uncanny space, not least because the viewer is given clear coordinates as to where the action takes place (we know this because Paul buys a T-shirt with his town's name on it upon arriving back home). Rather than infusing this nightclub with any kind of mystery, the film makes rather transparent jokes at the expense of the provincial *Mief* (stale air). The song playing throughout the disco scene is the 1980s Johnny O hit 'Fantasy Girl' and the *Indiana Jones* and *Back-to-the Future* pinball games also suggest the 1980s and conjure up the discomfit of this and any future trips back to hometown discos. Lacking any nondiegetic music, *Bungalow* takes advantage of the music and décor of the disco setting to undermine any potential pangs of nostalgia, drawing attention to the cultural emptiness of the *Dorfdisko* and its utter inability to become a location of realizable fantasy, sexual or otherwise.

See BOREDOM

See AMBIENT SOUND

In all of these films, an understated, yet keenly attentive cinematic eye casts its gaze on the disco as setting and backdrop, drawing viewers' attention to unremarkable, out-of-the-way lifeworlds. Affects of mourning, disenchantment, apprehension, and embarrassment predominate rather than the frisson of sexual connection or personal conflict. Each of these

Fig. 41: *Bungalow*.

films positions the camera inside *Dorfdiskos*, but each at varying levels of reflective distance from the dance floor; these films do not draw the viewer in through the vicarious excitement of watching young, beautiful people or by narratives of dramatic liberation or conflict that organizes more conventional music videos and advertisement. Instead, we are encouraged to watch figures perform the inconspicuousness of their lives and milieus, dancing in front of a camera that at times does not even mind if anyone remains within the frame at all.

See FRAMINGS

SF

Notes

1 Hochhäusler writes, 'It cannot be our task to cosy [*sic*] up to the media industry—at the beginning there must be a necessity to let a thought or an emotion become film. Setting, budget, cast, format, broadcast slot—those are things that have to follow at the end of the creative process.' See Christophe [*sic*] Hochhäusler, 'A Cinema of Challenge,' *Vertigo* 3.5, Spring 2007, http://www.closeupfilmcentre.com/vertigo_magazine/volume-3-issue-5-spring-2007/a-cinema-of-challenge/.

2 Although we do learn from the credits that some of the film was filmed in the lower Austrian town of Reichenau an der Rax, internet research also reveals that the disco scene was shot in the Reichenauer 'Tanz- und Eventlokal' called Der Preiner-Stadl.

Eclectic Affinities

When the German film journal *Cargo* asked the director Benjamin Heisenberg what films he had recently seen, he named Michel Franco's *Daniel y Ana/Daniel and Ana* (Mexico, 2009) and added, 'It is interesting how Mexican cinema makes use of a style which we in Germany would label "Berliner Schule," but which is obviously simply an internationally accepted form of storytelling, of a certain perspective on reality, and of dealing with the viewer.'[1] At a 2011 panel discussion at Dartmouth College, Christoph Hochhäusler underscored these transnational forms of alignment by stating, 'It is misleading to stress the Germanness of this movement [i.e., the Berlin School].'[2]

While I do not intend to question that a preoccupation with things German is front and center for many Berlin School films, I do contend that, following Heisenberg and Hochhäusler, the Berlin School of German cinema can be profitably situated within the broader context of international independent filmmaking. Taking issue with Olaf Möller's apodictic claim that a search for resemblances leads to a 'Gleichmacherei' ('leveling down') that ultimately erodes local specificity and historical uniqueness, I insist that such comparisons are a necessary first step that help us articulate what ultimately sets the Berlin School apart from other national or regional cinemas.[3]

Almost by definition, all contemporary independent filmmakers work in pronounced contrast, if not outright opposition to the dominant modes of storytelling and audience address. In the process of working outside the system, they are also creating new forms of production, distribution, and consumption. Hollywood, with its global reach, high production values, and immense advertising budgets, is the dominant cinema in most regions of the earth and thus the common measure against which—but also at times *through* which—other national or regional cinemas define themselves. At the same time, the new means of dissemination provided by the Internet (including blogs, online journals, YouTube, Mubi, Fandor, on-demand screening, etc.) and the ever-expanding festival circuit increasingly allow international filmmakers to become more closely interconnected and better aware of what's out there beyond Hollywood. It should therefore come as no surprise that, when we follow these filmmakers' efforts to find alternate ways of telling a story, we come upon parallels, similarities, and convergences among them in the aesthetic choices that they make to have their films stand out.

The Berlin School maintains a number of eclectic affinities with their contemporaries on other continents. In a variety of individual interviews, as well as in the pages of the German film magazine *Revolver*, these filmmakers have repeatedly cited important precursors and influences, including Italian neorealism, the second generation of the French New Wave, Hollywood renegades, selected directors from the New German Cinema, and numerous European directors like Lars von Trier, the Dardenne Brothers, Michael Haneke, Ulrich Seidl, and Harun Farocki.

See PREDECESSORS

Heisenberg's statement, which is noteworthy for reasons beyond the obvious ones, establishes ties—and demarcates differences—that few critics have so far noted. On the one hand, *Daniel and Ana* is a surprising choice because it is in many ways more conventional than many Berlin School films. Perhaps this simply reflects the fact that Heisenberg's own films have at times been considered to be more mainstream than the more restrained works of Angela Schanelec and Thomas Arslan. Cristina Nord, for example, chided *Sleeper* for relying on plot points that are standard fare in scriptwriting seminars at film schools.[4] Heisenberg's second feature, *The Robber*, employs the kind of fast editing and pulsating rock soundtrack that are found nowhere else in the films of his cohort **[Fig. 42]**. But more importantly, there *are* a number of Mexican and Latin American films in which the affinities with the aesthetics of the Berlin School are far more

Fig. 42: *The Robber*.

pronounced. One notable example is *Lake Tahoe* (2008), by the Mexican director Fernando Eimbcke.

Lake Tahoe follows the teenager Juan as he wanders about town after crashing the family Nissan into a telephone pole. He meets a cast of odd characters, including a car mechanic accompanied by a beloved boxer hound, a young mother who dreams of punk stardom, and a martial-arts obsessive. Set in a remote rural town in the Yucatan—and not in California's Sierra Nevada mountains, as one might expect—the film captures the emotional inertia of its protagonist in wide-angle static shots that are periodically interrupted by black screens, as if its characters needed time to pause and reflect. Like the never-shown but crucially important assault in Schanelec's *Marseille*, we do not actually see the accident, but only hear it—in both films the violence is explicitly withheld from the viewer. Only slowly, when, late in the film, Juan asks his brother what the word 'condolences' means, is the family tragedy revealed that led up to the accident. Eimbcke's shots of windswept spaces and geometric architecture, edited at a siesta pace, evoke art photography, not the feverish frenzy of an Iñarritu nor the transgressive imagination of a del Toro (but, it should be noted, they are also still far more aestheticized than the static shots of, say, the Polish-German border in *This Very Moment*). Using static vignettes and some deadpan humor reminiscent of Aki Kaurismäki, but also found in Ulrich Köhler's *Bungalow* and *Windows on Monday*, *Lake Tahoe* off sets the tragic undertones, as it depicts a day in a life suddenly out of joint and a young protagonist struggling to come to terms with something beyond his comprehension. The use of minimalist dialogue powerfully conveys that the real burden of trauma is that it defies articulation and blocks expression.

See VIOLENCE

A number of other Latin American film directors display similar tendencies, including Argentinians Lucretia Martel and Lisandro Alonso. Despite important differences, both heavily emphasize a sense of place, often a particular region (while still emphasizing the sense of being in nowhere-land, as so many Berlin School directors do), location shooting, and the use of nonactors, while they also display a propensity for the long take (often taken to extremes by Alonso) to document the incursion of the everyday. While Martel, like many Berlin School filmmakers, is interested in making the familiar look different or strange, Alonso's 'slow cinema' puts a premium on bringing to life the drabness, monotony, and latent violence in the daily routines of the working poor in the Argentinian hinterland.

See LANDSCAPES

See LONG TAKES

An affinity with the Berlin School can also be found in the subject matter and formal properties of films by such American indie directors as Jeff Nichols, Greg Mottola, Craig Brewe, and Lance Hammer. Kelly Reichardt's *Old Joy* (2006), *Wendy and Lucy* (2008), and *Meek's Cutoff* (2011), a loose trilogy about the mythology of the American West, provide especially fruitful comparisons. All three films tell simple and austere stories, predominantly recorded in long takes, and in all three the screenplay leaves the characters' psychological makeup underdeveloped, denying us access to the protagonists' interiority. Reichardt is averse to what Thomas Arslan has called the 'dramaturgy of overbearance' (*Überwältigungsdramaturgie*), and these films eschew the melodramatic devices that guide audience members' reactions and instead emphasize the viewer's agency in creating meaning.[5] Thus *Wendy and Lucy* tells the story of a young woman who has fallen on hard times and now travels to the Pacific Northwest in hopes of finding work in Alaska. Her background story, in true Berlin School fashion, is never explained. While the promise of going west to better one's situation is a particularly American scenario that has no equivalent in the German imaginary, which typically assigns government the responsibility for dealing with (economic) failure, the film's intricate portrayal of how precarious and contingent life can be is at the center of many Berlin School films (just think of *Yella* or *Orly*). Set in Portland, Oregon, which is framed to look like the middle of nowhere—Reichardt operates without traditional establishing shots and carefully hides any identifiable markers; much like the Berlin of *Ghosts*, the Hanover of *Yella*, or the Munich of *Sleeper*, *Wendy and Lucy* explores the unglamorous byways of U.S. urban areas in order to tell a story of downward mobility. Here we witness prime examples of what Marc Augé has called the creative destruction of space—the big box shopping centers, immense parking lots, and decentered working and living environments that can turn the loss of an automobile, or of mobility in general, into an existential crisis.[6] The film first presents itself as the story of a young woman whose best friend is a dog; both the title and the poster raise expectations of sentimentality and melodrama. Then, however, the film resolutely refuses to meet these expectations. As portrait of a certain time and place—a post-Katrina scenario that renders palpable the erasure of governmental intervention that marked the years of the George W. Bush administration—it resembles the Berlin School's portrayal of post-unification Germany, when neoliberalism eroded the welfare state, and successive German presidents urged their fellow countrymen to become geographically more mobile in order to meet the demands of a radically changed labor market. With its focus on capturing a social reality from the ground level, *Wendy and Lucy* is the kind of political film that Ulrich Köhler would approve of.

See ANTI-HAUPTSTADT

See INTERIORITY

Kelly Reichardt and Fernando Eimbcke seem to have remained outside the orbit of many Berlin School filmmakers, even though *Wendy and Lucy* has been released by Fahrenheit 451, which also sells most of the films by Schanelec, Hochhäusler, Köhler, Arslan, Maria Speth, Pia Marais, and Isabelle Stever. The films of Apichatpong Weerasethakul, by contrast, have been firmly on the radar of *Revolver*, which first published an interview with him, then published his essay 'Geister in der Dunkelheit' ('Ghosts in the Darkness'), and also issued his film *Sud sanaeha/Blissfully Yours* (2002) as one of the first five DVDs on its own label. If we can find significant parallels to the Berlin School in Reichardt's and Eimbcke's aesthetics and particularly in their conceptualization of space, Apichatpong's film serves to illustrate an altogether different relationship, one that might be called a convergence through difference.

Like Christoph Hochhäusler, Apichatpong Weerasethakul first studied to become an architect, and both directors describe their films as spaces into which the viewers enter; and like Heisenberg, who trained as a sculptor and creates installations, Apichatpong frequently exhibits his video and film art in museums. Indeed, these installations complement and closely interact with his feature films, making them all of a piece, rather than different branches of artistic pursuit. His feature films are all characterized by elliptical narratives, a durational camera style, the absence of shot-countershot editing, and an emphasis on the incidental and the everyday—all elements that we regularly find in the Berlin School films. And yet Apichatpong's *Loong Boonmee raleuk chat/Uncle Boonmee Who Can Recall His Past Lives* (2010), to take as an example his most recent and accessible film, is of a very different nature altogether. Its story, which in this case may be too strong of a word, revolves around Boonmee, a farmer dying from kidney failure, who, on the eve of death, is visited by his long-deceased wife and a red-eyed monkey ghost, which serve as the spectral reincarnation of their long-lost son. With the notable exception of the ending to Köhler's *Sleeping Sickness,* which is a direct homage to Apichatpong's film, one looks in vain for elements of spiritualism, animalism, or reincarnation in the films of the Berlin School. However, *Uncle Boonmee* evinces a certain modesty discernible in the works of Valeska Grisebach or Maren Ade. Particularly Grisebach's *Longing* is also at times oblique, with little character development, and conveys a contemplative mood, drawing out the mysteries of ordinary existence. When J. Hoberman describes *Uncle Boonmee* as 'at once sophisticated and artless, mysterious and matter-of-fact,'[7] he implicitly points to how Apichatpong's film would be attractive to many Berlin School directors, precisely because it not only underscores certain affinities but also transcends them. While *Uncle Boonmee*'s absurdist humor and surrealism certainly point in a direction not taken by German filmmakers, it does seem like the (ir-)rational next step to take for many of them. Yet like the protagonists of Berlin School films, who are very much the products of a here and now, Apichatpong's characters do not live in a realm of their own. They often seem to stare into some off-screen space that does not belong to the realm of fiction in which they exist, but to our, the viewers', reality. The surreal ending of Maren Ade's *The Forest for the Trees* is perhaps the one sequence that most approximates Apichatpong's sensibility.

See DISENGAGEMENT

Heisenberg's comment that the style of *Daniel and Ana* and other such films is now 'an internationally accepted form storytelling' also implies that by virtue of its 'success,' the novelty of alternate modes of storytelling has worn off, or that it soon will. One can take this to mean that success creates its own problems, but it's certainly a nice problem to have. More recent films such as Arslan's *In the Shadows,* Schanelec's *Orly*, Köhler's *Sleeping Sickness*, and Hochhäusler's *The City Below* confirm that these directors are moving in new and excitingly different directions. Still new affinities may be in the offing.

GG

Notes

1 Benjamin Heisenberg, 'Zuletzt gesehen: 5 Filme von Benjamin Heisenberg,' *Cargo* 6 (2010): 80.
2 Christoph Hochhäusler, Panel Discusssion: 'The Berlin School: Newest Films from Germany,' Dartmouth College, May 13, 2011. DVD-recording of this event is available through Jones Media Center, Dartmouth College.
3 Olaf Möller, 'Das Mögliche machen, so Weiteres möglich machen,' *new filmkritik*, July 7, 2007, http://newfilmkritik.de/archiv/2007-07/das-mogliche-machen-so-weiteres-moglich-machen/.
4 Christina Nord, 'Notizen zur Berliner Schule,' *new filmkritik*, July 7, 2007, http://newfilmkritik.de/archiv/2007-07/notizen-zur-berliner-schule.
5 For a discussion of Arslan's use of the term *Überwältigungsdramaturgie*, see Kristin Kopp, 'Christoph Hochhäusler's *This Very Moment*: The Berlin School and the Politics of Spatial Aesthetics in the German-Polish Borderlands,' *The Collapse of the Conventional: German Film and its Politics at the Turn of the Twenty-First Century*, eds Jaimey Fisher and Brad Prager (Detroit: Wayne State University Press, 2010), 285–308; here, 287–92.

6 Marc Augé, *Non-Places: Introduction to an Anthropology of Supermodernity* (London: Verso, 1995).

7 J. Hoberman, 'Spirits in the Material World in *Uncle Boonmee*,' *The Village Voice*, March 2, 2011, http://www.villagevoice.com/2011-03-02/film/spirits-in-the-material-world-in-uncle-boonmee/.

Endings

Christian Petzold's *Ghosts* takes detours, periodically steering away from conventional narrative emplotment. The film's winding path may owe itself to the influence of Harun Farocki, with whom Petzold collaborated on the screenplay, and whose films, which have in some cases been exhibited as installations, are hardly known for their conventional storylines. *Ghosts*'s interludes include a long and strangely subdued monologue at a casting call as well as an extended sequence in which Petzold's camera accompanies Pierre, one of the protagonists, while he drives and listens to Bach. It thus comes as no surprise that when the film reaches its end and the credits roll, the denouement has been less than climactic. Petzold's pace hardly promises an explosive finish or even a resolution. Nina sits with Françoise in her hotel, and she is willing to accept that the woman seated in front of her is her mother. Nina has a signifying scar on her ankle, and based on the expression on Toni's face when she inspected Nina's back, it seems that she may also possess a telltale heart shaped birthmark. When Pierre finally intervenes, Nina is already crying out: 'I want my mother,' but Pierre is exhausted from routinely extracting his wife from similar situations, and he is having none of it. 'Marie is dead,' he reports bluntly to Nina as though it were a matter of fact. This may indeed be the case; it could be a secret truth that he hides from his wife, or one that she is unwilling to hear. The film has not said with certainty whether Nina is in fact the abducted Marie, but Pierre's intractability prompts her to leave. Outside the hotel she wanders in the direction of a grassy crossroads similar to the space where the film began. She recalls that Françoise's stolen wallet was discarded in a nearby trashcan, and she reaches in. Nina finds some photos in the nearly empty object, and the lost daughter's image, in what must be a computer-generated reconstruction, is strikingly similar to her own **[Fig. 43]**. The viewer must conclude that what would be impossible in life—that Françoise has fortuitously stumbled upon her abducted daughter—is possible in narrative. Petzold, however, offers no supplemental judgment. Nina drifts into the park and,

See CARS

Fig. 43: *Ghosts.*

although the exit music begins, the artificiality of the transition only accentuates the film's final equivocations.

In analyzing the events as they are put in sequence—the *fabula*—some would maintain that Nina, because of her scar, should in fact be taken for Françoise's daughter, and that the film is about dashed hopes and squandered opportunities. Insofar as it centers on a communicative failure (here between a potential daughter and her possible mother), the film is typical of the Berlin School. Alternative postulations, however, come to mind: the storyline is not meant to be resolved. The events in the film are, after all, narrative and not life. What has happened and whether Nina was the lost daughter of Françoise remains uncertain only insofar as the film's events have all been, in any case, a fiction. Its 'facts' have no referent and can be scripted to accommodate any outcome. *Ghosts* thereby comments on the limits of what storytelling itself is obligated to offer.

But why the open-form dramaturgy? Why would Petzold deny his audience the indulgence of a clear conclusion? Deducing a film's outcome is half the fun. The truest hallmark of Hollywood cinema is that it delivers an ending, and for German filmmakers '*das Happy End*' has long been a reliable US export and a recognizable idiom. Either the evil aliens are conquered and the planet is saved, or the film seamlessly incorporates death, the logic of sacrifice and the prospect of a proper farewell. For this reason, however, Hollywood cinema is so forgettable. Whether endings are cheerful or wretched, they tell spectators precisely what happened as well as its meaning, and as the dark gap between the final shots and the end credits appears, the viewer begins, with the studio's blessing, to disremember the images on screen. Berlin School films, by contrast, refuse resolutions, suppressing details, explanations and facts, and instead force their audiences to reconsider events upon exiting the theater. Through acts of withholding—by avoiding all expository conclusions—Berlin School films engage in a self-conscious mode of stylization that expresses itself most intensely in how the films transition between the final moments (their very last images) and the closing credits.

Toward the end of Benjamin Heisenberg's *Sleeper*, Farid and Johannes, who are colleagues in a laboratory and rivals for the same woman's affections, walk home after an evening's activities. Johannes parts with Farid in front of his apartment, where Farid is quickly and surreptitiously swept up by waiting policemen who believe him to be an Iranian terrorist **[see Fig. 64—FRAMINGS]**. The camera lingers on Johannes, whose expression tells us nothing with certainty: has he deceitfully incriminated his colleague to get him out of the way, or has the surprise of the secretive raid left him dazed and speechless? Johannes is alone with his feelings, but the protracted stillness indicates that Heisenberg does not intend to elaborate. The silence on the character's part echoes the director's elusiveness where the 'facts' that belie the elements of this fictional plot are concerned.

See FRAMINGS

After his return home, Frau Wasser, a government agent, questions Johannes. It may be that Farid has been telling the truth in his own defense, and Johannes could help him by confirming his alibi, but Frau Wasser offers a path of less resistance: 'If you remain silent,' she says, 'I will take that as a "no."' He remains silent, she takes it as a 'no,' and with a nongesture—with an absence of expression—Johannes has eliminated his competition both in the lab and in his love life. Then, in the film's final scene, he sits at the bedside of his aged and ailing grandmother. He is filmed from a low angle, in close-up, and dark shadows fall across his face **[see Fig. 89—LANGUAGE]**. The portrait alludes to the intimacy and honesty of the confessional, and all signs suggest that Johannes feels guilt and culpability. Heisenberg gives no ground. He does not disclose the full extent to which Johannes has cooperated. Questions linger while he quietly recites the Lord's Prayer, which is supposed to be said almost soundlessly. Following the low-voiced supplication, which falls only on the unresponsive ears of his grandmother, the film's audio transitions from the ambient noise in the house to the absolute silence accompanying its end credits. Farid's arrest was a consequence of insinuation and innuendo, and, to represent that logic, the film refuses to provide a comprehensive account. Unlike Heisenberg's subsequent *The Robber*, in which a bank robber courts conflict with the police in order to have a worthy opponent away from whom he can flee, the specifics surrounding Johannes's actions remain obscure, both in his consciousness, and in the text of a writer-director, who declines to state exactly what has happened and when.

When it comes to unresolved endings, Ulrich Köhler is particularly adept. The final fate of Nina and Frieder, the couple at the center of *Windows on Monday*, is a matter of speculation. The two intend to attend a funeral following the untimely death of a neighborhood boy. They arrive late and decide to wait out the ceremony in their van. In the midst of their marital troubles they end up alone together. Nina strokes Frieder's back, he makes a romantic advance, but—despite the warmly intentioned caresses—their encounter grows hopeless **[see Fig. 12—BAD SEX]**. They fumble, she chuckles, and the fun quickly turns unerotic. She makes another obliging attempt and reaches into his pants, but by now he has lost interest, and, at the film's last moment they find themselves discouraged. Köhler cuts to black, offering no apparent assessment as to whether the two will find a resolution. Time marches forward; their relationship may continue, and as in Maren Ade's strikingly similar *Everyone Else*, the couple reaches no decision. Their married life is an ongoing deferral of gratification, and it is far from clear that another state, a pleasant or unpleasant future, awaits them. Is there an outside—an elsewhere—beyond their marital purgatory? The hush over the credits mirrors acoustically that unanswered question.

See BAD SEX

Will Nina and Frieder stay together? To what extent did Heisenberg's Johannes intentionally incriminate Farid? In each case, the silence that suffuses the final moments signals the writer-director's reticence and can be seen as a refusal to render things transparent. Such instances suggest the Berlin School's conviction that conventional cinema, where it provides sense-making endings and clings to the concept of closure, sells reality short. That film and existence are distinct does not mean that film has to strive for falsity. Whether it concerns the messiness of marriage or how the state imbricates its subjects in its espionage investigations, their films emphasize indeterminacy and incorporate signature gestures that suggest the various directors' self-aware acts of withholding. Valeska Grisebach's *Longing* provides a good example for this aesthetics of irresolution. Near the end of her film, after what appears to have been an awful accident more or less directly related to Markus's extramarital affair—an accident that has hospitalized his lover—he attempts to reconcile with his wife, or at least to beg her forgiveness. During the encounter, which is governed largely by its silences, Markus pleads with Ella, 'don't leave me alone,' and 'I didn't want to hurt you.' Ella's reply is scripted with an ear for ambiguity. She says, 'I never thought that I would experience such feelings for you.' The intensifier 'such,' in this case, simultaneously bespeaks her profound love and her anger. Without providing the couple with a resolution, Grisebach then transitions to Markus's workshop, where

Fig. 44: *Longing*.

the echoing sounds of power tools underscore his isolation. Markus embraces his pet rabbit, which tenderly rests on his shoulder, loads his shotgun and shoots himself through the heart **[Fig. 44]**. Grisebach deliberately cuts to the action a half-second after the trigger is pulled, making it impossible to describe Markus's suicidal intention with absolute certainty.

See AMBIENT SOUND

Filmed from a low angle, down on the ground, Markus's evacuation by helicopter alludes to a totalizing and transcendent aerial view that Grisebach's insistently intimate film will not provide. *Longing* then cuts to a series of images of wind rustling through bushes and trees, an empty sporting green, and finally to a small town playground, where adolescents idle on a jungle gym **[Fig. 45]**. One of them seems to be telling the story of the film, which, she adds, is 'really true' and happened 'near here.' She

See WIND

Fig. 45: *Longing*.

relates the whole tale, and, in so doing, she treats the narrative *as* narrative. Reflecting on the story from within the story, or diegetically, the children are distinct from a classical chorus. Appropriating from the German Romantic tradition rather than from antiquity, they stand for a manner of Romantic irony connected with Ludwig Tieck's *Der gestiefelte Kater/ Puss in Boots* (1797): they go beyond merely commenting on the action, remarking instead on how they themselves would write it. Although they register opinions about what has transpired, and poll one another as to whether someone would have been foolish or courageous to have attempted suicide in similar circumstances, they also attempt to reshape the storyline, offering theories as to which of the women would have taken Markus back. The conceit that *Longing* has been a true story teasingly insinuates that there is a truth to know; yet it is only acknowledged that this is a true story in the space of the fiction itself. Even if there had been historical facts to which one could refer, these would change little insofar as the young girl who leads the discussion—who, with her straight strawberry-blonde hair similar to Grisebach's own, serves as a playful stand-in for the director—takes in the speculations about possible endings and responds to them with a simple but coy, 'ah, yes' ('Ja'). Does she, with this act of withholding, mean to say that one cannot know (which would be surprising insofar as the story took place 'near here'), or that one conjecture as to whether and why Markus returned to his wife or lover is more correct than others? If the story is a fabrication, then, as Grisebach is aware and as far as the viewer is concerned, there is no undisclosed truth at its core.

The presence of the children on the jungle gym is itself an ironic comment on film form and on the seductions of narrative. It evokes questions as to what it might mean for a director to leave a narrative open. Akin to the ending of Köhler's *Bungalow*—did Paul, the AWOL soldier, ride away in the truck or the jeep?—we are left wondering **[see Fig. 91—LONG TAKES]**. On this point, however, Grisebach does not remain completely silent. She cuts from a shot of the children walking away from the camera (a concluding image that suggests the rolling road at the end of Christoph Hochhäusler's *This Very Moment*) to the credits **[see Fig. 49—FAMILIAR PLACES]**, and the music that accompanies the closing scroll is an instrumental version of Grauzone's New Wave song 'Eisbär' ('Polar Bear,' 1980). In the original recording of the song, the singer yearns to be an arctic polar bear, intoning, 'then I wouldn't have to scream/ everything would be so clear.' Grauzone's song expresses a longing for a place free of strong emotions, and it concludes with the repeated line, 'Polar bears need never cry.' Moreover, as though this longing were not a clear enough comment on the major themes of the film (the double-edged fantasy that one could be disburdened of '*such* feelings'), the version of the song Grisebach has chosen is instrumental. The absence of words—of lyrics—suggests that language is so insufficient, that here too it fails. What words could Markus have said to his wife to make things right? Even if Grisebach refuses closure, as though she herself were the adolescent in the playground who knows the ending but will not tell, she, at this moment, tacitly reasserts the film's key thematic contention concerning the limits of language. See LANGUAGE

The protagonist of Angela Schanelec's *Marseille*, Sophie, makes her return at the end of the film to the eponymous French city where the story began. It is not entirely clear what she is seeking there or what she is fleeing, but as her train approaches Marseille she takes the time to appreciate the wind falling on her face, and possibly hints at a smile **[Fig. 46]**. Upon arrival she makes her way to a seemingly unpopulated street and ventures deep into the shot, away from the motionless camera. The frame remains steady and, as at many moments in Michael Haneke's *Caché/Hidden* (2005), the still image calls for further inspection. One stares, yet observes little, apart from a streetlight that changes to red. Then, suddenly and abruptly, Schanelec cuts to a police station. In the space of the editorial ellipsis something, an act of violence, has taken place. Sophie sits, looking downcast despite the bright canary yellow dress that may have been presented to her by the police subsequent to the appropriation of her clothes as evidence **[see Fig. 27—BOREDOM]**. Through a narrow doorframe and via an interpreter, an inquest is taking place. About the criminal she apparently encountered, she is asked, 'You knew what he

See WIND

See VIOLENCE

Fig. 46: *Marseille*.

wanted, even though he didn't speak to you?' She replies: 'There wasn't much to understand.' Her affect indicates that there has been a crime, yet the details, apart from their exchange of clothes, remain unclear. Something is unspoken. Sophie answers questions in two languages, but what is clearest about her response to the situation is extralingual; now she is crying about something else, to which she cannot or will not refer.

In that same yellow dress, Sophie later walks alongside the lapping Mediterranean waters **[see Fig. 50—FAMILIAR PLACES]**. The ambient sound, which underscores the absence of interlocutors, continues as the otherwise silent end credits begin. Key plot points remain unclear: Was the violence more severe than she stated (were there unreported aspects of the assault?), or was her interaction with this criminal, whom she understood without language (that is, even 'though he didn't speak to her'), reminiscent of the silences that suffuse her German life, and which she had hoped to leave behind? She may have been attracted to Ivan, her best friend Hanna's muted partner, or she may have left Berlin for fear of falling, like the two of them, into a life of quiet desperation. And again, the acoustic cue, as the sound carries over to the end credits, is expressive. The echoes of the water splashing, and the exclamations of people at play, are familiar. Similar ones have been heard before, at poolside, where they filled the long silence after Hanna severely accused Sophie of caring more for Ivan and her son Anton than for her. Is the lapping water at the end meant to connect this ending back to that earlier scene? Does it suggest that the troubles she left behind in Berlin are bound to resurface?

Similar to *Longing*, Schanelec's *Marseille* also withholds. Details pertaining to the attack as well as to Sophie's inmost feelings—as was true of Johannes in *Sleeper*—remain unspoken. Where the films do not provide specific accounts, however, no additional knowledge is to be had; where fiction is concerned, that which is unwritten is surely unknown. As in other works by Berlin School filmmakers, these films adhere to their aesthetics of irresolution and reserve. Their persistent refusal mirrors their content. In life as in art, much remains a question of inference and innuendo or at least, of interpretation. Most evident, however, is that this refusal has become a repeated and fundamental feature of the filmmakers' signatures. They each have slightly different means of signing their names with a knowing refusal, but, one after the next, they self-consciously avoid endings that are sense-making and thus forgettable.

See INTERIORITY

BP

Familiar Places

In each of the first three shots of Thomas Arslan's film *Vacation*, the camera holds between seven and ten seconds on an empty space around the country home where most of the film takes place **[Fig. 47]**. The first looks out from a path through the woods onto a field near the house. The second shows a small outdoor table and four chairs on a patio next to the house. The third is of a bench up against a tree in another part of the field. In the fourth shot, we see Anna seated alone at a larger table, this one out in the field away from the house.

These places along with a few others, including the dirt road leading to the house, a beach at a small lake nearby, a rustic dinner table inside the house, a bench along the path in the woods, beds in two rooms of the house and a ping-pong table in the field, are the main locations where we see family members interact throughout the film. At various times during the film there are also shots of these places without any characters present. In a few instances the shot starts without anyone in the frame, remains fixed while people enter and exit and then remains empty for the last few seconds of the take. Through this Berlin School approach to mise-en-scène, the key spots around the family house in *Vacation* become *familiar places*.

Berlin School directors generally avoid iconic sites that viewers would recognize as landmarks of particular cities or regions. Rather, they favor generic settings that are familiar from everyday experiences. Locations that appear frequently include small towns, city parks, apartment complexes, country residences, motels or small-town hotels, local roads, highway rest stops, and swimming pools. They select and shoot these sites so that there are no unusual or prominent features that mark them with a particular significance or that might explain why they were chosen. They are for the most part unspecified locations, what we might term *anywhere places*.

See ANTI-HAUPTSTADT

The choice of general locations that are *anywhere places* and the framing of individual settings as *familiar places* foster an alternative relation to the image in Berlin School films. The recurring shots of select places near the country home in *Vacation* breed a sense of familiarity. Each time

FIG. 47: *Vacation.*

the camera returns to one of these spots the viewer recognizes it purely visually, rather than through plot associations or thematic connections. In the course of the film, these places become familiar to the viewer less in the cognitive sense of 'I know that place' than through a bodily awareness that suggests 'I have been here before.' To establish this relation to each place, the camera lingers on it and, at times, even more *in* it, without narrative elements intruding and attracting attention to the story. Initial shots with no characters present invite the viewer to explore the location for its own sake and not as a setting for narrative events. This evokes a sense of presence and generates a stronger sensorimotor engagement with the environs, a different bodily attitude toward the image. Embodied participation in the moving image increases, and the preoccupation with narrative becomes less controlling.

See LONG TAKES

Berlin School filmmakers have regularly employed this strategy with respect to place, adapting it to the style and theme of their films. In *Bungalow*, Ulrich Köhler has much of the action—or, more to the point, *nonaction*—take place in the small area on the patio around the swimming pool outside the family's bungalow-style house **[see Fig. 93—POOLS]**. The easy, free-flowing transition between interior and exterior (a prominent architectural feature of bungalows) creates a film space well adapted to Paul's languid mental and physical bearing. As the viewer settles into this setting, the tendency is not to identify with Paul as a character so much as to assume his physical demeanor and bodily rhythm. To this end, Köhler strives to invoke a sense of simply being there on the patio with the film characters. As the film progresses without any compelling action, the viewer becomes used to inhabiting the space in and outside the bungalow and gradually abandons the idea of it as a film location.

See POOLS

This aesthetics of place that emphasizes presence over performance serves various thematic functions in Berlin School films. In *Marseille*, Angela Schanelec shoots the scenes in Sophie's Berlin apartment in long takes from only a few fixed points of view. Even when taken together, these shots offer no idea about the layout of the apartment or how large it is. The restricted perspectives, dim natural light and limited movement in these scenes convey a feeling of being confined and cramped that mirrors the mental state of Sophie and her sister. The long takes in *This Very Moment* of the two children walking along deserted rural roads impart a very different sense of space **[Fig. 48]**. Filmed in medium-long to long shots and showing the brother and sister on different sides of the road, these images also tend to draw the viewer into the scene.

FIG. 48: *This Very Moment.*

In contrast to the spatial strategies that bring the viewer together with the protagonists in *Bungalow* and *Marseille*, these scenes channel isolation. The vast open space and the distance between the children evoke the feeling of being alone and adrift. Hochhäusler thus conveys the tribulation of the children in this fairy tale-like film without resorting to conventional narrative elements such as a schematic story line or emotional identification. In their place, an aesthetics of presence physically situates the viewer in the children's predicament.

This approach is perhaps most readily characterized via its opposition to the spatial practices of mainstream narrative cinema. Berlin School filmmakers defy the established rules for creating spatial continuity. The four films discussed here avoid establishing shots that could provide a visual sense of the larger space in which the film transpires. In *Vacation* there is not even a single long or medium shot of the exterior of the house. There is also no indication of how the frequently visited settings in and around the house correspond to one another spatially. The camera captures each of them from different angles, but we never get a sense of how they intersect with each other. That is, we are not able to stitch them together into a continuous, integrated whole. The coordination between the different sites in *Marseille* is more radically disjunctive. Not only does Schanelec not offer establishing shots for the specific localities where much of the film is shot, such as the apartments in Berlin and Marseille or the factory floor of the plant where Ivan works, but she also fails to provide them for the major shifts in location. In the most disorienting moment in the film, there is an abrupt cut from Sophie at a bar in Marseille at night to her on a street in Berlin, also at night. Schanelec provides no signal that the change is coming or that it has occurred, either visually or in the dialogue. When we see her on the street, we have no way of knowing where she is or even that she has left Marseille.

See THE CUT

This strategy of spatial (dis)orientation serves to disrupt the hold of narrative with respect to content as well. By beginning scenes *in medias res*, both spatially and with respect to the story, Berlin School directors prime the viewer to accept what is shown *prima facie*, rather than as part of a prefabricated narrative whole. Their films also end on this note, finishing with shots of places or scenes that reinforce a sense of presence but fail to satisfy the conventional desire for narrative closure. *Vacation* closes the same way it began, with a series of three shots of empty places, places now well known to the viewer—the bench out in the field, the dirt road and the path in the woods. The final shot of *This Very Moment* looks down a rural road as the two children walk away from the camera, becoming ever smaller until they become undetectably small dots before vanishing altogether, leaving a final shot of an empty landscape **[Fig. 49]**. *Marseille* ends in a strikingly similar fashion. The last four shots are long takes of Sophie on the Marseille city beach, each a long shot from a different angle and taken at a progressively later stage of dusk. In each subsequent image, it gets more difficult to see her on the beach, both because of the distance and the advancing darkness, until we are not sure whether she is actually there in the final shot **[Fig. 50]**. In each of these cases, the ending puts a

See ENDINGS

See LANDSCAPES

FIG. 49: *This Very Moment.*

FIG. 50: *Marseille.*

final touch on the dominant strategy of place that had sought to engage the viewer more immediately through a sense of presence rather than strictly on the level of cognitively grasped representation.

One final example of a Berlin School film that constructs filmic space according to these principles will serve to illustrate the intricate ways that familiarity with location can function in this scheme. In *Longing*, Valeska Grisebach adheres painstakingly to the Berlin School strategy of not providing a visual sense of the larger space in which the film takes place. Markus and Ella, the married couple, live in an ordinary house on an unpaved road in a small village. Several scenes take place in and around the house, the yard and the adjoining workshop and fields. Although most of the film is set in this small area, there are no establishing shots that offer a clear sense of how their house is situated with respect to those nearby or the village as a whole. Grisebach positions the camera to offer only a limited view of both the interior and exterior spaces, constantly changing the point of view such that they cannot be pieced together to provide a visuospatial overview of the house and its environs. Nor does the visual landscape reveal any particular features that are out of the ordinary. The house and village are like many others throughout rural Germany, and the film presents them as a consummate *anywhere place*.

The characters and the story in *Longing* also fit this pattern of unadorned realism. We see them going through the simple routines of their daily lives with no dramatic intensity. As the film follows them through mundane and seemingly unimportant moments in their everyday reality, the classic tale of a tragic love triangle begins to emerge, at first almost imperceptibly. The film carries through with this story in the same nondramatic fashion until the climatic moment, when Markus puts the barrel of a shotgun to his chest in his workshop and pulls the trigger. At this point, what had been a definitive example of Berlin School realism seems to have morphed into an almost generic love story. But rather than following through decisively in either one form or the other, Grisebach ends the film with an ambiguous final scene that seems to nod in both directions. A closer look will suggest how she tips the scales back toward an aesthetic of presence by re-establishing the sense of being in a familiar place.

The scene opens with a group of children sitting around a play structure. Neither the playground nor any of the children had appeared earlier in the film. One of the girls tells the story of Markus's tragic love that has just played out on screen. Her version suggests that it has become something of a legendary story passed on by word of mouth, and we might imagine

FIG. 51a: *Longing.*

that these are children from a nearby village to which the story had spread. This final scene of the film functions much like the final installment of a frame story, only there is no corresponding opening frame scene. Until this point, the viewer has simply been positioned as being present at different moments in Markus and Ella's lives, with no extrascenic knowledge of how an episode might fit into a narrative whole. Thus, the ending signals a radical reversal in the tenor of the film and the viewer orientation that had dominated throughout. It seems to suggest that we should read *Longing* as a modern version of an archetypal love story; the film seems to have taken a 180-degree turn, from a work of embedded realism to a schematic tale of romantic love.

In what is the final shot of the movie, the girl who told the story and two of the boys walk away from the camera down an unpaved village road. In its perspective, stationary camera and duration (circa 30 seconds) the shot recalls the ending of *This Very Moment*. The setting is unremarkable, typical of the anonymous sense of location that had characterized the film as a whole. The retelling of the story in the final scene seems to suggest that the setting has shifted to a town that did not appear previously in the movie. However, one unremarkable element in the final shot returns

FIG. 51b: *Longing.*

with inexplicable force. In the lower right corner of the frame, a small section of a green and yellow fence becomes visible. This is the fence that separates Markus and Ella's house from the road. It is an ordinary fence, but its somewhat garish green and yellow colors stand out amidst the drab earth tones that dominate in the shots of the house and village. The fence had appeared previously in only two scenes, in each case just as Markus returned home after spending time with his new lover. And in both instances Grisebach subtly directs the viewer's eye to it. In the first, the fire truck that has dropped Markus off pulls away, revealing it almost as if a curtain were being pulled aside. In the second, the headlights of his truck, serving as a spotlight, illuminate it as he turns into the driveway **[Fig. 51]**.

The green and yellow fence has no narrative or symbolic purpose—it merely catches the eye in an incidental manner. And yet, when it reappears in the last scene **[Fig. 52]** it provides the sudden revelation that we are still in the same village and even right next to Markus and Ella's house. It restores a sense of presence and immediacy and dispels the notion that the events experienced throughout the film have been subsumed by a generic narrative. Stirred by the familiar color, resistance to the formal reading of the film as text occurs at a precognitive level of affect. It does not depend on

FIG. 52: *Longing.*

recognition and awareness, but rather on the affective force of the location that had been generated in the course of the film. The small piece of fence in the final shot turns the *anywhere place* of a final frame story back into the *familiar place* that had fostered a sense of presence and participation throughout the film.

RFC

Forests

Given the historical prominence of wooded environs in the German cultural imagination, what stands out in *This Very Moment*, *Windows on Monday*, and *Hotel* is more what the forest does *not* signify. In these films, the woods do not function as symbols of German or Austrian identity; they are associated neither with a realm of natural innocence and mystery heralded by the Romantics nor with idealized rural settings *qua Heimat*; and none of the films reference ecological disasters such as forest 'dieback' (*Waldsterben*). Furthermore, these films do not rely on the visual language of the sublime, eschewing images of both natural grandeur and melancholic meditation most commonly associated with the work of Caspar David Friedrich. They do not recapitulate Romantic ideas about the forest, but rather engage with and reject Romantic tropes in favor of enigmatic representations that favor the mundane and the inscrutable over both the conventionally beautiful and the foreboding.

Berlin School films unsentimentally depict people's forest experiences as continuous with the everyday worlds in which they work and live. The fact that characters overwhelmingly enter and exit the woods by automobile underscores this continuity. The car symbolizes the self-containment of the modern subject, and it is a quintessential extension of the larger social and economic system of individualism and private property. In contrast to earlier modes of travel, the car allows easy access to the forest, compressing the distance between natural and urban spaces. Likewise, these films equate forests with human habitations of varying levels of transitoriness, including family homes, vacation hotels, and roadside truckstops. Rather than establishing a strong division between nature and culture, the films explore homologies between forests and other settings. Experiences in forests are neither redemptive nor transformative; they only extend and carry over difficulties from other parts of life.

See CARS

See HOTELS

Christoph Hochhäusler's *This Very Moment* draws on Romantic themes most directly, not least because it is based on the Grimm fairy tale 'Hansel and Gretel.' The director calls his film a 'realistic fairy tale,' suggesting that

Fig. 53: *This Very Moment.*

it takes up an arch-Germanic forest mythology.[1] The story centers on two siblings, Lea and Konstantin, who are abandoned by their stepmother, Sylvia—her name synonymous with the woods themselves—on the Polish side of the German-Polish border. The children wander through a forest, where they meet a Polish man named Kuba whose job is to restock truck stops with cleaning supplies out of a van, which here stands in as the rough equivalent of the witch's fairy tale cottage **[Fig. 53]**. The film also tracks the father's attempts to locate the children and the stepmother's physical collapse after Kuba promises to deliver them. In its focus on wandering siblings it plainly recalls 'Hansel and Gretel,' leaving us to wonder whether we should interpret the setting of Lea and Konstantin's travails as analogous to the fairy tale's realm of foreign mystery.

See SIBLINGS

See BORDERS

Why are cars omnipresent in this otherwise sylvan story? *This Very Moment* opens with Sylvia picking up the children up as they walk home from school. The confined space of the car is a cage that intensifies the tensions of an already strained family life, but it also offers Sylvia the illusory chance for the freedom of the open road. In a burst of exasperation she throws Lea and Konstantin out of the car and drives on into the forest, where she witnesses a stork crossing directly in front of her in the grass-covered road. Is the stork a symbol of fertility, infancy, or perhaps a different family constellation? Evocative and dreamlike yet opaque, Sylvia's wildlife sighting suggests a moment of potential transformation, but one with few further consequences: her earlier anxieties are only heightened when she returns to fetch the children, who have wandered off.

The automobile remains central to the narrative, as the children come across Kuba resting near his van in the forest. The van is both a threatening space and an indication of the relative proximity of civilization. The children's initial sojourn through the woods ends with this encounter, as Kuba ferries them back to populated areas.

While the forest is a gateway to an unfamiliar realm, passing through it leads the children into spaces surprisingly similar to the landscape they leave behind. Vaguely frightened yet also curious, they wander through the back hallways and parking lots of roadside hotels and restaurants, through temporary fairgrounds and bus stations. These transitory spaces mirror their unfinished family home back in Germany, and they are also homologous to the forest as a foreign and unknown site. The homology is underlined by images of Sylvia in these three realms, equally fugitive in each. As much as Poland represents an uncanny location much like the *unheimlich* (uncanny) Romantic forest, such that 'the fairy tale's dual spatial order (the everyday world of home vs. the magical space of the forest) [is transposed] over a contemporary national divide,'[2] the children's troubles straddle both the German-Polish border and the boundary between forest and civilization. While the children meet new adventures and dangers upon crossing the national border and entering the forest, their family home does not stand as a symbol of stability and comfort as it might in a fairy tale. This contiguity of different realms connects the fate of contemporary Germany and Poland through 'a shared set of challenges and anxieties.'[3] The 'forest' is both everywhere and nowhere, because danger and adventure cannot be contained. The closing scene confirms this idea, as Kuba expels the children from his van after Lea tries to poison him. They are abandoned to walk along the road in the Polish countryside just as they did in Germany at the film's outset [**see Fig. 48—FAMILIAR PLACES**].

Ulrich Köhler's *Windows on Monday* similarly calls into question the boundaries between natural environs and domestic spaces while thematizing family tensions through metaphors of a house under construction and a journey into the woods. In the process the film exudes a particularly flat affective register conveyed through the characters' actions, the actors' delivery of their lines, and the visual style of the film itself. This flatness extends to depictions of nature as unremarkable, boring, and altogether unsublime.

The film follows Nina, a doctor in her late thirties or early forties, as she breaks with her daily routine of work and family. *Windows on Monday* would be simply about the collapse of a marriage were it not for the strange, unsettling apathy of all the characters. Nina's strained family life is magnified by the unfinished state of the family home, which her husband

See RENOVATION

Fig. 54: *Windows on Monday.*

is renovating largely by himself. Without telling anyone, Nina drives alone into the nearby Harz Mountains. She arrives at night, using her headlights to guide her way, and she spends the night at a family cabin with her brother and his girlfriend. Once again a character enters the forest by car, and our first glimpse of the forest is through a windshield, illuminated only by headlights. Initially, the forest might be seen as a refuge, and upon arrival Nina smokes a joint with her brother, something she hasn't done 'since Berlin.' At the same time, the woods do not conform to expectations of natural beauty, and Nina is not in search of nature's reinvigoration. This forest, a downhill ski area in the winter, has undergone extensive logging and is riddled with stumps and recently harvested trees stacked in neat piles. Nature is something managed and profited from, rather than something kept in a pristine state untouched by development.

The viewer then follows Nina as she bikes to the ski resort **[Fig. 54]**. Though she does not traverse the forest by car as before, her bike trip indicates an intention to reach a destination rather than to soak in the forest as a place of calm and rejuvenation. As in earlier scenes, the camera follows her as she moves through space and time, but we are not sure where she is going or why. Like other locations that she passes through (including her town, the surroundings as she drove to the mountains) the forest is entirely unremarkable, and viewers do not have a sense of the place as any kind of end goal, even after realizing that she has arrived somewhere. Nina makes her way to the resort hotel, where she wanders aimlessly, almost ghostlike. She is detached but at the same time vaguely curious. Why does she go there? What is she looking for? What is she feeling? What is going on in the hotel itself? The film offers no explicit answers to these questions and often seems even to thwart them deliberately.

In the meantime, Nina's husband agonizes about her disappearance, while continuing construction on their home. The title of the film refers to a planned date for installing new windows; with carpenters poised for installation, the husband calls the job off after realizing that they have brought windows made from the wrong kind of wood. Insisting on frames built from Oregon pine, the husband makes do with plastic sheeting as temporary window covers, adding to the house's fragility (something that recalls the residence under construction in *This Very Moment*). The husband's search for an elemental trace of nature that can complete human domesticity fails: the windows don't come and the house remains incomplete. In contrast to Nina's ennui, the husband's predominant affect is disappointment. Presenting his do-it-yourself idealism as a failure, the film rejects a quasi-Romantic vision of harmonizing the natural and the domestic. Does Nina's gaze represent an alternative way of looking at the world, disenchanted, bored, yet vaguely open to whatever comes next?

The film ends with the couple pausing at the lightly wooded outskirts of a cemetery as they make one final, unsuccessful bid to rekindle mutual sexual attraction; here again, the cars meet the woods. It is unclear, however, whether this sexual nonevent in the back of their van will be the norm of their continuing relationship or its conclusive demise. There is no untamed, regenerative force in this filmic world—neither in the outdoors nor in personal intimacy—that can deliver its inhabitants from boredom and disaffection.

See BAD SEX

See BOREDOM

Like *This Very Moment* and *Windows on Monday*, Jessica Hausner's *Hotel* juxtaposes domestic and forest environments. More so than the other two films, *Hotel* plays with depictions of forests and hotels as similarly uncanny or haunted, suggesting at first glance a standard Romantic vision of forest mystery and *Unheimlichkeit*. In addition, the film engages with generic conventions related to plot, camera movement, and the representation of space, all familiar from mainstream horror movies or thrillers. However, even while taking up these literary and filmic conventions, the film presents both forest and nonforest environments as lacking any deep discernable meaning, bringing viewers to linger on the act of seeing above all else.

Irene, a young woman who has recently taken up a service position at a resort ('Hotel Waldhaus') in the Austrian mountains, discovers

Fig. 55: *Hotel.*

that her predecessor Eva disappeared under mysterious circumstances. Strange things start happening to Irene: her eyeglasses are broken and she temporarily wears Eva's, her cross necklace goes missing, and she hears a scream emerge from the forest. Furthermore, Irene does not get along with her coworkers, some of whom take callous pleasure in tormenting her. According to regional folk legend, a woman of the woods or a witch (*Waldfrau*) is rumored to live in nearby mountain caves **[Fig. 55]**, and when Irene disappears into the forest with a scream at the film's end **[Fig. 56]** it is unclear what has happened to her: has she been abducted

Fig. 56: *Hotel.*

Fig. 57: *Hotel.*

by the *Waldfrau*, by her sadistic, potentially Satanist coworkers, or is it all just a dream?

The forest and hotel are both spaces that seem to bear some kind of secret. Despite offering Irene certain possibilities—the hotel as a new professional beginning and the forest as a site for solitary reflection—both places become constricting and claustrophobic. In scenes in the woods, the camera remains low to the ground and attends to drab underbrush and dead tree limbs rather than to majestic vistas **[Fig. 57]**. As in *Windows on Monday*, the film also depicts nighttime scenes of the forest illuminated by headlights. Lit via the flat 'vision' of the car rather than by a more penetrating form of depth perception, the forest cannot be seen into and remains all surface. The social world of the hotel is equally inscrutable, not least because it is unclear whether Irene is being disturbed by supernatural forces or by her coworkers. A psychosexual interpretation might help parse this uncanniness: is the film an allegory of a young woman's sexual awakening and concomitant anxiety? Scenes showing Irene's free time activities might support such a reading: she goes to and from the local disco through the forest at night, and has a first kiss with a creepy new boyfriend in a woodland cave. Additionally, Irene's predecessor was named Eva, suggesting an archetypal quality to these enigmatic events.

At the same time, both forest and hotel remain fundamentally flat and impenetrable, blocking any resolution of symptom into pathology, of surface

Fig. 58: *Hotel*.

into depth, of image into lasting meaning. The film achieves this not least through parallel shots of Irene gazing alternately into woods and indoor spaces. In the forest, she sees little more than the trees closest to the hotel, illuminated by the hotel's lights **[Fig. 58]**, but when she is indoors, she either gazes or walks into an unknown darkness. In focalizing the audience's gaze through Irene, these carefully composed shots set up structural similarities between interior and exterior spaces. The images echo Friedrich's style of self-referential meditation on the viewing subject, but in contrast to Friedrich's expansive landscapes, the object of Irene's gaze always seems to evade her. By thwarting both her and our desire to see into the depth and forcing the protagonist and the viewer to remain on the surface level of what is before them, the film occasions a reflection on attentiveness, curiosity, and interest. It is characteristic of the aesthetics of Berlin School films more generally that they aim to bring viewers to reflect upon the terms of their own viewing; the homologies that *Hotel* establishes between interior and exterior spaces pursues this aim in a particularly compelling manner. At one point Irene asks a hotel guest if he would prefer a room with a 'valley view' or a 'forest view.' The film's provocation is to suggest there really is no difference between sylvan and nonsylvan ways of seeing. Neither can access depth or deeper meaning; one can neither see these towns for the roads, nor the forests for their trees.

See LANDSCAPE

SF

Notes

1 See the interview with Christoph Hochhäusler on the *This Very Moment* DVD.
2 Kristin Kopp, 'Christoph Hochhäusler's *This Very Moment*: The Berlin School and the Politics of Spatial Aesthetics in the German-Polish Borderland,' *The Collapse of the Conventional: German Film and its Politics at the Turn of the Twenty-First Century*, eds Jaimey Fisher and Brad Prager (Detroit: Wayne State University Press, 2010), 285–308; here 285.
3 Kopp, 'Christoph Hochhäusler's *This Very Moment*,' 306.

Framings

When, in 1933, art historian and film theorist Rudolf Arnheim set out to explore film's potential as an art form, he revisited the medium's most basic limitations, among them, the delimitation of the picture. Simply put, all composition was beholden to the axes of the frame's 'two vertical and two horizontal lines.'[1] In keeping with Arnheim's larger thesis that cinema's formal constraints—its marked difference from life or profilmic reality—enabled the development of film art, he attributed the possibility of film-aesthetic expression to the frame's inherent duality: first, as a mimetic space of narrative action in depth and, second, as a two-dimensional canvas for the arrangement of pictorial elements. More recently, the cineastes of the new wave in German and Austrian film have made a practice of drawing attention to the boundaries of the image. Filmmakers like Valeska Grisebach, Angela Schanelec, Ulrich Köhler, and Benjamin Heisenberg have turned against narrative and aesthetic conventions of spatial contiguity, emotional identification, and classical editorial continuity in favor of greater ambiguity in setting, character, and narrative progression. With a predilection for long, static takes, exact compositions, complexly choreographed mobility, and unusual camera placement, these directors unsettle narrative and spectatorial expectations and resist the frame's correspondence to the institutional frameworks of a state-funded cinema that often favors commercial potential (and narrative economy) over artistic experimentation (a challenge to this economy).

See LONG TAKES

See ENDINGS

The Berlin School's rigorous attention to form frames contemporary lives full of uncertainty, vulnerability, and moral frailty. This controlling cinematographic attitude or behavior toward imperfect, often inscrutable protagonists and the spaces they inhabit can be explored in a brief typology: (1) the imprisoning frame; (2) the antisocial frame; (3) the frame of passage; and (4) the judgmental frame. The following cases are by no means exhaustive; rather, they are meant to provide some orientation in the ways that Germany and Austria's new auteurs exploit and insist upon the 'hardscape' of the frame's architecture. Rather than pretending that the diegetic world obeys a logic of spectatorial interest, the Berlin School frame maintains a didactic presence, often resisting this logic and debunking its assumptions.

The Imprisoning Frame. The imprisoning frame rejects the spatial contiguity traced by a mobile camera. French film critic and theorist André Bazin once extolled 1940s Italian Neorealist filmmakers' propensity to shoot in crowded, moving vehicles. What impressed him was their ability to create 'density' within 'the framework' and thus to keep a cinematic action within its 'material context.'[2] In this version of realism, the narrative fiction was embedded in nonfictional surroundings, and the porous boundaries of the frame, filled by the contingencies of life, promised its potentially infinite access to the 'real' world. Though the diegetic world of the Berlin School films also extends beyond the boundaries of a given shot, access to offscreen space is often withheld. Instead, a character is placed, often alone, in the visual field with his or her body caged by the static edges of the frame and a rear wall. Limited to a fixed performance space, the body is subject to the camera's unwavering stare and to a temporal continuity unbroken by cuts and variations in shot scale.

See DORFDISKOS

In the dance scenes in Valeska Grisebach's *Be My Star* and Angela Schanelec's *Passing Summer*, bodies left to emote at a distance become bearers of angst and frustration. *Be My Star* is set in the milieu of streetwise, working-class Berlin teenagers, caught in awkward fluctuations of persistent adolescence and precocious adulthood. The young Nicole, just dumped by her boyfriend, dances by herself in a club. As she moves repetitively to electronic music at the center of the image, a DJ stands unobtrusively to the right of the frame. Strobing and pulsing white and red lights underscore the music's regular beats as her head appears to intersect a diagonal line on the rear wall. Graphic elements literally 'in tune' with a stable background, Nicole's limbs keep time but do not alter her environment. The wide, frontal shot accentuates, rather, the solitude of her exposed and inescapable vulnerability.

See STRIESOW, DEVID

In *Passing Summer*, Valerie, who lives in Berlin, has traveled home to help her brother, played by Devid Striesow, deal with their father's illness. Their dance at the local *Dorfdisko* couples frustration and nostalgia with a rite of passage to a new phase in adult life. When the two siblings, standing at the bar, move off frame to go dance, Schanelec cuts to a shot of a pathetically empty dance floor. The framed space precedes the event that is supposed to take place within it. Despite the acoustically implied proximity of the two spaces, there is no smooth cut on action from the bar to the dance floor. This requires the two figures to 'enter' the frame as if stepping onto a stage. Once they begin dancing, they occasionally move beyond the edge of the frame. The camera does not, however, pan to adjust to these transgressions; rather, it is as though the space itself is aligned with the camera **[Fig. 59]**. Schanelec does not interrupt the highly personal gesticulations that accompany this dual performance (of the actors dancing their characters' dance) with an anthropocentric shot breakdown of privileged close-ups and pointed detail. Instead Valerie and her brother's slightly clumsy movements, like those of Nicole in *Be My Star*, occur both *in* and *to* the space before the camera. The otherwise kinesthetic qualities of dance, often conveyed by editing and mobile framing, are tempered by the fixed camera distance, the frame's immobility and the shot's duration. Acts of self-expression, even liberation, thus remain caged within the dual architectures of the set and the frame.

See DISENGAGEMENT

The Antisocial Frame. Elsewhere, the architecture of the frame disciplines spectatorial expectations through a refusal to 'cover' continuity cues such as eyeline matches, matches on action and shot/reverse shot patterns. By avoiding the clarity that these cues usually establish between two characters or between characters and setting, the filmmakers of the Berlin School introduce a frame that might be termed 'antisocial.' As if disinterested in mere action, the antisocial frame often selects reaction over action. This interrupts the process of making inferences about character behavior and substitutes complexity and uncertainty for unequivocal information.

Fig. 59: *Passing Summer.*

In *Passing Summer*, a series of interlaced vignettes of a 'passing summer' in Berlin, the child Clara, who shares an apartment with her parents and Valerie, asks her babysitter Maria to dance to some music. The two are sitting on a couch facing the camera. When Maria moves out of frame, the camera remains focused on Clara. In an acoustic off, implied by Maria's question, 'What kind of music?' and confirmed by Clara's glance in that direction, Maria indulges Clara's request to hear 'Der Erlkönig' (1815), but insists that 'one cannot dance to' it. Juxtaposed to this claim are, however, the music itself and Clara's absorption in the off-screen space. Clara's question, 'Why not?' is answered by the first bars of Schubert's scoring of Goethe's ballad, a text, rich in imagery, about a worried father trying to save his sick son. Though the young girl's eyes seem to register an off-screen movement, Schanelec withholds a shot/reverse shot pattern. If, indeed, Maria attempts to dance to 'Erlkönig,' this performance is denied the spectator. Instead, it is Clara's face that bares the ambiguity of this invisible action. Does she watch Maria dance, exchange a long glance with her babysitter and listen raptly to the ballad's narrative, or is Clara's attention focused solely on the music and its *un*-dancer-*ly* qualities? **[Fig. 60]**

Schanelec further cultivates this antisocial frame in *Afternoon*, a loose adaptation of Chekhov's *Chayka/The Seagull* (1895), in which the summer ennui of a lake house at the outskirts of Berlin sets the scene for familial and artistic frustrations and general lethargy. The immobile frame or frame of limited, even reluctant motion provides a visual approximation for the estranged intimacy of the depressed young writer Konstantin, the son of a successful actress (played by Schanelec), and his childhood friend Agnes,

Fig. 60: *Passing Summer.*

who is back from school. In one scene they lie on his bed, but despite their spatial proximity and shared history, they are prone to miscommunication. Agnes is framed in close-up, her head sideways against a dark blue blanket. Konstantin enters this static frame both acoustically and visually as first his footsteps, then his blue shorts, announce his arrival to a position just above Agnes's head **[Fig. 61]**. All the while, she fiddles with her necklace and does not look up. When she finally rolls over in his direction, the camera tilts just slightly to reframe the shot and reveal more of his legs. She asks him why everybody is sleeping and tells him not to fall asleep. When there is no response, she gets off the bed. At first, the camera pans left with her movement, but once she exits the frame, it remains fixed on Konstantin, who, in a sense, 'inherits' the space of action. His eyes follow Agnes as they converse, but neither he nor the camera moves toward her. The next shot, a delayed reverse shot, shows Agnes at Konstantin's computer. He then replaces her in the acoustic off.

In addition to the duration of individual poses within Reinhold Vorschneider's complexly static and haltingly mobile cinematography in *Afternoon*, the temporal lag of the reverse shots emphasizes a disjunction between the communication on the audio track and the limited interaction of the characters on the visual track. Once again, actions are denied reactions, and the close quarters of Konstantin's bedroom are undercut by the filmic separation of bodies. It is as if Agnes and Konstantin, in this scene, can neither remain in the same frame, nor participate in a classically continuous dialogue. This cinematographic evocation of a lack of curiosity

Fig. 61: *Afternoon*.

(i.e., a camera that does not want to look) once again inverts a classical trope at the site of its dramatic necessity. Schanelec's resistance to showing it all enriches the function of off-screen space while also suggesting a cinematographic evocation of boredom. At the same time, the bored camera portrays some of narrative cinema's blind spots—the very emotional residue lost in the strict informational economy of the continuity system.

See BOREDOM

The Frame of Passage. In Ulrich Köhler's films, the camera's mobility has a punch line. Much less a function of the Neorealists' roving camera, linking the diegesis to a quotidian milieu, Köhler's mobile framing, his frame of passage, explores the dangerous revelations inherent in spatial contiguity. Because these shots change meaning in the midst of their execution and lead to unexpected end points, they emphasize the gap between apparent truths and actual states.

Bungalow depicts a young *Bundeswehr* soldier who goes AWOL. Spontaneously opting out of his required military service, 19-year-old Paul revisits his bourgeois family's vacation home. His refusal of social responsibility coincides with a regression to an earlier life of ease and asserts, as well, a strong sense of individuality and desire for personal freedom. The film opens with a close-up of a young man in a military transport vehicle. His glance off camera is followed by a pan along a row of sleeping soldiers. Another military truck is visible on the receding highway behind them. After the title appears against a black background, a single long take charts the convoy's progression along an exit ramp and into the parking lot of an Esso rest area. At first, the trucks pass rather anonymously through this unidentified rural landscape. A steady pan tracks their arrival at this travel center (which could be anywhere), but it is not yet clear what this combination of factors—military convoy and highway rest stop—will yield. The trucks park, and the camera, temporarily static, frames the soldiers disembarking in long shot and then pans left as they enter a Burger King **[Fig. 62]**. The camera remains outside, positioned on the veranda as the pan resumes laterally along some outdoor tables. Gradually the camera's motion rejoins the soldiers, and one in particular, exiting the restaurant. Paul becomes a point of interest as the camera follows his movement to a table. Off camera, a voice calls for the soldiers to reboard the trucks. An older man at his table looks at him questioningly, but Paul does not budge.

In this sequence, Patrick Orth's virtuoso cinematography links the repetition and anonymity of the scene's fast food and gas station chains, unidentified countryside and uniformed collective to the specific narrative

Fig. 62: *Bungalow*.

action of one individual. While the film has not yet provided any motivation for Paul's desertion, the mobile frame demonstrates, through the complexity of its choreography, the difficulty of extracting one life or one story from these spaces of transit. In the camera's unbroken journey from the long shot of the highway to the medium shot of Paul at a table, the film preserves a level of narrative indeterminacy. Why should this truck, wending its way along Germany's Autobahn, lead to this young man's disaffection? In a continuous process of recontextualizing visual information, the mobile frame thwarts premature spectatorial assumptions. Only when movement ceases does the reason for this trajectory become clear.

In *Windows on Monday* even shorter camera movements destabilize identification and narrative clarity. Soon after moving from Berlin to a new house in a smaller town, Nina runs away from her estranged husband Frieder, her young daughter and the disarray of home remodeling to her family's cabin in the woods to join her brother and his girlfriend. After a call from Frieder, who is looking for her, Nina sets out through the hilly forest on a bicycle **[see Fig. 54—FORESTS]**. A long shot of her breaking for an acoustically implied flat tire is followed immediately by an elevated shot of the treetops taken from a cable car. At first, this seems like an establishing shot, offering a wider perspective of the very forest in which Nina was just biking. A car creeps along a mountain road, and it seems possible that Nina, too, will emerge in the distance. As the cable car continues its climb, the camera pans to follow the car, a minivan like the one Frieder drives, in its ascent. This, too, appears to be unembodied narrative information

See RENOVATION

for the benefit of the spectator. A subsequent cut to Nina's face places her, however, in the cable car and recodes the camera's position and movements, in retrospect, as her point of view **[Fig. 63]**.

At the same time, this reversal of an eyeline match disrupts the correspondence between what the spectator sees and what Nina sees. It is not clear how much of the view from the cable car can be aligned with her subjective gaze. The route of passage of a single pan, which might otherwise promise spatial and temporal continuity, accentuates, instead, Nina's alienation from her environment. This phantom-like shifting of subjective and objective gazes helps to structure Nina's odd encounters with an anachronous resort hotel, where she seeks temporary refuge from her marriage. Köhler's cinematographic routes offer means of rebellion and fantasy for protagonists who desire 'time out' of the social networks and mores that entrap them.

The Judgmental Frame. The final frame in this Berlin School typology is one of judgment, in which careful composition and blocking interpret the actions of a character. Beyond the frame of passage, in which mobility salvages individuality, the motion and placement of the judgmental frame maintain a relationship of distrust between the spectator and the protagonist. That is, there is a second, distancing frame (or perspective) structuring access to the fictional world. Benjamin Heisenberg's *Sleeper* thematizes surveillance, social distrust, and ethnic profiling in the wake of the terror attacks of September 11, 2001, and Islamic extremist cells

Fig. 63: *Windows on Monday*.

discovered in Germany. A film about the disjunction between seeing and knowing, *Sleeper* provides a catalogue of potentially surveillance-generated views: long shots of corridors, doorways and windows; shots of streets and parks; public as well as institutional spaces scanned for clues of radicalism. When the virologist Farid is arrested, his colleague, friend, and romantic and professional rival Johannes, who has collaborated with the authorities, looks on from a distance.

See SURVEILLANCE

The camera tracks laterally toward the right as the two men part for the evening. While Farid walks away from the camera into the deep space of the frame, Johannes proceeds parallel to the camera's path. Just when the camera begins to track Johannes at closer range, men in the side street on the left side of the frame begin running toward the sidewalk where Farid had been. Johannes looks back and then returns, accompanied by the camera, to the spot where he had left his colleague. Shooting Johannes from behind as he watches plainclothes agents handcuff Farid, the camera maintains an independent point of view, one in which Johannes's silence and inaction are part of the record **[Fig. 64]**. Even when a subsequent set of shot/reverse shots present Farid's arrest from Johannes's perspective, a final shot undercuts this personalization by reverting to a position behind his back, a place where the spectator's knowledge and capacity for judgment exceed that of the protagonist. By complicating Farid's arrest through this duality of frames, Heisenberg effectively forces a rupture between identification (with someone else's mistake) and either coresponsibility or condemnation for any injustice that Johannes may have perpetrated. The judgmental frame eschews alignment with the psychology of a single character and ultimately

Fig. 64: *Sleeper*.

invests the image with layered and dynamic possibilities for interpretation of character behavior.

The cinema of the Berlin School takes form seriously, and as a closer study of framing strategies makes clear, the revision, inversion, and subversion of classical narrative continuity distinguishes these works from more commercial emphases on informational and emotional economies of storytelling. Nearly all the films associated with this style take on the German, Austrian, or European present. Most confront the conflicted lifestyles of the affluent and educated classes. Yet the difference these films make within the contemporary German and Austrian film landscape often comes down to how they picture the present, to the frame that makes their diegetic worlds visible in the first place. These worlds of houses and families, relationships and moral transgressions, and self-articulation and stagnation are not as stable as they seem at first glance. Architecture imprisons, lovers fail to communicate, certainties and friendships collapse, and images themselves cannot be trusted. Sometimes, the frame entreats us to notice banality; at other times, we are forced to endure the excessive vulnerability of characters onscreen. At still other moments, we are curious about the secrets hidden beyond the frame's edges and startled by the new information revealed in a pan or a tilt. The characters in these worlds are as complicated and nuanced as the frames that enclose them. As the filmmakers of the Berlin School revitalize the art house strain of German-language cinema, their approach to the frame is also political. If, as Arnheim suggests, *cinema* is a matter of what one does with the frame, then these films' critiques of contemporary society are cinematic arguments, made between 'two vertical and two horizontal lines.'

BW

Notes

1 Rudolf Arnheim, *Film As Art* (Berkeley: University of California Press, 1957), 74.

2 André Bazin, *What Is Cinema?*, vol. 2, trans. Hugh Gray (Berkeley: University of California Press, 1971), 38.

Ghosts

Any discussion of the 'ghost' in the corpus of Berlin School films must focus on Christian Petzold's 'Ghost Trilogy': *The State I Am In*, *Ghosts*, and *Yella*. Petzold's trilogy, in classically modernist fashion, appeals to ghostly figures, because they are reminders of capitalism's exclusions, and especially of those individuals it leaves behind. In this sense, ghosts represent the mobility, rootlessness, and resulting alienation of modern life. As his interest in the figure of the ghost suggests, then, Petzold's three films are deeply engaged in our late capitalist modernity and the spectral nature of its relationships, transactions, and exchanges. His Ghost Trilogy explores in detail how such processes are played out in the cities and on the highways of post-Wall Germany, depicted as one region in a vast geospatial network.

The State I Am In and *Yella*, in different ways, each represent nonsynchronicity (what Ernst Bloch describes as *Ungleichzeitigkeit*), or worlds out of step with their own pasts, ones that render ghostly those persons caught in between. Nonsynchronicity brings to light a certain unevenness in development. The German title of *The State I Am In*—*Die innere Sicherheit*—translates literally as 'Internal Security' and thus resonates with the concepts of inland or homeland security. That title is particularly apt given that the film's protagonists are a pair of former RAF-type radicals and their adolescent daughter. Clara, Hans, and Jeanne have been on the lam for 15 years, traveling the highways of the New Europe as they await the chance to flee to South America. The parents are ghosts of the old Cold War Europe, having outlived the relevance of their political crimes and the project to which they had devoted their lives. Leftovers from a history which most people wish to forget, they are out of step with the present, uncanny reminders of imagined futures that never came to pass. As for the authorities, they will indeed track the former radicals down, but not because their leftist politics (however little these are explicitly thematized in the film) threaten the established order—a new order—but rather because they represent an unrealized historical trajectory, a specter of what might have been, in a sociopolitical milieu that likes to imagine it has no history.

Fig. 65: *The State I Am In.*

In *The State I Am In*, then, to be a remnant of history is not to be mythologized, nor does it make one celebrated or legendary. Clara and Hans, who once threatened the Cold War state, instead join the shadowy ranks of petty criminals, outcasts, and illegal aliens. For Petzold, New Europe's 'criminal' is an abstraction, a totalizing category that, like the 'terrorist,' potentially includes any nonnormative subject. Petzold emphasizes this point in the scenes in which the radical outlaws brush with the forces of order, or with other criminals. The beginning of their flight from a coastal Portuguese resort town takes place when they are the victims of an unglamorous thief who preys on tourists. The petty thief and this family are perceived as more similar than different, as a provincial policeman's treatment of Hans makes clear. Similarly, when a former comrade, still committed to the old ideals, but shifty and shadowy, tries to help the family by getting them needed cash, he is apprehended by black-helmeted Special Forces moments before their meeting [**Fig. 65**]. Caught on tape paying off a prostitute or perhaps a drug dealer moments before his rendezvous with the family, Petzold suggests that the former comrade's capture might have nothing to do with the outlaws after all. Indeed, the family, waiting only steps away from the gas station where the police raid takes place, manages to get away despite the presence of a helicopter, high-tech surveillance equipment, and scores of black-helmeted personnel.

The ambiguity of the family's 'security,' referred to in the title, also alludes to post-Wall Europe's new organization, its definition of subjectivity, and its postnational apparatuses of population control. Because of the couple's past crimes against the state, Hans, Clara, and Jeanne have been rendered 'stateless,' exceptional subjects who are without any legal rights. Their lives are determined by the new post-Wall European state, by apparatuses of control that are shadowed and invisible, but still absolute. The state of the stateless is slyly evoked in a scene that takes place on the French/German border, where the family stops for a brief rest. The ghost of national boundaries is now marked by three symbols: the German and French flags, and the EU flag upon which Jeanne gazes [**Fig. 66**]. Her focus rests on the German flag, a cipher of her own cultural and national identity [**see Fig. 120—WIND**]. Increasingly vestigial and fictive, national identity in the European Union is a mystery not only for Jeanne. At the same time the EU flag's suggestion of a cosmopolitan future identity provides no new solutions for the family, even though all of Europe becomes their 'country' as they can more freely cross borders undetected, both a blessing and a curse. In fact, Clara and Hans are figures that reinforce the nation, even if negatively. Their target has been the nation-state, an easily identifiable institution and form of power. Without this enemy, their life's work is irrelevant. Their generation did not succeed in achieving a wholesale overthrow of the authoritarian state; on the contrary, if anything it created a more clever and insidious one. Furthermore, though Clara wears dark glasses and seems to embrace her identity as leftist radical outlaw, being white, German (and middle-aged with a child) grants the family a certain privilege, made clear in a scene in which

See BORDERS

See WIND

Fig. 66: *The State I Am In.*

Fig. 67: *The State I Am In.*

they witness a group of illegal Albanian immigrants, fellow ghosts, rounded up by the police. As the family tensely waits to see who will be the target of the police crackdown, they inevitably identify with the 'aliens.' Yet, when the police start to chase down and haul away these illegal border crossers, the family seems to exhibit, along with relief, a slight sense of shame at both their own irrelevance—the police state has other targets now—and the privilege that their white skin and German tongue grant them. On the highways of the New Europe, Hans and Clara are also ghostly because they blend in almost too well; invisible and irrelevant, their life has lost its meaning.

In order to get to Brazil, Hans and Clara eventually rob a bank, but on the eve of their departure, Clara tells their story to Henry, the young man with whom she has fallen in love. Henry tips off the police. Yet as the end of the film shows, the apprehension of Hans and Clara will not be the occasion for a theatrical climax, a political debate, nor a meditation on Germany's past. There will be no press, no cameras, no trial. Clara and Hans are simply eliminated when their car is run off the highway—mafia style—by unmarked black vehicles. Their death made to look like an accident, they are finally erased from history. Jeanne is the sole survivor, and the film ends with her looking down the highway, perhaps the only witness of her generation who might eventually decide to attest to the existence of another past with different ideals and imagined futures **[Fig. 67]**.

Another film that deals with the nonsynchronicity of late-modern temporalities and histories, *Yella* is the only film of the Ghost Trilogy that represents this theme with supernatural narrative elements. In many ways it is a true ghost story or horror film insofar as it explicitly draws its tone and major plot points from Herk Harvey's *Carnival of Souls* (1962). The young woman of the title, an accountant from a dying East German town, at the moment of her death is able to glimpse how life would be were she to survive the suicide/homicide (by car crash) engineered by her ex-boyfriend, Ben. A meditation on the definition of 'success' for those (East Germans) who have just been brought into Europe's new globalized economy, *Yella* reveals that the rapidity of change and the sudden possibility of vertiginous social mobility has meant that 'life' can signify nothing else. 'Death' is to be immobile, inert, and shut out of the realm of high-speed, high-stakes capital. Death is to be trapped in the past of those East German cities left off the map of the new global economy. In *Yella*, globalization has passed over cities like Wittenberg and Dessau, now ghost towns whose only residents are the old and dying or the invalid, the loser, the n'er-do-well.

On one level, then, Yella is a ghost by virtue of literally being caught in a purgatory between life and death. On the other, though, this supernatural state is of course a metaphor for her plight: the film's opening sequence shows a train traveling back to Wittenberg (it traverses the screen from right to left), a journey back in time, reinforced by the view from the train's windows: countryside followed by aging infrastructure and the absence of people and cars. We later learn that Yella is briefly returning home to Wittenberg from Hanover, where she has finally found a job as an accountant. She will stay just long enough to pack her things and say goodbye to her father. We see Yella exit the train station, and walk with cold determination through Wittenberg's shabby streets. Her gaze fixed in front of her, she steers clear of Ben, her former boyfriend and business partner, who has, it seems, lost everything. Ben appears from out of nowhere like a ghost from the past, to stalk, jeer, and taunt her with reminders of what she refuses to become: like him, a failure **[Fig. 68]**. Throughout the film, Ben appears from behind the shadows calling Yella back to the deadly life she so fears. Thus, following the car crash when an unconscious Yella suddenly jerks awake at the sound of a crow, she merely exhibits another example of the superhuman determination that we have already witnessed: to escape mediocrity, invisibility, and her own immobility in a failing East German town. *Yella* then meditates upon the ghostly status accorded to the losers in a winner-takes-all global economy and suggests that it is a fear of nonbeing, of 'death,' rather than simple ambition, that drives women like Yella to succeed. Ben is again the constant reminder of the ghostly existence from which Yella flees: his start-up company failed, he has nothing but his company-owned car to show for his former status and freedom, an ironic symbol given his utter immobility and entrapment.

With Kafka-esque humor Petzold includes several references in *Yella* to a company called the 'The Dissolve Group.' The latter is the undertaker,

Fig. 68: *Yella*.

the ragpicker of dead companies; it exploits the bankrupt, who need all the liquidity they can get. 'Dissolve' has bought the leftover IT equipment from Ben and Yella's company at fire-sale prices. 'Dissolve' also appears in the accounting pages of the company that Yella and her new partner in Hanover, Philipp, are assessing for investment purposes. The name 'Dissolve Group' indicates the moribund. But the Dissolve Group also symbolizes capitalism's inadequate solutions to the problem of its losers, the bankrupt subjects who stall and disrupt the endless transfers and exchanges, and who work against the flexibility late capitalism requires. In *Yella*, when the Dissolve Group seeks to remove those insolvent subjects from the system, they resist in a sense by taking their dissolution one step further and committing suicide by drowning, as does Ben, who tries to take Yella with him. And the film's climax takes place when Yella, to save Philipp from his own dissolution by getting him 200,000 Euros, blackmails a client, who then drowns himself in despair, anticipating, we can assume, the inevitable arrival of the Dissolve Group. At a meeting where they await the man so that they can close the deal, Yella suddenly sees his corpse, dripping wet, eyes closed **[Fig. 69]**. These drowned bodies, ghosts made flesh, insist, then, that the Dissolve Group produces a fiction, because it can never succeed in eliminating the materiality, the biological life upon which the whole system finally depends.

After she locates the drowned man in the pond behind his home, the film's final sequence cuts to Yella silently weeping in the backseat of a police car, and another cut returns her, once again, to Ben's car on the bridge **[see Fig. 7—AMBIENT SOUND]**. Returning to the fateful moment just

Fig. 69: *Yella*.

before the end, this time Yella does not scream out or try to stop Ben as he turns the wheel toward the river. The final shot of the film shows the police covering up Yella's own dead body. Exhausted by her own future, in which 'life' is an endless flight from the 'death' of financial failure, Yella's acceptance of her drowning is a gesture of solidarity with the other 'ghosts,' who have refused their invisibility, the fiction of dematerialization, and dissolution.

In the new globalized spaces represented in Petzold's films, connections—familial, affective, biological—are random, fragmentary, and, owing to the gaps that separate capitalism's subjects from one another, inevitably narcissistic. Surveillance cameras are at once symptoms of this alienation and one means by which connections are maintained. In *Ghosts* surveillance videotape is the only record of the abduction of a French couple's child from a Berlin supermarket **[see Fig. 97—PREDECESSORS]**. The tape memorializes the moment of loss when the mother, Françoise, looked away, the moment when flesh and blood was transformed into a ghostliness that forever haunts the present. As if replaying the tape again and again Françoise compulsively returns to Berlin, where she accosts adolescent girls, each of whom she believes is her lost child. Prosperous and mobile, Françoise can afford to become herself the one who surveils, a kind of stalker who attempts to give her ghost daughters embodiment, only to abandon them anew once they become flesh and blood. In one scene, a high angle shot reveals her gaze as she looks down from her Berlin hotel room after her husband Pierre has fetched her from a mental institute. As she spies the teenage girls Nina and Toni, her eyes flicker, and the ritual begins again. Nina is the random

See HOTELS

See SURVEILLANCE

target of her attention, and the montage that depicts Nina and Françoise's first meeting suggests that class difference permits Françoise to track down her ghosts: possessing the powerful gaze of the mother, of the wealthy, Françoise watches before she strikes. Thus, the surveillance tape recording Nina shoplifting is linked to the tape of the baby's abduction through the gaze of the wealthy French woman, who has taken a dubious control over her own traumatic memory by manipulating others. As Nina exits the store with her stolen clothes, we expect the hand that accosts her to be that of the store security guard. Instead, the camera reveals that Françoise chases down the frightened girl so that, staring deep into her eyes, she can ritualistically list the physical markings that will allow her to claim this unwanted child as a daughter **[Fig. 70]**. Never knowing when the ghost of the child, Marie, will appear, Françoise deals with the eruption of her trauma by repeatedly replaying with a difference the scene of loss: this time she will watch, and she will instigate the separation.

Nina is indeed ghostly in the sense of being a not fully (economically) legitimate subject. Off the radar, she wanders Berlin as an outcast and a ward of the state. Nonetheless, Nina is a flesh-and-blood subject, herself possessed by a loss and by the compulsion to repeat the primal scene that haunts her. As she quietly picks up trash with other community laborers, she witnesses a young woman, Toni, being beaten up by a pair of men who leave her disheveled and bloody-mouthed. Nina falls instantly in love with the untrustworthy and street-smart Toni, who convinces her to audition for a reality television show called 'Freundinnen' ('Girl Friends'), which

Fig. 70: *Ghosts.*

Fig. 71: *Ghosts.*

requires two teenaged best-friends-forever to tell the story of their meeting, the more fancifully the better. At the audition, Toni stumbles through a series of clichés about their first meeting (shreds of which seem to refer to Toni's own ghostly scene of primal loss); she is on the verge of bungling her big chance, when Nina begins in a halting voice to recount 'their' story, a fantasy version of what was likely her own abduction and rape as a child **[Fig. 71]**.

Nina states that when she saw Toni she realized that she was the girl in her dreams, the dream she always has in which she watches powerlessly as a beautiful young girl is raped in a car in the woods by two men. Nina recounts how in the dream the girl's screams subside as she stares back at Nina and their gazes remain locked. In this fantasy, Nina doubles herself and watches her own traumatic injury from a distance. The power of her own gaze is self-healing, a gaze of empathy, and one that empowers her without requiring a disempowered stand-in, or someone upon whom to project her memories. The authenticity of Nina's telling and the strange erotic beauty of the story impress the producer and the girls are invited to a party. Toni abandons Nina there, which underscores Nina's isolation and potentially edges her back in the direction of Françoise.

Nina then returns to the place where she met Françoise, and the two pick up where they left off. Pierre, however, merely touches his wife's hand and that is enough to call Françoise back to her senses. Françoise withdraws her gaze, abandoning Nina (perhaps for a second time). When Pierre tries to give Nina money, Nina refuses her own exploitation, and insists on the physical proof of her identity—a heart-shaped mole on her back—and thus on her right to claim the status of legitimate daughter, to which he replies coldly, 'Marie is dead.' Whether he means literally or figuratively, we don't know, and although Nina bears the physical markings as evidence of her rightful identity, the French couple turns her into a ghost, negates her, and returns her to the land of the walking dead. Indeed, Françoise and Pierre's relationship is dependent upon having a ghostly and not a real daughter. Earlier, Françoise is surprised to learn that her husband has made a business appointment in Berlin, suggesting that his trips to retrieve his ill wife have become commonplace. Worse, he seems to encourage her to repeat her compulsive forays to seek out the ghostly daughter. For his part, Pierre has replaced the loss of his daughter with the compulsion to repeat the loss and recovery of his wife. Françoise and Pierre have the means to play out their compulsive repetitions, rituals that depend upon the ghostly status and the quasi-invisibility of the homeless teenager, the runaway, the orphan, the ward of the state.

The film ends with Nina retracing her steps from the day before until she discovers Françoise's wallet, which Toni stole and discarded. Inside the wallet, Nina discovers a baby picture and an artist's rendering of Marie's face as it matures over the years **[see Fig. 43—ENDINGS]**. The final image is almost unmistakably that of the adolescent Nina. *Ghosts* is thus a cautionary tale: Françoise is too attached to the ghostly memory—she loves her ghost so much that she is unable to recognize and accept the real thing. But Nina, as revealed in her half-real and half-fictive story about Toni, understands that our chosen love objects are always simultaneously ghosts and also Others with their own losses, traumas, and stories. Nina also seeks out her ghosts, but she is willing to step into the fantasies of others, to play the ghost; such reciprocity can potentially lead to pain (the loss of Toni and of Françoise, for example) but it opens up a space of future possibility and allows one to escape the death of endless repetition.

See ENDINGS

The ghosts of Petzold's trilogy symbolically map the terrain of late-modern subjectivities, spaces, and histories, both personal and political. Often seeking to be off the radar screen of the New Europe, with its apparatuses of control and containment, Petzold's ghosts, like Nina, point toward new ways of living with dislocation, fragmentation, and alienation.

See INTERIORITY

VK

Hotels

In the films of the Berlin School, hotel visits and stays are rampant. In the hotel, these films foreground and thematize a pivotal icon of modernity, common in cinema at least since the 1920s. These recurring images of the hotel point to some of the spatial characteristics of these works, underscoring both the importance and negotiation of space in the narrative and technical approach of the Berlin School. In the existing scholarship on literary and (more rarely) cinematic representations of hotels, the public and private spheres tend to be the central tropes, that is, the narratively and spatially structuring principle. But analyzing the hotel as vacillating between the private and public spheres reveals very little about the refracted structure of contemporary desire that Berlin School films explore. Rather than merely offering the intersection or entwinement of the public and private, the Berlin School hotels manifest much more a recurring dialectic of business-dominated/alienated space symptomatic of modern mobility and personally invested and meaningful place. And the films memorably explore deformation of desires and fantasies that arise from the negotiation of these dialectical spaces in the contemporary lifeworld.

With respect to alienating spaces, hotels suggest what Henri Lefebvre has termed 'abstract space' and Marc Augé has called 'non-places.'[1] Petzold, for instance, has emphasized the influence of Augé on *Yella*, and Lefebvre's influence is palpable in Augé's anthropology of contemporary spaces. At the core of Lefebvre's abstract spaces and Augé's non-places is the manner in which largely abstract economic processes increasingly dominate the planning and living of human space. Lefebvre traces how the aesthetic visions of earlier urban design were increasingly dispensed with in favor of profit maximization. For Lefebvre, this means that 'reproducibility, repetition and reproduction of social relationships' attain clear precedence over nature.[2] Lefebvre gives the extended example of a city grid as the deliberate production of abstract space, and, indeed, the contrast between lower Manhattan's snaking alleys and its uptown grids materializes the historical development and conquering of earlier, less abstract spatial organization.[3] In their repetitive rooms, long corridors, and general logical layout, hotel spaces are structured by business rationale at some remove from the conventional private home.

The Berlin-School films' critiques of built environments structured by profit maximization hint at the generic precedents for some of these films. The hotels of these films indicate how the works of the Berlin School, rather like Sophia Coppola's *Somewhere* (2010), engage with and critique modern spaces as they were developed not only in films during the 1920s, but also in modernist classics by Michelangelo Antonioni (e.g., *L'avventura* [1960]) and Alain Resnais (e.g., *L'année dernière à Marienbad/Last Year at Marienbad* [1961]). *L'avventura*, in particular, as Dominik Graf has observed, seems influential for the Berlin School. And, indeed, one can see the influence of these films in the many Berlin School films that deploy the hotel: Jessica Hausner's *Hotel*, Christoph Hochhäusler's *This Very Moment*, Ulrich Köhler's *Windows on Monday* as well as *Bungalow*; Pia Marais's *Im Alter von Ellen/At Ellen's Age* (2010); Birgit Moeller's *Valerie*; and Petzold's *The State I Am In*, *Ghosts*, *Yella*, and *Beats Being Dead*.

Yet a trenchant critique of these symptomatic spaces of our contemporary society is only part of the story. A deeper disquiet comes when the films See INTERIORITY reveal how the hotel has colonized human fantasy, along with its ability to desire and imagine as it yearns for something better. This tendency becomes clear in how the hotels in these films do not merely represent these abstract spaces and non-places, but also depict them as potentially emancipatory places away from the home—or at least they function as imaginarily emancipatory spaces that demonstrate the desire to get away from conventional homes. To cite Gilles Deleuze, one of Petzold's stated influences, reterritorializing tendencies manifest themselves alongside the clearly nomadic protagonists and deterritorializing processes of contemporary economy.[4] Scholars writing about hotels have tended to cite the motto 'home away from home' ironically, underscoring the putative impossibility of the place of a home in the abstract spaces of the hotel. In these films, however, the hotel serves ambiguously, not only as abstract space of estrangement, of deformed experience and maimed humanity, but also somewhat emancipatorily as a place vested and producing personal meaning and social ritual away from the home. They are not simply alienating amidst and via estranged spaces—they are fantasized as See FAMILIAR PLACES something quite the opposite, as meaningful and longed-for places.

In these ways, the hotel seems to house a spatial dialectic between the deterritorialized alienation of modern life (as one finds it in *L'avventura* or *One Minute of Darkness*) and a recurring longing for place that manifests itself in often distorted fantasies of a private house (as in Petzold's *Pilotinnen/ Pilots* [1995] or *Yella*). This tension between the abstract, modern space of the hotel and the hotel as a symptom of an atavistic longing for place recurs throughout the films. The question for these narrative films is how characters, that is, individual subjects, negotiate such abstract spaces and non-places—to look at them from the point of view of subjects, not only at the macrolevel of design and planning. The films, particularly Petzold's, Hausner's, and Köhler's, seem to unfold from the perspective of the characters in what Petzold has called a 'bubble' or parallel world.[5] The hotel turns out to be a hermetic world in which individual subjects relate to one another, desire, and display affect, all without mediating back to any larger scale project or collective political project (hence the 'bubble'). Kracauer emphasized how the hotel lobby was a place of smoothness and depthlessness, a collective space increasingly hollowed out of tensions inherent in striving for a different, better community—instead, individuals' desires become paramount. In his chapter 'Hotel Lobby,' Kracauer contrasts the church community, with its tensions between earthly strictures and divine yearning, to the hotel lobby, which is completely uniform, empty, and flat.[6] There is no utopian project here in the hotel the hotel itself, as the bubble or parallel world, underscores the postlapsarian nature of the very concept of utopia. It is precisely the combination of a spatialized study plus a sensitivity for fantasy and the subjective that mark the hotels in the films.

Details from just three of the films cited above confirm the hotel as housing this ongoing dynamic of deterritorializing, modern space, and a reterritorializing longing for place. I choose these three films not least because they operate in significantly different stylistic and tonal registers: Moeller's *Valerie* is a film that seems different from most Berlin School works due to its more familiar style and narrative approach—it would seem to belong to a series of stylistically and narratively less challenging Berlin-School films like Elke Hauck's *Karger* (2007) or Marais's *At Ellen's Age*. *Valerie* was, however, shot in contemporary Berlin—like Petzold's *Ghosts*, largely at Potsdamer Platz—and it explores many of the recurring themes of the Berlin School (under- and unemployment, financial struggles, and subsequent metaphysical estrangement in the contemporary Berlin Republic). Featuring less mainstream approaches and styles, the other two films, Hausner's *Hotel* and Petzold's *Yella*, deploy the hotel to recast horror classics. In these quasi-horror films, the hotel becomes a kind of mental space emblematic of modern alienation and unfulfilled longing.

Hotel seems directly engaged with, and certainly cites, Stanley Kubrick's *The Shining* (1980), while *Yella* opaquely recasts a psychological horror classic, *Carnival of Souls* (Herk Harvey, 1962), to depict the employment travails (and travels) of its ghost-like heroine at some distance from mainstream character identification. Although the three films vary in their representational and narrative styles, they all use the space of hotels in remarkably similar ways, as emblematic of contemporary alienation and as symptomatic of the maimed fantasy of the individuals suffering under it.

In *Valerie*, when the audience first encounters the eponymous protagonist—a Polish fashion model—she has been staying in the Grand Hyatt at Potsdamer Platz, accommodations indicative of her lifestyle and career in general, including her studied postures, extravagant couture clothes and vintage sports car. She attends parties, goes to photo shoots in SoHo-style lofts, and meets with her modeling agency handler at a sushi bar near the Hyatt. The hotel is thus a paradigmatic and constituent aspect of contemporary work life, in its normative mobility and required 'flexibility.' But it rapidly becomes clear that this lifestyle is transpiring, soon expiring, on borrowed time: her jobs, even escort assignments, are drying up; her photographer-boyfriend is moving on to a younger, suspiciously similar-looking woman; and her friends are oblivious to her suffering, even as she desperately begins to eye a large kitchen knife.

When she can no longer afford the hotel room she occupies in the film's first 20 minutes, she is left to sleep in her car in the hotel's underground parking lot, where an attendant at first scolds her and then befriends her. Her hotel bubble space, part and parcel of both her career and fantasies about it, has been significantly downgraded. The film tellingly takes place over a few days during Christmas. Valerie celebrates this holiday that is normally spent with loving family and friends in a dark and dirty corner bar (an *Eckkneipe*), with strangers at far socioeconomic remove from the hotel and then with the parking garage attendants in their festively decorated subterranean booth. Deep space, deep focus shots of the hotel corridors and parking garage are combined with shallow focus, close-ups of the heroine as she tries to ignore the growing assaults of her increasingly hostile hotel surroundings. She is trying to block out the encroaching brutality of contemporary life and work, materialized in the oppressive architecture of the postmodern hotel.

See DISENGAGEMENT, INTERPELLATION

In both the younger model now occupying her photographer-boyfriend's bed and in a homeless woman at the bar who declares Valerie and her own run-down self to be sisters, *Valerie* plays out one of the central anxieties manifest in the hotel film as well as in many films of the Berlin School: that of the fundamental and thoroughgoing seriality of people in modern life. Individuals in contemporary society are not only imminently replaceable, but also, perhaps more disturbingly, are always replacing someone else who has been dismissed, disappeared and/or disposed of. The hotel, with its revolving roster of guests and rooms, offers an eerie architectural paradigm for this seriality and exchangeability of human life.

This seriality and exchangeability in the modern workplace are central themes of Hausner's quasi-horror film *Hotel*, which resets Kubrick's horror (and hotel-centered) classic *The Shining* to a rural Austrian hotel. Here, however, the protagonist is not a middle-aged father and would-be writer but rather a young woman, the earnest but perpetually spooked Irene, trying to enter the workforce. Although Hausner's *Hotel* derives more drama from her interaction with the (living) hotel staff and guests than *The Shining*, both films emphasize how the contradictory spaces of the hotel, as simultaneously homey and emphatically uncanny, can lead to hallucinations and horror. In both films, the hotels' serial architecture—as well as its beautiful natural context—start to impinge on the thoughts, dreams, and fears of the protagonist, such that the repeating rooms down endless corridors become a menacing mental as well as physical space **[Fig. 72]**. In both films, there is the dawning sense that the perpetually serial turnover of the hotel hints at an elusive, terrifying past and the ghosts it generates. Irene, in *Hotel*, begins to realize (like Jack in *The Shining*) that a predecessor disappeared under mysterious and likely criminal

See VIOLENCE

FIG. 72: *Hotel*.

circumstances. Despite the familiar horror effects of the hotel corridor and its surrounding landscape and forest, Hausner's *Hotel* does not go very far in developing the crime plot—the investigating policemen remain at the fringes of the narrative—and opts instead to make the hotel and its ghosts a metaphor for the struggles of the contemporary workplace.

See GHOSTS

A hotel, the appearance of ghosts, and the uncanniness of the contemporary workplace constitute the thematic constellation of Petzold's *Yella* as well. In *Valerie*, Devid Striesow plays the kindly hotel garage attendant who helps the protagonist navigate her lonely holiday, and he returns to the hotel in *Yella*, in which he plays the man whom Yella (another eponymous protagonist) meets in that film's eerily lit hotel restaurant. In *Yella*, he plays Philipp, a traveling venture-capital analyst/ love interest whose memorable pick-up line to Yella in the hotel restaurant queries her interest in financial statements. Such a mélange of romance and business is a telling inquiry for a hotel that seems to have little other purpose than to house transient traveler-workers, as there are no sights or cities nearby. Like Valerie and Irene, Yella is an economic immigrant, who left her home (both Valerie and Yella are from the former Eastern Bloc) in the pursuit of professional fantasies that the hotel will ambiguously house and undercut. Much as in *Valerie* and *Hotel*, there is uncertainty about a young professional woman's finances and future, staged in all the films as the fading fortunes of a last job opportunity and a semi-handsome stranger who might help, professionally, emotionally, or both. Deep-focus, deep-space shots of hotel corridors foreground, as in *Valerie*

See STRIESOW, DEVID

FIG. 73: *Hotel*.

FIG. 74: *Yella.*

and *Hotel*, the serial nature of both work and of life in general at this historical moment (for example, when Valerie searches the corridor for a door left accidentally open, when *Hotel*'s Irene peers down a corridor into the abyss [**Fig. 73**] or when Yella dashes down the hotel hallway after seeing her estranged Ben suddenly appear in her room [**Fig. 74**]). It is a disquieting seriality that might, on the other hand, be undercut by fundamentally meeting the right person at the hotel: figured, in all the films, by the image of a door menacingly ajar that breaks the monotony of the corridor. Here again, through its use of mise-en-scène, the fantasy of found love and social mobility has been evacuated by an abstract non-place associated with the post-unification era. As the larger settings—the hotels' surroundings—turn bleaker, the characters' gestures become more desperate, and the films' conclusions grow ever colder.

JF

Notes

1 See Henri Lefebvre, *The Production of Space*, trans. Donald Nicholson-Smith (Malden, MA: Blackwell, 1991); and Marc Augé, *Non-Places: Introduction to an Anthropology of Supermodernity* (London: Verso, 1995).

2 Henri Lefebvre, *Introduction to Modernity: Twelve Preludes, September 1959-May 1961*, trans. John Moore (London: Verso, 1995), 120.

3 Lefebvre, *Production of Space*, 150–58.

4 'Civilized modern societies are defined by processes of decoding and deterritorialization. But *what they deterritorialize with one hand, they reterritorialize with the other*. . . for example, deterritorialization of the flows of finance, but reterritorialization of purchasing power and the means of payment.' Gilles Deleuze and Félix Guattari, *Anti-Oedipus* (London: Continuum, 2004), 279–80.

5 Christian Petzold, '*Gespenster*: Ein ausführliches Booklet' (Berlin: Piffl Medien, 2006), booklet accompanying DVD.

6 Siegfried Kracauer, 'The Hotel Lobby,' *The Mass Ornament: Weimar Essays*, trans. Thomas Y. Levin (Cambridge, MA: Harvard University Press, 1995), 173–86.

Interiority

Where are we going?—Home, always
(*Wo gehn wir denn hin?—Immer nach Hause*)
Novalis, *Heinrich von Ofterdingen*

In contrast to Lars von Trier and the rule-bound cinema of *Dogma 95*, the Berlin School never developed a programmatic vision of what constitutes the '*nouvelle vague allemande*.' Yet the Berlin School was clearly conceived as—and still remains—an antimainstream cinema opposed to the dramatic effects and moralizing stories that characterize the 'cinema of good intentions' (*Kino der guten Absichten*) and its aesthetics of 'identificatory emotionalization.'[1] The Berlin School instead develops what might be called an 'aesthetics of reduction,' exemplified in its long takes, static camera, sparse editing, and almost complete absence of close-ups and establishing shots, all of which serve to undermine the audience's ability to identify with or get close to the protagonists. Both stylistically and narratively, the protagonists are portrayed from the outside, so to speak, and their actions often remain unexplained—if not inexplicable—in psychological terms. Why does Rita decide to kill her parents in Jessica Hausner's *Lovely Rita?* (Indeed, Hausner's story is reminiscent of Rainer Werner Fassbinder's *Warum läuft Herr R. amok?/Why Does Herr R. Run Amok?* [1970]—except that this earlier film, unlike Hausner's, aims to provide a coherent answer to the question posed by its title). Why does Paul in Ulrich Köhler's *Bungalow* decide to go AWOL and risk criminal charges? What exactly is Sophie looking for as she roams the streets of Marseille in Angela Schanelec's *Marseille*, and what is the specific nature of Markus's sadness that drives him to attempt suicide in Valeska Grisebach's *Longing*?

These seem to be the wrong questions to ask, not only because they inevitably lead back to the identificatory mode of viewing the Berlin School hopes to transcend, but also because their films deliberately thwart the viewers' expectations and their search for meaning. Rather than trying to dissect its protagonists, to understand their motives and interpret their behavior, the directors seem content with recording their characters' mundane existence and daily lives—at home or at work, strolling in the park or navigating busy city streets. The characters, we might say, literally act (themselves) out; yet they nonetheless lack a center of gravity—a proper self—able to keep these acts together over time. This poses significant interpretative challenges for the audience. Psychoanalytic discourse, for one, has little to say about characters who refuse to talk, much like deconstruction or traditional hermeneutics has trouble operating on a cinematic surface that seeks to bypass the entire signifier–signified dynamic altogether in favor of producing a flat cinema Benjamin Heisenberg calls 'devoid of content' (*ein inhaltsleeres Kino*).

At the same time, however, questions about human intentionality are difficult to avoid not only due to our customary interpretive habits, but also because the Berlin School refuses to entertain them in the first place. We cannot help but look for clues that give meaning to what we see, and the more enigmatic the object under investigation, the more intense this search becomes. This dialectic sustains both art and aesthetics—a truism made evident in the marvelous closing sequence of Grisebach's *Longing* that shows a group of kids narrating and joyfully commenting on the film's story: 'Courageous, courageous'—'Stupidity, complete stupidity'—'Somehow that is also romantic'—'Cool.' They also speculate on what might have happened after Markus's attempted suicide: does he reunite with his wife or his lover? Does true love really exist—is it fate or fantasy, real or imagined? *Longing* makes clear that the story never ends as long as there are human minds left to ponder it.

See ENDINGS

Given this premise, what are we to make of the Berlin School's focus on the human body: its affects, its gestures and its physical movement through space? My central argument is that these films unfold psychology in(to) geography. Human subjectivity, in other words, is depicted as a possible effect of bodily movement rather than posited as its original cause. Movement matters precisely because it ontologically precedes the elusive subjectivity the protagonists hope to find. This spatial unfolding of the human mind also explains why traditional psychological models fail to signify in these films. Neither behaviorism, which interprets behavior as willful acts of autonomous individuals, nor evolutionary psychology, which explains behavior in terms of genetic predispositions and innate mental structures beyond individual control, can help explain the protagonists' erratic behavior: one theory presupposes human subjectivity, and the other denies it. Neither is able to elucidate the individual's *struggle for subjectivity*.

What we see on screen are less embodied minds than minding bodies—bodies still searching for a proper mind to call their own.

Berlin School cinema connects the (Freudian) topology of the subject's inner mind with a (Bayesian) topography of its bodily movement through external space. This simply means that the protagonists' restless search for self-identity serves to delineate the spatial continuum between the two poles of body and mind. This 'in-between' space, by its very nature, must remain ambiguous: it encompasses both concrete (geographical) locations and the abstract (conceptual) realm of the human mind. It is both a literal and a metaphorical space, because this very distinction itself is at stake in these movies. Cognitive science, in fact, teaches us that our mental apparatus—including, above all, our sense of subjectivity—operates on the basis of primary metaphors grounded in physical experience: 'There is now very strong evidence that essentially all of our cultural, abstract, and theoretical concepts derive their meanings by mapping, through *metaphor*, to the embodied experiential concepts,' claims Jerome Feldman.[2] Once we recognize concepts as metaphors that map bodily experience onto mental space (e.g. 'up is more' and 'down is less'), the metaphysical binary between real (geographical) space and abstract (mental) space collapses, because everything takes place between the two. This incessant movement between spaces characterizes Berlin School cinema.

In methodological terms, this means that each individual case is less significant than the overall patterns of behavior that arise across a representative sample of these films. Although we must pay close attention to each individual scene, our interpretation must also reflect the stylistic and narrative configurations that bind this cinematic movement together and testify to the close collaboration between its core members. This perspective gives rise to a spatial topography that provides important clues for how to read these films. For one, it highlights the economic stratification that divides different (national) territories: in *This Very Moment*, Sylvia crosses the Polish border 'to go shopping' because things are cheaper there, much like Yella moves from East to West Germany in search of a career she was unable to launch at home. See BORDERS

Moreover, these economic-spatial differences are rooted in—and point to—larger historical and sociocultural shifts: Yella, for example, See INTERPELLATION leaves behind not only her old father and her bankrupt husband, but also the antiquated world to which these figures belong, that is, the world of local business and an orientation toward productivity (i.e., the father's restaurant and the husband's bankrupt heating business). What she finds and embraces in Hanover, by contrast, is the twenty-first-century world of high finance and venture capitalism, whose spatial parameters are global, not local, and whose products are virtual, not material. Indeed, the main objective of Philipp's and Yella's business negotiations is to predict the future yield of an early investment into a nascent company or product that does not yet exist. They primarily deal in speculation: what matters is the future economic viability of their clients' *ideas* as opposed to their current material *assets*. The potential monetary yield of these ideas can only be assessed indirectly through their mode of presentation, which includes not only material values and numerical balance sheets, but human behavior and psychological tricks as well. 'It's a packaging question,' Yella responds to Philipp's own idea about how to sell cheap antibreak devices to big oil companies at hyperinflated prices. Yella instinctively understands that the 'material' value inside the box depends upon how it is wrapped and perceived from the outside. There is, so to speak, nothing inside the box until they are able to convince their customers to the contrary.

The same dynamic applies to many other Berlin School films, whose main characters often reinvent themselves in and through the stories they tell, like Jeanne and Achim in *The State I Am In*, or Toni and Nina in *Ghosts*, or Armin in *I Am Guilty*. In the end, however, it is up to their audience—both on the intra- and the extradiegetic levels—to decide what, if anything, hides inside the box. Obviously, such (aesthetic) judgments are risky because they always remain speculative. On the other hand, they are hardly more so than the (economic) judgments behind the financial transactions depicted in *Yella*. Both require an investment of sorts—be it thoughtful reflection or monetary transfer—in order to yield something in return: critical insight for the viewer or economic profit for the entrepreneur. Cultural critique, not unlike capitalist profiteering, presupposes the willingness to invest (oneself) into an idea. Both activities remain, by their very nature, speculative. One may lament this parallelism as evidence for the increasing economization of the cultural sphere in late capitalism—as 'the becoming cultural of the economic and the becoming economic of the cultural'—that no longer leaves any space for aesthetic reflection.[3] One may also welcome it as a reminder that ideas always matter, because all things remain, to some degree, virtual, and 'purely actual objects do not exist,' neither in art nor anywhere else.[4]

Whichever perspective one chooses, the cinematic world depicted in Berlin School films is clearly one in which (conceptual and territorial) borders have dissolved into a flat surface crisscrossed by the incessant flow of various (physical, libidinal, fiscal, etc) forces—'everything solid melts into the air,' as the young Marx had predicted almost two centuries ago. The precarious state of human subjectivity that results from these movements becomes evident in the scarcity and inhospitality of the protagonists' private living spaces, many of which they inhabit either illegally, as in *The State I Am In*, or temporarily, as in Schanelec's films, where people housesit for friends or swap apartments with strangers. Equally significant are the numerous hotel rooms, boarding houses or unoccupied buildings that play a crucial role in Köhler's and Petzold's films. The human self, much like its temporary home, is thus depicted as an alien, impersonal, empty body—a foreign object literally under construction. To be sure, some of these homes are uncanny (*unheimlich*) in the strict, Freudian sense: they are sites of bourgeois repression that prompt violent outbursts or other symptoms of escapism, as in *Lovely Rita* and *I Am Guilty*. Others, however, are literally wrapped in plastic, still waiting to be unpacked, as in *This Very Moment* and *Windows on Monday*. These houses are unhomely in the more literal sense that their inhabitants are not at home even if they happen to live there. *This Very Moment* provides a perfect example—one among many—in the scene when Kuba tries to contact the children's parents. As the phone keeps ringing, the film first cuts to an external view of the family's sterile home before moving inside and from room to room in a series of static shots utterly devoid of life **[Fig. 75]**. Reminiscent of Fritz Lang's famous sequence in *M* (1931)—the mother anxiously calling out the name of her child as the camera cuts from one empty space to another—Hochhäusler's montage of static and photographic images signifies, above all, absence; it culminates in the view of Sylvia sleeping motionless on the bed, blinds drawn and hands folded as if she were lying in a coffin. This house, like many others in Berlin School cinema, resembles a tomb more than a home, because the people living there, though still shown breathing, are already dead inside.

See HOTELS

See FAMILIAR PLACES, RENOVATION

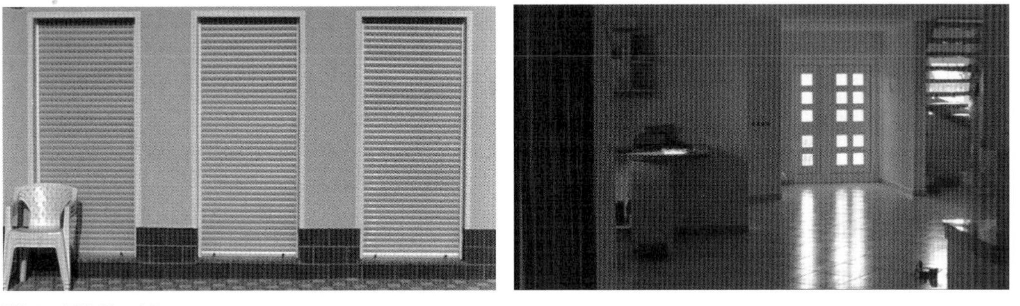

FIG. 75: *This Very Moment.*

Stylistically, the lifelessness of these interior spaces is emphasized through square angles and horizontal lines that frame the protagonists as if to lend structural support to their fragile selves. This aesthetics reflects—or might even be directly influenced by—the works of several contemporary photographers trained in the Düsseldorfer Kunstakademie (Düsseldorf Academy of Art) under Hilla and Bernd Becher in the 1980s and 1990s. Like the Berlin School, the Becher School favors an aesthetics of reduction and repetition that provides ample opportunities for the study of visual patterns: the Bechers' original works from the 1970s feature photographic series of similar objects (like windmills, water towers, or industrial plants all shown from the same perspective). Their students, meanwhile, have modified this approach to include interior spaces (Andreas Gursky; Candida Höfer), empty streets (Thomas Struth), and human faces (Thomas Ruff). These photographs not only mirror the compositional pattern of the most prevalent shots in Berlin School cinema, but also raise similar questions about their specific meaning and the limits of interpretation. Although I cannot examine the parallelism between these two schools any further in this essay, the two juxtapositions of images below might help clarify my point **[Figs. 76 and 77]**.

My central claim has been that Berlin School cinema depicts human characters in search of a proper identity so their restless bodies can find a home. I have also suggested that these films require a considerable amount of emotional, intellectual and hermeneutic investment from their audience in order to yield any critical insight into the current geopolitical situation. This last claim can be substantiated with reference to closing shots—shared by so many Berlin School films—of protagonists heading away from the

FIG. 76a: Candida Höfer, *Bank Oldenburg.*

FIG. 76b: *Ghosts.*

FIG. 77a: Candida Höfer, *Bauhaus Dessau.*

FIG. 77b: *Hotel.*

camera and into an uncertain future until they literally vanish from sight. In Hochhäusler's *This Very Moment* Lea and Konstantin disappear into the horizon **[see Fig. 49—FAMILIAR PLACES]**; in Hausner's *Hotel*, Irene fades into the dark forest **[see Fig. 56—FORESTS]**; and Paul performs a miraculous vanishing act at the end of Köhler's *Bungalow* **[see Fig. 91—LONG TAKES]**. How are we to interpret these shots? Are they allegories of physical dying or of spiritual self-transcendence? Is this the end or a new beginning—or maybe both?

See ENDINGS

The same ambiguity haunts the final scenes of Petzold's 'Ghost Trilogy': Does Jeanne's surreal awakening after the car crash—her fingers stirring in the earth, her body bathed in sunlight to the sound of chirping birds in a green field under blue skies—symbolize her rebirth as a new person liberated from the yoke of her previous (self-)alienation? Or does her bloody face and dazed stare into the (off-screen) distance betray anxiety about her own fate and that of her parents? **[see Fig. 67—GHOSTS]**. Does Nina ultimately refuse or accept her (possible) identity as Françoise's daughter when we see her discarding the photographs and walking off into the distance? Is Yella's decision *not* to grab the steering wheel of Ben's car at the end of the movie a sign of resignation and despair—a passive acceptance of death? Or is it instead a conscious act of resistance that, finally, renders her a true 'subject' precisely by refusing to accept the capitalist modes of exchange—a 'becoming human' that would be utterly at odds with Deleuze and Guattari's philosophy? I, for one, would loathe to trade places with any of these characters, nor am I inspired by the escapism of so many others whose search for self-identity terminates in police custody (as in Hochhäusler's *I Am Guilty*), religious belief (as in Heisenberg's *Sleeper*), or death (as in Grisebach's *Longing* and Petzold's *Yella*). At the same time, there seems no better place to be than among the group of kids at the end of *Longing*, and I would love to be able to join them in the final scene, joking and laughing in the street on their way back home.

CS

Notes

1 Benjamin Heisenberg, 'Revolver Selbstgespräch,' in *Revolver: Kino muss gefährlich sein*, ed. Marcus Seibert (Frankfurt am Main: Verlag der Autoren, 2006), 9–30; here 19.
2 Jerome A. Feldman, *From Molecule to Metaphor: A Neural Theory of Language* (Cambridge, MA: MIT Press, 2006), 199.
3 Frederic Jameson, *The Cultural Turn: Selected Writings on the Postmodern, 1983–1998* (London: Verso, 1998), 73.
4 Gilles Deleuze and Claire Parnet, *Dialogues II* (New York: Columbia University Press, 2002), 148.

Interpellation

While the acting style of many films of the Berlin School tends toward the nontheatrical and minimalist (limited affect, minimal dialogue, restrained bodily gestures, etc.), 'acting' itself is often highlighted, not as a craft or art, but as a figure representing the process of interpellation. In an oft-quoted essay, Louis Althusser defines 'interpellation' as the process through which individuals recognize themselves as subjects of a society's guiding ideological apparatuses. Ideology, according to Althusser, exists materially in the gestures and rituals of everyday life; and is embodied in institutions such as schools, churches, and states. To be interpellated is to be 'recruited' for or 'transformed' by such apparatuses, and to accept one's subjection so that '[one] shall make the gestures and actions of . . . subjection all by himself.'[1] The paradox, for Althusser, is that the acting out of such prescribed roles 'guarantee[s] for us that we are indeed concrete, individual, distinguishable and (naturally) irreplaceable subjects.'[2] On the other hand, to be outside of ideology, that is, to remain 'free' of subjection and interpellation, means to forfeit possible recognition, to accede to invisibility and nonbeing.

In Christoph Hochhäusler's *I Am Guilty* and Jessica Hausner's *Lovely Rita*, we encounter young protagonists struggling with this paradox. In both films, late adolescence is a moment of clarity as these subjects on the cusp of independence realize that they must choose between two equally untenable possibilities: conformity and a false form of recognition or renunciation and invisibility. In both films, the young protagonists solve their dilemma by performing acts of violence that will allow them both to be seen and to remain outsiders. What both films add to the well-worn trope of the criminal teen is an almost ethnographic attention to the tiny gestures and speech acts of everyday life through which processes of normalization and interpellation take place.

Lovely Rita focuses on how such processes play out for young women. The film's narrative involves Rita's attempts to resist the kinds of roles and gestures that she is required to perform. As the 'dutiful daughter,' she must kiss her father goodbye each day and pour wine at tableside like a trained server, though she is ill-equipped to do so. When Rita sulks, she is berated for her 'sour face,' for not fully embracing her interpellated role. Indeed, in this middle-class home, such gestures of *politesse* mask a violence that both literally and figuratively lurks underground. The first shot of the film shows a body target riddled with bullet holes, a prop that adorns a wall in the family basement, where Norbert, Rita's father, practices his shooting skills. While she is not threatened with the father's gun, Rita is regularly locked in her bedroom like a prisoner, usually for not putting down the toilet seat cover, a gesture she stubbornly refuses to learn though she is forced to perform it repeatedly before her parents' watchful gaze. One brief scene offers a window onto Rita's past, as we watch her older sister force her toddler-aged daughter to perform a song. When Rita's father giggles, scoffing at the child's anxiety and fear, which causes her to urinate on the floor, her exasperated mother halts the performance **[Fig. 78]**. The intensity of the child's response and the mother's anger at this 'failure' suggests that performance in *Lovely Rita* is never just for fun.

See VIOLENCE

But the theme of role-playing as disciplining and interpellation is principally evoked in scenes in which Rita rehearses in a school production of A. J. Priestley's 1945 play *When an Inspector Calls*. The scene that the young actors perform involves polite conversation at cocktail hour in the bourgeois home (not unlike the scene at Rita's home). Their awkward and halting English and their struggle to recall their lines reveals the artificiality of this ritual of social intercourse. Requiring memorization

FIG. 78: *Lovely Rita*.

and rehearsing, playacting here reinforces the sense that the dinner table is a training ground for learning the gestures that must be adopted by 'normal' disciplined subjects. As in everyday life, the actors play roles. Thematizing her subordinate status in her own family, Rita plays the maid, Edna, a character who has no lines. Edna is a double for the play's structuring absence, Daisy, the maid who has committed suicide, following mistreatment by her employers. Priestley's play is a socialist classic, and it appears ironically on the stage of the conservative Catholic school, where it serves as a ritual for rehearsing the gestures of normalcy and containment that the original play in fact attempts to critique. But in a sense reclaiming the play's critique of the bourgeoisie, Rita refuses her assigned role, and, during one rehearsal, breaks from the script to recite the lines of the character Sheila, the play's young ingénue, because the actress, Rita's classmate with whom she is trapped in a rivalry, forgets them. For the play's premiere, Rita—replaying the violence she has learned at home—locks the actress into a basement dressing room. She proceeds to steal her costume and the role of Sheila, and then make her entrance on stage to the shock of the other actors **[Fig. 79]**. Claiming lines and a subject position to which she has not been authorized, Rita stages a mini revolution. The other adolescent actors all wear stylized white mime makeup, the school production's attempt to represent the play's critique of bourgeois conformity. Appearing on stage without the makeup, Rita performs the role she wishes to play: that of the woman who speaks and who is served (a role she attempts to assume off-stage by wearing gaudy makeup and having an affair with an older bus

FIG. 79: *Lovely Rita.*

driver). Rita also hijacks the play's climax: in this particular scene, Sheila, like other family members before her, admits her complicity in Daisy's suicide. Resisting her real-life victimization by stepping into the shoes of the 'master,' Rita is empowered to speak and to command others. What she doesn't realize is that this role, too, is a mask that suffocates.

Rita's 'off-stage' rebellion involves cutting school to ride the bus of a sympathetic driver, with whom she eventually has sex, and to sleep with a young sickly neighbor boy, himself a prisoner of his family's worry and overbearing care. Refusing the familiar adolescent role of the masochistic girl who trusts the wrong men, *Lovely Rita* represents Rita's choices as authentic, dignified, and real. The glittery lipstick and blue eye shadow that she wears for her tryst with the bus driver is a masquerade that, similar to stealing the role of Sheila, is also an act of freedom. Rita's rebellions against interpellation into polite society are not meant so much to draw attention, but to initiate radical change. The tragedy of her life, though, is that nothing happens. When Rita kidnaps her young love to save him from the abuses of his mother, the hospital, and the world that will soon entrap them both, her punishment is unremarkable. Silently, her parents fetch her at the police station. Her act of kidnapping apparently on the same level as her refusal to lower the toilet seat, they once again imprison her in her bedroom. Once released from 'prison' and returned to the family bosom on the occasion of her father's birthday, her father opines, 'look how sweet she can be.' But sweetness is another prison, the nonbeing of the interpellated subject, and Rita refuses to adopt the violent forgetting that this subjection would require. Like many teenage cinema rebels before her, Rita decides it would be better to kill, and she descends one evening into the basement target range to shoot her father with his own gun. She finishes off her mother off-screen. Returning home after fleeing the scene of the crime for a single night, Rita discovers that her actions have once again had no effect. In the film's final scene, Rita sits on the couch in front of the TV just as her mother had, and she is slightly startled when a table lamp, on an automatic timer, suddenly illuminates. Everything continues to work as before, as though on remote control, and for Rita, there may be no escape from the world of numbing performances.

In *Lovely Rita*, interpellation is thematized as role-playing on a literal theater stage, while in *I Am Guilty* interpellation as performance takes place in the public 'theater' of the self-help seminar, the corporate conference room, and even the supermarket. Armin is a sheltered young man who lives with his parents in a bleak suburb. His parents hover about worried that he will squander his 'head start,' the big break of not having been called up for compulsory military service. But Armin is subject to a different kind of initiation, one no less brutal than the boot camp from which he has been spared. We watch Armin as he submits to a series of job interviews for entry-level positions in the cold offices of a technology company, a travel agency, and other interchangeable spaces where work is performed. We observe how Armin, ill at ease in his skin, is scrutinized by the button-down male employers, who, rather than inquire about his skills, want to know 'who he really is.' But Armin cannot quite figure it out, and he perceives dimly that this coveted 'inner self' is merely a script that must be learned and adopted in order to gain admission into a rather unappealing professional world, an initiation that signifies the achievement of the fully formed 'self.' Personal development and self-help are indeed the buzzwords of the corporate culture and ideology that *I Am Guilty* critiques.

See INTERIORITY

Job interviews are represented as humiliating tests that determine the state of the individual's 'self,' that is, his or her fitness to adopt the proper gestures and words of the 'company.' While he is assured by one employer that there are no right or wrong answers, clearly there are, and Armin stumbles and mumbles while the interviewers respond with questions like, 'But what do you personally find interesting about Curtec? . . . In your own words if possible?' The scene that most obviously represents the job interview as a ritual of interpellation depicts Armin undergoing a personality test in which the interviewer asks a series of questions designed to elicit an 'immediate, spontaneous' response. When Armin 'fails,' the interviewer, Herr Klein, shows him a series of images. Armin's anxiety increases until his gaze alights upon a photo of marching SS soldiers, and he asks Klein what *he* would say.

> Klein: 'I don't know … that my grandfather was a Nazi.'
> Armin: '*Was* your grandfather a Nazi?'
> Klein: 'Yes, but that's not the point!'

In fact, this *is* the point. But in the dominant ideology represented in *I Am Guilty*, memory and history are the enemies of the ideal corporate self, so much 'clutter' that masks one's 'truth,' one's 'essence.' As Katja, Armin's object of fantasy and desire, tells it, 'The self is a kind of mental space and the first job is to tidy it up. You have to imagine that your memory is filled with junk and it's left lying around.'

FIG. 80: *I Am Guilty.*

Katja has learned this script in a motivational self-help seminar that trains *I Am Guilty*'s young people in the gestures that they must master in order to be happy successful adults. Armin himself attends one of the seminars, and in a surreal scene that could appear in a science fiction movie, he wears a stark white expressionless mask with eye and breathing holes to signify the blank slate that one must become in order to build the proper 'self' **[Fig. 80]**. As pressure mounts at home, Armin submits to this training in a white-walled computer lab, where participants, all donning the identical white masks, are paired in conversation: 'What's your favorite color?' 'What are your favorite hobbies?' The participants rehearse appropriate responses to questions that are meant to elicit their personal, individual truth, an authenticity that paradoxically must be scripted.

While the subjected and interpellated 'self' is formed through learning a particular script, through replaying an accepted set of phrases and gestures, *I Am Guilty* represents Armin's 'real life' as defined by its silence. The film opens with Armin quietly surveying the smoking wreckage of a car, an accident for which he later claims responsibility by writing anonymous letters to the local newspaper. Cinematic form takes over here, as shots and reverse shots linger on Armin's gaze, then on the bloodied face of the dead driver, then on the lone auto fragment that Armin claims as a souvenir of his supposed crime (it remains unclear whether he has in fact engineered the accident). Armin's fascination with the real, palpable consequences of violence is connected to a homoerotic fantasy life, the shadowed other of the rigid exchanges of the job interviews. Here the men in suits are replaced by a leather-clad motorcycle gang that Armin meets in a roadside men's bathroom. The film here references a cinematic tradition (perhaps most importantly represented by Kenneth Anger's 1964 *Scorpio Rising*) that fetishizes biker subculture and its leather-

See LANGUAGE

FIG. 81: *I Am Guilty.*

clad rebels. In one scene, Armin participates in a silent ritual in which the helmeted men—anonymous like the white-masked seminar participants—help him choose the man who will initiate him into sexual pleasure as the others watch **[Fig. 81]**. Unlike the cold interviewers, one of the men rests a paternal arm on Armin's shoulder, and Armin smiles as he later rides on the back of his motorcycle. A steady sound of droning automobiles on a highway connects these rituals to the moment of discovering the car crash, all three moments suggesting a 'real' or at least a sense of freedom that lies outside the coerced performances of Armin's daily life. At the film's close, Armin's anonymous confessions for a variety of crimes catch up with him, and the police chase him down in his parents' home. The boy has chosen the identity of the rebel, and noticing Katja watching, he smiles in satisfaction as he is led, handcuffed, to the police car **[Fig. 82]**.

Several other Berlin School films represent forms of performance as rituals of interpellation as well. In Christian Petzold's *Ghosts*, two teenage

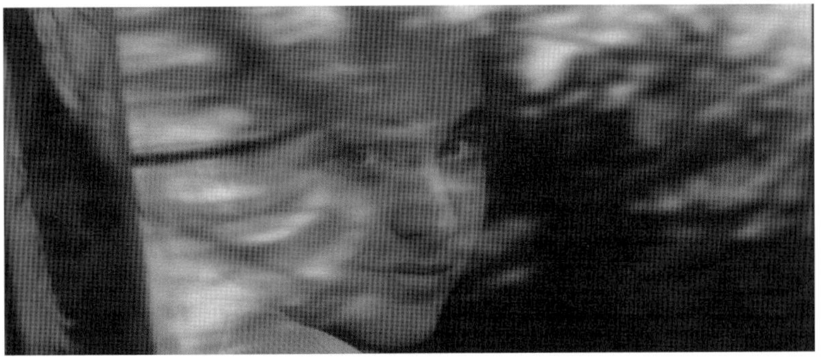

FIG. 82: *I Am Guilty.*

FIG. 83: *Marseille.*

runaways, Nina and Toni, compete to appear on a reality TV show. They win when Nina tells a fantastic romance tale of her meeting with Toni **[see Fig. 71—GHOSTS]**, a story that is more emotionally 'true' than the conventional story that they had planned. However, her public revelation of the 'truth,' a triumph of recognition, leads to her new friend's betrayal. In Angela Schanelec's *Marseille*, a central scene of interpellation comes when the protagonist, a photographer's assistant, helps to take portraits of factory women who describe how much their identities, their 'selves,' are tied to how they pose before the camera **[Fig. 83]**. Again and again Berlin School films view the learned language of gestures as a trap that debases the selves who are caught and forced to unhappily embrace it.

See BORDERS, BOREDOM

VK

Notes

1 Louis Althusser, 'Ideology and Ideological State Apparatuses (Notes towards an Investigation),' *Lenin and Philosophy and Other Essays*, trans. Ben Brewster (New York: The Monthly Review Press, 1971), 102.
2 Althusser, 'Ideology and Ideological State Apparatuses,' 170.

Landscape

Large portions of many Berlin School films take place outdoors, and even the most urban of those films—including *Ghosts* and *Marseille*—still offer drawn-out moments depicting stretches of green grass and trees, blue water, and sandy brown beachfronts. We watch as the children in *This Very Moment*, for example, walk along a gently rolling road at the film's beginning and as they disappear over a hill at its end **[see Fig. 49—FAMILIAR PLACES]**. In *Windows on Monday*, Nina drives through darkened woods one night, and subsequently rides (and walks) her bicycle through the same woods by daylight the following morning **[see Fig. 54—FORESTS]**. Armin in *I Am Guilty* stashes his interview clothes in a field before heading on to his world of fantasy. The multiple characters of *Vacation* reach their quiet, open, rural home by walking or driving along worn paths that cut through the country, and for *Hotel's* Irene the woods both cause fear and provide potential answers **[see Figs. 55, 56, 57—FORESTS]**. Landscape becomes an extended stage for the characters' lives, offering the viewer lush colors while also focusing his or her attention on the characters themselves. The characters become bound up within their own microcosms of problems, and the enduring presence of the landscapes brings those problems into relief.

The relative minimalism of expansive fields, interminably redundant tree lines, and even the gentle ripples in lakes serve as quiet backgrounds for characters' stories. Because stretches of green frequently stand empty or nearly empty, broad expanses accentuate how the world stands still around the films' characters. Even the smallest or most mundane details of their lives rise to the foreground, as if the rest of the world has grown mute in order that their day-to-day problems can emerge. The characters reflect on their own individual troubles, whether these include vexed marriages, a desire for escape from the routine, or questions about which path should be taken for the future. The camera's static gaze serves to accentuate the plainly defined frames through which we view the characters. In *Vacation*, for example, we frequently experience frames so still that they seem to be photographs that are only now and again brought to life

FIG. 84: *Passing Summer.*

[see Fig. 47—FAMILIAR PLACES]. The characters alone determine any movement beyond the slight swaying of branches. As two children play in the yard, the camera remains stationary, allowing them to enter and leave the frame along with their toys. The motion associated with toys tossed into the frame from a shed takes on a comic tone owing to the overall lack of motion in the landscape. In *Passing Summer* the camera watches from afar as the characters walk down a long path **[Fig. 84]**. There is playfulness in the juxtaposition between these characters and the director's highly controlled camera. At first it is as if the characters push the frame further with their continued steps, but eventually they stop and the camera rolls on without them, moving at its steady pace along its path. We are reminded that the landscape exists with or without them; it extends beyond the frame and well beyond their relatively small spheres of influence.

See FRAMINGS

The swaths of natural space, which paradoxically cause the films' characters to stand out, call to mind long-established natural cycles, whether in the form of seasons or life spans. The spans of these cycles serve to foreground the impermanence of whatever angst a character may be experiencing, no matter how trivial or profound. We are reminded that the natural spaces of the Berlin School films have been around longer than the characters into whose lives we are meant to become absorbed. In *Hotel*, Irene and Eric walk through the woods surrounding the hotel in order to visit a famous cave. Once there, Irene stands outside of it with her back to Eric as she reads about the area's woman of the forest (*Waldfrau*) who, according to legend, once lived in the cave. Because we view Irene from

See FORESTS

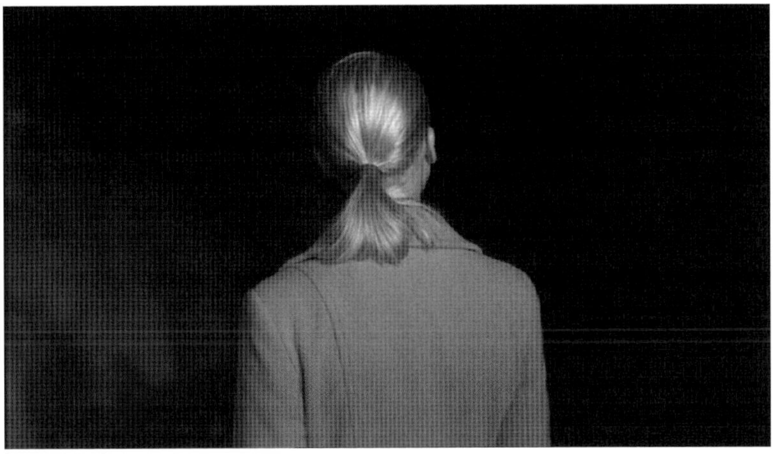

FIG. 85: *Hotel.*

the back, as one sees a *Rückenfigur* ('back figure') in Romantic painting, the scene is suspenseful [**Fig. 85**]. The viewer is more aware of Irene's own vulnerability than she is. Eric suggests entering the cave; Irene agrees and follows him in. The camera at first stays outside, and Irene seems to have been swallowed up completely. She reappears only after the camera jumps to a scene from within the cave, where she is illuminated and kissing Eric rather than being harmed. The camera jumps again to a view of Irene from behind; she has left the cave and is reading the names of multiple pairs of lovers that have been carved into the bark of a nearby tree over time. Her tone of voice switches from happy and playful to quiet and concerned as she realizes that she has just read the name of the woman who had interned before her at the hotel. Irene has been hired because Eva needed to be replaced, and now she has entered into the hotel's cycle. The camera cuts again, this time taking the viewer to where a nearby body of water is dredged, hinting at her predecessor's probable fate. Woods take years and years to grow, natural coastlines change only gradually, and even fields rely on seasons of dormancy. The physical and temporal scale recalls the slow, even languid pace at which lives, institutions, and the characters' surrounding lifeworlds are altered.

An underlying sense of cyclical time pervades the films: this has been and will come again, even if some things are perceived and felt in the moment as unique. While individual problems become all-consuming for characters, we as viewers are continuously reminded of the larger frame.

FIG. 86: *This Very Moment.*

In *This Very Moment*, Lea and Konstantin head off on their own after being ordered out of the car by Sylvia. They may feel at this point that they know where they are headed, but their fate is already foreshadowed when they seem to disappear among the reeds at a field's edge. Akin to Irene in *Hotel*, their forms seem absorbed or eaten whole by the landscape **[Fig. 86]**. When Sylvia returns, the children have essentially disappeared, leaving her to move back and forth between moments of relief and panic at their absence. Lea and Konstantin travel further and further into the landscape, wandering first somewhat happily through fields, but eventually, after getting lost, being scooped up by Kuba, who will determine their trajectory for the remainder of the film. We are brought back to the mythical, transformative nature of the fairy tale. And as in a fairy tale, Lea and Konstantin, upon being finally returned to the constructed landscape and its open road, are altered. Something has happened to Konstantin, and Lea no longer seems to be in control of her environment. They have grown up in reverse: the adult world turned self-confident children into fearful ones. In what is almost certainly an echo of the film's opening shot, the camera's wide and seemingly interminable view of the endless road captures the sight of the children walking an unknown path until they disappear from view **[see Fig. 49—FAMILIAR PLACES]**.

See BEGINNINGS, ENDINGS

Inasmuch as Lea and Konstantin wind up at the film's end in a spot that recalls the film's beginning, many Berlin School characters permanently find themselves in states of suspension; they are neither here nor there. *Longing*'s Markus, for example, physically travels between two tiny villages as he considers the possibility of life with two different women. In *Falling* Nicole is really only out on a temporary leave from prison. These characters, like so many Berlin School characters, are caught in long-lasting moments of indecision or uncertainty. The way that the characters interact with their natural environments corresponds to this state of being-in-between. In *Bungalow* Paul is on the run from the *Bundeswehr*, a commitment that is already only temporary. Similarly to Armin of *I Am Guilty*, Paul struggles as the younger brother of a successful, assertive sibling. His struggles, both to decide what he really wants in life and to avoid his would-be captors, are drawn out. They happen in slow motion because they feel so futile. He seems to be fighting an Oedipal battle we know he can never win as he pushes against all structures around him, even seeking refuge on his parents' patio, one eye to the interior of the house, the other to the fields beyond the backyard. Within multiple scenes in *Bungalow*, the landscape is depicted as a flat surface, neither beautiful nor sublime but nearly as vacant as an empty cinematic frame. When an explosion takes place in the distance, Paul and Max decide to go to the grocery store to see what happened. Rather than showing a dramatic scene—an action sequence, for example, in which the landscape races by rapidly and dramatically—the camera instead depicts Paul and Max standing outside their car, watching as a ribbon of cars and semi-trucks attempts to snake down a congested hill **[Fig. 87]**. The landscape sits in the background as though it were a piece of paper upon which the slowly moving cars etch their lines; it could just as easily be a painted theater backdrop. Likewise, when Paul secretly

See ECLECTIC AFFINITIES

See SIBLINGS

FIG. 87: *Bungalow*.

returns to his parents' house after being dropped off by Max at the train station, his presence is signaled to Lene by the buzzing noise of a model airplane. The airplane is the only thing that is not static within the frame; everything else seems to stand still as we watch the plane fly across the sky, soaring at first but ultimately plummeting to the ground with a crash. Paths are traced or cut through the atmosphere, but despite the motion, the surrounding frame remains unchanged.

In Berlin School films, characters seek refuge in the landscape, yet they seem only as at home in the natural world as they are in their built spaces—which is to say, not at all at home. The characters occasionally seek answers there, but they never find them. The landscape's long and slowly shifting natural history, when seen in connection with the often vain and circular movements depicted in the films, underscores the protagonists' nearly permanent inability to effect lasting changes in their lives.

See DISENGAGEMENT

AJF

Language (Absence Thereof)

In the opening scene of Christoph Hochhäusler's *This Very Moment*, Sylvia throws her stepchildren out of the car after a fight during a shopping trip near the German-Polish border and drives off. When she returns a little later, the children have disappeared. While the film now unfolds as the story of the family's failure to reunite, Sylvia never finds words for what happened. When her husband comes home, she initiates a nonverbal sexual communication; afterwards, a stuttered 'Josef?—I . . .' seems to constitute an attempt at confessing, but then she fails to answer his (short) reply: 'What?' Later, Sylvia calls a friend who apparently doesn't have time to talk. After making a plea for being listened to just for a moment ('a sec . . .'), Sylvia herself realizes: 'No, I don't think I can tell you.' From here on, she more and more sinks into complete silence. Many times, the camera will capture her face in close-ups while she fails to articulate herself; at moments, it also zooms in on Josef's return silence as they exchange stares that are painful to watch **[Fig. 88]**.

The effect, and arguably function, of this loss, absence, and/or inadequacy of language in this and other Berlin School films is twofold. On a thematic level,

FIG. 88: *This Very Moment*.

it facilitates a fairly straightforward critique of the state of communication in society and, especially, the nuclear family. Initially, Josef keeps shooting questions at Sylvia about the disappearance of the kids, but his tone, body language, and simultaneous engagement in other activities signal that he neither expects nor even desires an answer. The one slightly more developed verbal exchange they have culminates in her reproach: 'You have no idea what goes on around here.' The film thus presents the (heterosexual, bourgeois) family as a brutally dysfunctional unit in its bare, characteristically unfinished house somewhere in an unspecified East German suburbia. In *Windows on Monday*, where the title already announces an analogous crisis of family home construction, Nina just puts down her renovation tools and leaves; she, too, will never find words to explain her impulsive decision. Reviewers interpreted her 'wordless flight from the daily grind' ('wortlose Flucht aus dem Alltag') and the film's reliance on 'the loud muteness of moods' ('die laute Stummheit der Stimmungen') in terms of communication failures between disconnected individuals.[1]

See RENOVATION

At the same time, and to more complicated effect, this absence of linguistic motivation is part of the Berlin School films' phenomenological method, that is, their aesthetic techniques of bracketing social as well as psychological explanatory narratives altogether, and focusing instead on the phenomena directly visible on screen. These bracketing techniques have the effect of producing 'extremely ambiguous texts.'[2] In key respects, it often remains unclear exactly what kind of critique the films are developing. Film-historically, their procedure indicates the Berlin School directors' interest in the legacy of phenomenological modernisms, for example Siegfried Kracauer's aesthetics of film as the project of, as Christian Petzold refers to it, touching 'external reality.'[3] Kracauer presented this project in a media-theoretical frame: he designated the 'material continuum' of '[l]ife' as film's proper territory, as opposed to the 'mental continuum' explored by the modern novel.[4] In some respects, *This Very Moment* presents itself as a textbook case for Kracauer's programmatically antilinguistic modernist film aesthetics. Eschewing the 'definite' meanings produced by dialogue, *This Very Moment* clings 'to the surface of things' and presents (increasingly) indeterminate emotions, for example through bodily gesture.[5] In the beginning of the film, we may in fact still be able to thus make sense of Sylvia: her face, and her gestures in lighting a cigarette, indicates stress in response to the children's provocations in the car; when she returns to the place where she threw them out and repeatedly calls for them, her voice signals anxiety. But ultimately, the issue at stake in Berlin

See INTERIORITY

School films is not one of media difference, but of aesthetic design. Even the nonverbal sign system of body language, which supplements the function of dialogue in the audience's sense-making process, becomes increasingly indeterminate in the course of *This Very Moment,* as Sylvia's body seems to fall silent along with her speech. Can Sylvia's inexpressive appearance be explained by assuming that she is psychologically frozen—or is she the 'nonhuman' who, as her upset husband declares, must be responsible for the children's disappearance? ('I don't know who is responsible for this, but what human being would do something like this?'). In close-up we see her virtually unmoved face as she silently takes in that charge.

Similarly, the viewer of Petzold's *Yella* may struggle to understand exactly what motivates the protagonist's eagerness to delve into the world of high-risk capitalism. Because of the film's minimal use of dialogue, restrained acting technique, as well as the overall absence of subjective shots or subjectivizing music, we have to make do with few, and, worse, diverging clues. Does the film tell a story of social despair, as indicated by its protagonist's momentary emotional breakdown after the initial loss of her regular job prospect? If so, to what extent is it connected to her East German background? Or does the small smile that she later offers in response to Philipp's comment that she must be enjoying their joint business negotiations suggest a different interpretation of her character? Importantly, the relative absence of language both in the narrow sense and in the more general one of any readable sign system does not equal the cancellation of cultural scripts and established meanings. Yella's ex-husband Ben perceives her as a 'beautiful' woman, and some of the cultural associations attached to that label are indicated by the fact that he uses it as part of the charge that she left him because of his financial crisis, preferring to 'show her beautiful legs' in Hanover—that is, to realize her professional ambitions by using her femininity. A reviewer takes this reading of Yella in terms of established sociosymbolic templates a step further by describing her as a 'femme fatale,'[6] thus giving determinate meaning to the film's ambiguous images. In *This Very Moment*, the film's fairy-tale intertext may similarly seduce us into reading Sylvia as the evil stepmother from 'Hansel and Gretel.' And Kuba, her (human) competitor for the role of 'nonhuman' agency, whom the children encounter in the forest, would then turn into the witch. Whereas to all appearances, he initially intends to simply return the kids to their home, does Kuba's later desire to secure the reward money offered by Josef, in combination with his unexplained anxiousness about not involving the police, transform him into a kidnapper? In these cases,

See INTERPELLATION

the spectator's uncertainty about motivations is generated also by the film's aesthetic transposition of linguistic difference into inaccessibility: *This Very Moment* does not offer subtitles for its Polish conversations, and specifically the one Kuba has with his pregnant girlfriend while he watches the reward announcement on German-language TV. Even where technically present, language only produces surplus indeterminacy.

Scholarship on *This Very Moment* has critically cautioned that the film thus 'others' its Polish setting as 'a place of cultural opacity'[7] or a 'nonplace onto which childlike fantasies of the "Wild West" as well as visions of fairy-tale enchantment are projected.'[8] As I would rephrase, the film's phenomenological method does not *prevent* audience readings along the lines of cultural stereotypes. *This Very Moment* does *allow* alternative takes. Thus, the unknowability of Kuba, and by extension Poland, merely doubles the unknowability permeating the German family home: without its interrupted circuits of communication, including Sylvia's drug-induced sleep through Kuba's initial calls, the fairy-tale narrative of evil abduction would have never emerged in the first place. Nonetheless, because of the film's aesthetics of indeterminacy, we cannot be quite sure in the end: is the audience actually invited to reflect critically on the role of (old and new) fairy tales suturing the gap opened up by failing everyday communications? Or should we conclude that the film itself subterraneously surrenders to the temptations of simple fairy-tale scripts?

See BORDERS

A similar ambiguity is produced in Benjamin Heisenberg's *Sleeper* when at the end, the protagonist Johannes remains silent in response to the secret service agent's question whether he can give his colleague Farid an alibi for the night of the bombing in conjunction with which he has been arrested. Although the film's editing and overall narrative configuration seem to suggest that this was in fact the night the two of them spent in a club together, and that Johannes thus unethically fails to confirm the alibi after his rival has let him down once too often, doubts remain. (The different clothes Johannes wears in subsequent shots may contradict the editing's implication that it was the same night. And even if it were, would Farid's presence in the club prove he could not be involved in the terrorist act?) In the film's concluding scene, the camera then shows Johannes's face in an angled, slightly distorted—or martyr-like?—close-up as he recites the Lord's Prayer—a religious gesture that, as he explicitly told Farid earlier, he has previously performed only with his traditional grandmother **[Fig. 89]**. Thus, Johannes's silence is superimposed with a linguistic template enacting religious identification. In doing so, does the film suggest that he himself is the title-giving sleeper,

FIG. 89: *Sleeper.*

a previously closeted radical in the post-September 11 'war of cultures'? Or, rather, is the film itself retreating into the frontlines of this war, having failed to exculpate Farid beyond all doubt?

The Berlin School films' phenomenological aesthetics regularly refuses clear-cut answers to such questions. However, the individual films are also quite different from each other. Petzold's *Ghosts*, for example, probes an alternative approach to language. To be sure, this film was widely praised as a 'purely visual film' ('reiner Bilderfilm') too;[9] in Kracauer's spirit, the director elaborates on how he prefers physical expression over dialogue and intends to make images unfold as a richly overdetermined reservoir of correspondences rather than simply decodable signs.[10] Nonetheless, the film does not develop indeterminacy into opacity the way *This Very Moment* does. In Kracauer's terms, the key to this difference is how *Ghosts* includes the characters' *mental* world in its investigations; in doing so, it explores language (in different sign systems) as a medium less of determinacy than of imagination. *Ghosts* is a film about fantasies. At moments, these fantasies take the form of elaborate verbal stories including Nina's writing in her diary, and the scenarios both Toni and Nina develop at the film casting. Elsewhere, they are evoked simply by conversation fragments surrounding physical data, prominently when Nina and Françoise, who has lost her daughter, develop their shared fantasy of kinship through the investigation of Nina's birthmarks and scars. The film wins its power in visually exploring these fantasies, for example with the (pseudo-) documentary images that support Françoise's child-abduction story and later make us reluctant to

See SEEING AND SAYING

FIG. 90: *Ghosts.*

believe her husband when he harshly declares her ill. *Ghosts*, too, does not definitively resolve the status of the physical resemblances it evokes and thus plays with metaphysical ambiguity not altogether unlike *This Very Moment*. But in key respects, this matters very little. When at the end, Nina, by herself once again, throws the computer simulations of Françoise's grown child into a garbage bin, she definitively forfeits the fantasy which has, one way or the other, proven unrealizable **[Fig. 90]**. Nonetheless, the film's complex interweaving of images and words has explored the significance of such fantasy and now enables us, as the audience, to mourn it along with her. At a closer look, the (relative) absence of language in the Berlin School films thus enables a range of different (sociopolitical as well as aesthetic and philosophical) investigations. All of them, however, probe issues of communication—both in their diegetic worlds and with respect to the production of meaning in their audiences' minds.

CB

Notes

1 For these assessments, see reviews by Jean Lüdeke (originally in *film-zeit*), http://montag.451.eu/presse.html, and Simon Rothöhler (originally in *Polar*), http://montag.451.eu/presse.html.

2 See Bert O. States, 'The Phenomenological Attitude,' in *Critical Theory and Performance*, eds Janelle G. Reinelt and Joseph R. Roach. (Rev. and

enl. edn Ann Arbor: University of Michigan Press, 2007), 26–36; here 31. States is quoting from Umberto Eco, *A Theory of Semiotics* (Bloomington: Indiana University Press, 1979), 1.

3 Christina Nord, '"Mit geschlossenen Augen hören." Interview mit Christian Petzold,' *Taz,* February 15, 2005, http://www.taz.de/1/archiv/archiv/?dig=2005/02/15/a0230; see also Siegfried Kracauer, *Theory of Film: The Redemption of Physical Reality* (Princeton: Princeton University Press, 1997), 297.

4 See Kracauer, *Theory of Film*, 237.

5 Kracauer, *Theory of Film*, 104.

6 See Demetrios Matheou, 'Yella,' *Sight & Sound* 17.10 (October 2007): 82.

7 Randall Halle, 'Views from the German-Polish Border: The Exploration of Inter-national Space in *Halbe Treppe* und *Lichter*,' *The German Quarterly* 80.1 (2007): 77–96; here, 79.

8 Kristin Kopp, 'Christoph Hochhäusler's This Very Moment: The Berlin School and the Politics of Spatial Aesthetics in the German-Polish Borderlands,' *The Collapse of the Conventional: German Film and its Politics at the Turn of the Twenty-First Century*, eds Jaimey Fisher and Brad Prager (Detroit: Wayne State University Press, 2010), 285–308; here, 302.

9 Andreas Kilb, 'Berlinale. Stich der verborgenen Klinge,' *Frankfurter Allgemeine Zeitung* 39 (February 16, 2005): 40, http://www.faz.net/aktuell/feuilleton/kino/berlinale-stich-der-verborgenen-klinge-1103008.html.

10 Bettina Böhler, 'Interview mit Christian Petzold,' http://www.gespenster-der-film.de/html/interview.html.

Long Takes . . .

. . . are one of the decisive hallmarks of Berlin School filmmaking, radically decelerating the drive of narrative development and probing the audience's ability and patience to observe, bond to, anticipate, and recall the events (and nonevents) on screen. David Bordwell has described the accelerating pace of mainstream Hollywood filmmaking over the last few decades in terms of the rise of a new regime of intensified continuity: while most of the basic principles of classical visual storytelling might still be in place, feverish cutting practices, the shrinkage of average shot lengths and the use of ever shifting camera lenses have come to communicate a general sense of energy and excitement in order to demand the viewer's unconditional attention.[1] In synch with the temporal interventions of many international art directors throughout the past two decades, the aesthetic formalism of Berlin School films reveals little tolerance for the speed of contemporary mainstream storytelling. Whether they employ mobile or static cameras, extended shot durations here play a crucial role in deflating the frantic hype of dominant editing protocols, pushing linear or teleological forms of storytelling to the point of implosion, and recalibrating the viewer's sensory relationships to the cinematic image. Christian Petzold's relentless shots of solemn automobilists as they navigate urban or rural landscapes; Angela Schanelec's extended lateral tracking shots of characters in motion, at once opening and reaffirming the defining power of the cinematic frame; and Ulrich Köhler's unremitting tableaux shots situating the viewer as a seemingly detached observer—all clearly hope to suspend narrative cinema's current drive toward intensified continuity and, amid the ever-accelerating flows and transactions of our globalized present, to make the viewer contemplate cinematic images that no longer seem to want anything from them.

See ECLECTIC AFFINITIES

See CARS

In their efforts to stretch the pace of cinematic temporality, the films of Berlin School filmmakers at first recall the gestures of European auteurs of the 1960s and 1970s as they sought to challenge commercial filmmaking by developing a cinema of personal expressiveness and reduced narrative integration. Instead of merely using the long take as a bravura act to astonish viewers with technical skills and flowing perspectives, extended shot durations in the work of directors such as Theodoros Angelopoulos, Michelangelo Antonioni, and Miklós Jancsó aspired to unfetter the cinematic image in all its contingency from the burden of telling a story and thus invite the viewer to reflect upon the temporal nature of motion pictures in the first place, the fact that cinema does not simply represent time and motion but instead embodies time by means of showing and continually being in motion. Pier Paolo Pasolini's 1967 'Observations on the Long Take' offered one of the shrewdest ruminations about postwar art cinema's systematic refusal to cut.[2] For Pasolini, the long take represented cinema's at once modernist and paradoxical desire for the grace of unadulterated presentness; it defied the closure and death imposed by the violence of the cut, yet, in so doing, it also ran up against the very possibility of meaning-making, precisely because our ability to generate meaning, in Pasolini's understanding, cannot do without recall and retrospection, without us actively recognizing the finality that is death and that film allegorizes in the form of the cut.

See THE CUT

Following Pasolini's suggestion, the long-take aesthetic of postwar auteurs has often been conceptualized within a Bazinian framework, the auteur's resistance to cutting thereby understood as a method of challenging closure, probing presentness, and thus intensifying realism; of allowing spectators to peruse the screen according to their own measure and will; and of expressing the alienated, disillusioned, and blasé atmosphere of modern life. The Berlin School's long takes surely reference and recall the distended shot durations of earlier art house filmmakers. It has often been noted that Berlin School protagonists—reminiscent of auteur cinema's many antiheroes—are marked by a remarkable void of affect, their deadpan faces and automatized movements expressing a fundamental absence of expressiveness, their emotional exhaustion encoding the evacuation of interiority in an era of compulsive connectivity, and the utter commercialization of feelings. In causing viewers to pensively peruse faces, bodies, objects, and landscapes, the Berlin School's long takes therefore at first seem to reinforce this sense of an utter absence of sense and hence situate the viewer as a cold and critical observer of an even colder reality. In most cases, there is nothing here to decode, no insight to be gained, no deep reading required to penetrate the surface of the visible. You may look as long as you wish or as long as a shot will allow you: no visual exertion will uncover anything not already visible upon the first

See INTERIORITY

See DISENGAGEMENT

encounter. Disenchantment thus appears to reign triumphant, dooming us to contemplate the vanishing of any object worth contemplating. In their effort to communicate a sense of presentness, individual shots might roll on for minutes on end, but in their refusal to ever picture the present as a site of meaningful events or transformations, these long takes only seem to confirm that the Berlin School's protagonists, as much as their cinematic representations, are haunted by what Garrett Stewart calls 'the cadaverous,' that is, the fact that a film's basic unit remains to be a still frame after all, even though individual images in cinema will always be on the run and resist any attempt to be arrested.[3]

Consider, at this juncture, the final shot of Ulrich Köhler's 2002 *Bungalow*, a film that has very little to offer to gratify mainstream appetites for fast-cutting, constant lens changes and hypermobile camera work. The film tells the story of Paul, a young soldier unwilling to return to his service, yet not really able to make any meaningful connections as he spends his days at his parents' bungalow in a nondescript small town in Germany. The final sequence has Paul sleeping with his brother's girlfriend Lene in an equally nondescript hotel room, less in order to quench bursting desire than simply to mark the bland passing of time. The film's final three minutes begin with Paul pensively looking out of the hotel window before we cut to what we initially must assume to be his point of view—a static view through the window, its frame no longer visible, situating the viewer as a cool and detached witness to whatever may unfold within the visual field. We first see the car of Max, Paul's brother, as it approaches the camera and comes to stop on the hotel's parking lot. Max exits the car, moves a few steps toward the bottom of the frame only to meet Lene who has entered the frame at the same time from below. As they talk to each other, an army jeep pulls into the image and comes to a halt on the right **[Fig. 91]**. Two soldiers, eager to pick up the deserter, exit the car and move toward the right corner of the frame, Max following at a slight distance, Lene slowly approaching Max's car in the opposite direction. A few seconds after Max and the soldiers have left the frame, Paul suddenly enters the image from

See ENDINGS

See HOTELS

FIG. 91: *Bungalow*.

the left and first approaches Lene and then crosses the street to the jeep, awaiting the soldiers' imminent return as we must assume. A huge gasoline truck swiftly enters the image from the right; the driver leaves his vehicle such that, for a decisive minute or so, it will block our view of Paul and the jeep. A few seconds later, the soldiers and Max return; Max joins Lene again while the soldiers walk toward and around the truck in order to return to their jeep, presumably frustrated about having been unable to fulfill their mission. Meanwhile, the truck driver reenters his vehicle and drives off away from the camera, thus unblocking our view of the military jeep. Its doors already shut, the jeep will make a U-turn and drive off into the opposite direction from the truck, leaving Max and Lene as motionless witnesses to the final departures of both vehicles, and leaving us in a complete state of wonder about both the curious emptying of the frame and Paul's exact whereabouts.

In spite of its apparent detachment and theatrical tableaux, Köhler's final long take leaves the viewer with as many questions as it might have instead answered. The shot in fact is charged with remarkable reversals, inversions, and paradoxes, a rhetoric of choreographed ambiguity and inconclusiveness that stands in stark opposition to the camera's seemingly aloof posture of distance and objective noninvolvement. As if to transpose many of Béla Tarr's solemn opening shots, in which slowly tracking cameras retrospectively mark certain settings as being seen from a diegetic character's point of view, Köhler's final shot initially invites us to read the image through Paul's indifferent eye, yet then allows Paul to enter the image himself and hence disrupts our bodily and perspectival alignment, situating us as Paul's proxies without granting us his final sense of mobility. Left, as it were, in Paul's undesirable shoes, the viewer cannot but be challenged in his or her seemingly neutral distance by the drama that unfolds in the film's final minutes: the highly choreographed display of contradictory movements; the traversals, sudden intrusions upon and inconclusive exits from the frame; the final shot's graded emphasis on ever-shifting constellations of bodies and vehicles within the space of the visible. If mainstream cinema's intensified continuity today demands undivided attention, Köhler's long-take aesthetic in this and many other shots places the viewer in a rather impossible position. While the shot's pondering temporality clearly gives us time to peruse the image, contemplate the action on screen, and become absorbed by the protagonists' sense of temporal suspension, the theatrical aspects of Köhler's shot—its staging of ambivalence and contradiction—constantly remind us of our own act of looking, of being actively addressed by the framing power of the camera, of being positioned as a viewing subject eager to see something in the first place and to move along the protagonist's paths. At once pushed away and pulled into the long take's simultaneously static and animated image, we hover between a stance of contemplative distance and of projective engagement; we allow ourselves to get lost and forget ourselves in the shot's deliberate staging of movement, and we cannot but ignore that whatever we see is designed to be seen by us in the first place. Though seemingly aloof and utterly distant, then, we are struck by a profound feeling of wonder about what the shot itself—in spite of all its stress on visibility—refuses to show to us, an inquisitive amazement about what may have happened behind the truck and what has led to Paul's disappearance.

See FRAMINGS

While it is tempting to understand long takes such as this as a stylistic iteration of what celebrated auteur directors such as Antonioni sought to accomplish in the 1960s or the 1970s, there are many good reasons to insist on fundamental differences between the realist credo of the extended time images of postwar art cinema and the inherent logic of Petzold's, Schanelec's or Köhler's distended shots—their curious fusion of movement and standstill, the cinematic and the photographic, blandness and wonder. The return of the long take in the films of the Berlin School in fact deliberately pushes against and beyond the dual template of the postwar long take: the aspirations of Bazinian realism and the modernist demands for criticality and cognitive distantiation. In lockstep with (somewhat earlier) formalist interventions of East Asian filmmakers such as Hou Hsiao-Hsien, Tsai Ming-Liang, and Jia Zhangke, as well as with Eastern European art house directors such as Béla Tarr and Aleksandr Sokurov, the stretching of cinematic temporality in the films of the Berlin School often aspires to reclaim the most vehement of all human passions—the category of wonder—by picturing the equivocalness of reality itself, as much as it seeks to reclaim absorption, rather than criticality, as the most viable aesthetic relationship to the cinematic image in a time of mindless speed and willful mobility.

Let us consider this in greater detail.

As we have seen in the example from *Bungalow*, long-take strategies in Berlin School filmmaking, on the one hand, explore absorptive forms of looking (and hearing) as a critical corrective to the hastened pace of contemporary screen and online culture, yet not simply to return us to a time of uncontaminated celluloid and integrated storytelling, but frequently to probe the possibilities of representing our present moment as an indeterminate site of simultaneous rhythms, speeds, itineraries, and movements. In its opposition to narrative linearity and teleological causation, long-take photography in the films of Berlin School filmmakers often situates protagonists and viewers alike in a paradoxical state of aesthetic delay and suspension. It wants to hold our attention by suggesting the impending event of a discontinuous moment of change and wonder, 'wonder' here being understood not as a theological category but as the kind of vehement passion accompanying rare experiences and sparking inquiry, insight and knowledge. Yet, at the same time, long-take photography leaves little doubt about cinema's structural inability to ever really picture moments of wonder in the first place, because true wonder cannot unfold in and along time but would interrupt temporal flow altogether, and because any awaited wonder is no wonder at all. Rather than merely repeating how postwar cinema used long takes to express a sense of existential alienation and emotional exhaustion, then, the Berlin School's long takes tend to exhaust image and viewer in the paradoxical hope of reenergizing fantasy, the dreamlike and surreal, the indeterminate and open, and hence the possibility of unreserved passion in the form of a promise. It denies or endlessly delays the pleasures of wonder, not in the name of realism, but in the name of wonder itself.

On the other hand, long-take photography in Berlin School filmmaking, in stark contrast to the auteurs of the immediate postwar period, reckons with spectators largely accustomed to controlling the temporal and spatial terms of filmic consumption, whether they watch movies on handheld devices and on the move, or whether they actively navigate the order and speed of motion pictures with the help of remote controls and other random access technologies. Long takes such as Köhler's no longer believe in the perhaps most important dogma of twentieth-century modernist and avant-garde filmmaking: the mission of exposing the basic operations of the cinematic apparatus with the aim of activating the viewer. Rather than being seen and celebrated as the goal of good filmmaking, spectatorial activity and interactivity turn out to be the actual problem amid a contemporary culture demanding us to be always 'on.' Berlin School long takes therefore often invite us to question the normative divide between passive and active forms of viewership, and they know very well that former gestures of criticality, of foregrounding the operations of filmmaking itself, today amount to little less than preaching to the already converted. Köhler, Petzold, and Schanelec may often nostalgically recall a time in which cinema monopolized our exposure to moving images and did not find itself in ongoing competition with other media circulating pictures in motion. At the same time, however, rather than defining art cinema solely as a critical practice within and against commercial filmmaking, their long takes must be seen as being in ongoing conversation with other sites of moving image display, in particular the contemporary art museum with its ever-expanding video exhibitions and installation art galleries. Instead of merely challenging mainstream narrative cinema from within cinema itself, the Berlin School's long takes are part of a much larger aesthetic dynamic cutting across various sites of moving image display and projection; they join the efforts of many video artists today whose temporally expanded black box installations, in the midst of a historical moment of seemingly utter emotional functionalization and disenchanted willfulness, seek to reignite our sense of wonder.

'For the full experience of wonder,' writes Philip Fisher, 'there must be no description beforehand that will lead us to compare what we actually experience with what we were told . . . The object must be unexpectedly, instantaneously seen for the first time.'[4] Wonder cannot be willed. It resists controlled expectation and narrative unfolding. The long take in the work of the Berlin School, similar to its emblematic use in the Chinese art cinemas of the past two decades,[5] reminds us of the transformative power of wonder—a passion that both Plato and Descartes in fact celebrated as the origin of philosophy—precisely by not attempting to show that which, when shown, dilutes this passion in the first place. The long take's apparent void of affect and temporal drive here conjures, through its sheer negativity and in form of a promise, a world in which passion and wonder may once again return, a world in which we may recuperate our ability to be amazed by and whooshed up by whatever may unexpectedly unfold in front of our eyes independently of our own will. And, as we wait for what Berlin School filmmakers in the end can and will not show, we cannot but come to reconsider the value of spectatorial absorption itself—a category largely denigrated within modernist film practice as a sign of submissive passivity, yet certainly ripe for some conceptual overhaul in face not only of the critical evanescence of sustained attention today, but also of the nearly seamless integration of modernist techniques of self-reflexivity into the operations of mainstream cinema.

See SEEING AND SAYING

See INTERIORITY

In the *Encyclopédie* of 1751, Denis Diderot explained: 'To absorb expresses a general but successive action, which, beginning only in one part of the subject, continues thereafter and spreads over the whole. But to engulf indicates an action whose general effect is rapid, and seizes everything at the same time without breaking it up into parts.'[6] Though defined as an active state of attention, absorption required the subject to enter a certain state of obliviousness and unconsciousness, a ceding of self-awareness and willfulness. For art to appeal to the viewer's absorptive faculties, it had to do everything at its disposal not to acknowledge this viewer's presence in front of the painting or play; according to the encyclopedist, absorptive art had to represent human figures engrossed in certain activities while entertaining the fiction that possible audiences were not in existence.

In their aspiration to uphold the promise of wonder against the grain of today's intensified speed and willfulness, the long takes of the Berlin School seek nothing less than to reverse the modernist dismantling of absorption and explore this category's aesthetic and political productivity. As we have seen in Köhler's film, we should be careful not to misconstrue such a return to, or longing for, the absorptive as a retrograde search for aesthetic simplicity or a new jargon of authenticity. On the contrary, the quest for the absorptive in Berlin School filmmaking is far from naïve or nontheatrical, not least of all because it engages the hope for the rapture of wonder as something achieved not by fully denying but by partially recognizing our very act of looking. Long-take filmmaking here invites the viewer to *perform* absorption much more than it may actually grant it to us. While this might not sound like all too much in the perspective of those continually emphasizing the need for critical and activist forms of viewership, the Berlin School's long takes nevertheless offer valuable sites of aesthetic experience that unsettle not simply the templates of intensified continuity in mainstream filmmaking, but the regimes of spatiotemporal compression so rampant in contemporary society in general. To relearn how to yield to an image's thick, ambiguous, and ambivalent duration on screen and withstand our impatient desire for deep analysis and critical dissection might do much more to uphold our hope for a different future than to be recurrently reminded of what we all know anyway, namely that cinematic images construct impressions of the real rather than ever capturing reality in all its rawness.

LK

Notes

1 David Bordwell, *The Way Hollywood Tells It: Story and Style in Modern Movies* (Berkeley: University of California Press, 2006), 121–38.

2 Pier Paolo Pasolini, 'Observations of the Long Take,' trans. Norman Macafee and Craig Owens, *October* 13 (1980): 3–6.
3 Garrett Stewart, *Between Film and Screen: Modernism's Photo Synthesis* (Chicago: University of Chicago Press, 1999), 27–74.
4 Philip Fisher, *Wonder, the Rainbow, and the Aesthetics of Rare Experiences* (Cambridge, MA: Harvard University Press, 1998), 17.
5 Olivia Khoo and Sean Metzger, eds, *Futures of Chinese Cinema: Technologies and Temporalities in Chinese Screen Culture* (Bristol: Intellect, 2009); Jean Ma, *Melancholy Drift: Marking Time in Chinese Cinema* (Hong Kong: Hong Kong University Press, 2010).
6 Denis Diderot, *Encyclopédie* (Paris, 1771), s.v. 'Absorber,' quoted in Michael Fried, *Absorption and Theatricality: Painting and Beholder in the Age of Diderot* (Chicago: University of Chicago Press, 1980), 183–84.

Pools

Given the Berlin School's recurring themes of underemployment and the alienating character of contemporary labor, it is remarkable how often swimming pools appear in the films. In Christian Petzold's *The State I Am In*, the villa in which the family-on-the-run hides has an abandoned pool, a pale echo of the sparkling Portuguese coast where the film began; in his next work, *Something to Remember Me By*, the Hitchcockian opening scene features a municipal pool in which a couple fatefully (or not) meets; in Matthias Luthardt's *Pingpong* (2006), the upper-middle-class family with which the young protagonist is staying has a pool that plays a central role in the house pet's murder at the film's climax; in Jessica Hausner's *Hotel*, the protagonist Irene, a young woman starting a job at a rural hotel, tries to relax in the hotel's eerily abyssal pool; and in Ulrich Köhler's first two films, *Bungalow* and *Windows on Monday*, swimming pools play a subtle but central role in unraveling the films' elliptical and elusive thematic constellations.

Although not ostensibly relating to work, these films' pools nevertheless concretize the disciplining mechanisms of contemporary society that come to the thematic fore in many Berlin School films. If Foucault theorized the disciplining institutions of modern society—the factory, the prison, the school—the pool would seem to hold out the promise of at least temporary respite from such disciplining social institutions. In almost all of these films, the pool, at least initially, promises a break from the pressures of contemporary work. For instance, in *Hotel*, the protagonist Irene seeks to escape the oppressive and creepy atmosphere of the rural hotel where she works by asking to use the hotel pool to swim on off hours. Such pools seem to offer a different corporeal constellation than the ordered and ordering worlds of the workplace, the classroom or even the machine-dominated gym, offering, as pools do, a different structuring logic in their free-floating indulgence of near-naked bodies. This cultivated freedom, even anarchy, of the pool may be true particularly in German pool culture, which relies substantially less than US culture on using lanes in recreational swimming.

See INTERPELLATION

On the other hand, and in contrast with this potential for individual freedom, pools are artificial spaces, part of the built environment that has to be produced institutionally. They are products of large-scale construction that require significant and continuing deployment of financial resources.

Almost all the pools in these films are privately owned, either in homes or at private hotels. (An exception is Petzold's *Something to Remember Me By*, in which a municipal pool is transformed into the scene of a perverse, private fantasy.) The twilight of the municipal pool and the prevalence of private pools suggest the transition that Deleuze tracks in his 'Postscript: On the Societies of Control,' in which he describes the fading of the Foucauldian institutions (even as he pays homage to Foucault for analyzing them) and sketches instead the development of more individualized, even molecular modes of control—very much a central theme of Berlin School films.[1] The present and growing privatization of public institutions and spaces like schools and parks is only part of this broader story. For Deleuze, these developments away from the Foucauldian institutions are part of the twilight of mass-based institutions that might nevertheless be privately owned (like the factory): even such privately held institutions provided for collective experience on which, for instance, unions could then build. Now, in an economy and civic life built around the atomizing service industry, increasingly computer-based labor, and life in increasingly lavish, but insular homes (think of, for example, home theater), these mass experiences are fewer and farther between. In almost all of the films, the protagonists swim alone, and the pool becomes emblematic either of loneliness or of a collective to which the protagonist can no longer aspire. In Hausner's *Hotel*, for instance, Irene, though initially relieved to be swimming, is ordered by her supervisor to swim 'before 8 or after 8,' when there is sure to be no one else in the pool, and her isolation in the pool leads directly to the hallucinations that eventually overwhelm her **[Fig. 92]**.

In Köhler's first two features, one finds precisely this trajectory from the public, mass experience of the municipal swimming hall to the private pool that emphasizes the atomization and fading of social experience. In his debut film, *Bungalow*, late adolescent Paul deserts from the German army for no apparent reason and retreats to his parents' bungalow, where he spends most of the film meandering and moping aimlessly. His parents, conveniently, are on vacation in Italy, but his brother Max and his Danish girlfriend, Lene, have the same idea he does: to retreat to what they assume will be the empty bungalow for a few days before Lene has to go to Munich for an acting role. The weather is warm and the days lazy, aided and abetted by the

See DISENGAGEMENT

FIG. 92: *Hotel.*

private pool at the bungalow around which much of the action elliptically unfolds: Paul first sees Max and Lene as they start to have sex next to the pool, Paul flirts with his ex-girlfriend Kerstin there, and, in what expresses a curious fascination with swimwear, Paul tries on and then relaxes in Lene's bathing suit after she has apparently left for Munich **[Fig. 93]**. Orbiting the parents' pool in one or another way, all of the principles spend much of the film in various states of undress, underscoring the overarching malaise of swimsuited youthful idleness: Paul has abandoned his national post, his

FIG. 93: *Bungalow.*

brother Max is working slowly (if at all) on a dissertation, and Lene has been fired from her acting job (as an extraterrestrial with few lines) while vacationing at the bungalow.

If the private pool comes to reflect and produce their general laziness and detachment, one of the few hints at plot development involves a public pool: on the radio early in the film, when viewers are still seeking some hint of action to come, Paul and Max hear that there has been an explosion at the local municipal pool. Given Germany's history with domestic terrorism and the prevailing idyllic atmosphere in the film, which begs to be disrupted, viewers might suspect a terrorist attack. A publicity still of the swimsuited principals observing a plume of smoke in the distance seems to emphasize this possibility **[see Fig. 117—VIOLENCE]**. A visiting, former girlfriend of Max's, Dunja, conspicuously tries to engage the group in a discussion of what could have caused the pool explosion and what it could have meant. But the pool explosion proves another narrative dead end among many in the Berlin School: another radio report shortly thereafter recounts how the explosion was caused by faulty construction in the pool's boiler room. The frustrated promise of a more conventional narrative conflict is typical of Berlin School plotting, and the destruction of a municipal pool only underscores the detachment of the private pool from any kind of collective project. Much as Paul has abandoned the Foucauldian institution of the army for the privacy of the bungalow, the municipal pool has been destroyed by corruption and neglect in favor of the private pool. Aside from the army that is trying to reclaim Paul and the report about the municipal pool, no public institutions are even mentioned in the film.

The recurring pool-deck nakedness and Paul's modeling of women's swimwear underscore another aspect of the swimming pool hinted at above (as well as in Deleuze's understanding of the 'control society'), namely, the heightened relationship of people to their bodies, gender and sexuality. The Berlin School seems attuned to how, as Christian Petzold has put it, neoliberalism produces new forms of physicality as well as new bodies around these new forms.[2] Petzold's comments dovetail with the insights of theorists of neoliberalism like David Harvey, who regards the body as an unfinished product, one that continues to unfold in history as an emphatically relational 'thing' that must be seen as open to the 'spatiotemporal flux of multiple processes.'[3] As noted above, a swimming pool would seem to hold out the promise of contemporary bodies emancipated, bodies that could (potentially) act actively and perhaps resistively.[4] But, as in both *Hotel* and *Bungalow*, the emancipation of the body at poolside turns into a frustrated opportunity.

See INTERIORITY

Köhler's second film deploys the swimming pool to evoke the relationship of the control society to the body even more emphatically than in *Bungalow*. In *Windows on Monday*, Nina flees a domestic life that she finds oppressive: she is a working doctor-mother who is pregnant with a second child, renovating a middle-class house for her growing family and—perhaps most ominously where her feelings of confinement are concerned—new windows for the house are due to arrive on Monday. Abruptly, she abandons her husband Frieder and their daughter, Charlotte, and flees to a family vacation cabin in the woods where, in a spirit similar to that of *Bungalow*, her brother and his girlfriend are holed up. When her brother voices disapproval of her sudden flight from her husband and daughter, she goes on a bike-ride and then a tram-ride through some foggy woods **[Fig. 54—FORESTS; Fig. 63—FRAMINGS]**, which brings her to an enormous sport hotel in the middle of a forest. There, wandering the hallways in menacing handheld references to *The Shining*, she stumbles not upon terrifying murderers or a history of horror, bur rather upon a professional tennis demonstration for some affluent vacationers. A small crowd of well-heeled Germans stands next to an indoor tennis court where a late-middle-aged tennis professional from Eastern Europe, played by tennis personality Ille Nastase, but renamed here alternately David Ionescu or David Haase, defeats a local player. The variation in Nastase's character's name underscores how the hotel sequence, despite its length, may be at least partially fantasized. After the end of the match, the spectators, fully and expensively dressed, dive suddenly into the hotel pool. Many of them shed their suits and dresses in the pool and try to convince the tennis pro to join them.

See HOTELS

Nina observes the pool and these goings-on through a large picture window, like an anthropologist of the wealthy and bored; and, indeed, the scene reveals and underscores a number of the sociological meanings of the swimming pool outlined above **[Fig. 94]**. There is the link to the wealthy leisure culture of contemporary Germany that promises only consumerist emancipation: these Germans could think of nothing better than to be bussed in their finery to an aging sport hotel to watch an aging tennis player in a kind of private audience away from modern mass sports. The distance of the hotel and its lavish pool from conventional public and mass culture confirms the trajectory traced by Deleuze from the public to the private. The contrast between the sports hero in his suit and the wealthy Germans shedding their finery, changing into underwear and less, emphasizes the theme of lost corporeality which they attempt to regain in the swimming pool. In *Windows on Monday*, the image of the pool and

FIG. 94: *Windows on Monday*.

its putative but fruitless liberation of the body circles back to the viewers' first hint of Nina's discontent: in the first clue that something is wrong, an early scene presents her hiding out in the bathroom, bathing her feet in the sink and then concealing her indulgence when her husband knocks and enters **[Fig. 95]**. It is a casual lie, a disavowal of the pleasure of private bathing, one that, like the swimming pool in these films in general, veils deeper malaise.

NMA & JF

FIG. 95: *Windows on Monday*.

Notes

1 Gilles Deleuze, 'Postscript on Control Societies,' in *Negotiations*, trans. Martin Joughin (New York: Columbia University Press, 1995), 177–82.
2 Jaimey Fisher, 'A Ghostly Archeology,' in *Christian Petzold* (Champaign-Urbana, IL: University of Illinois, 2013).
3 David Harvey, *Spaces of Hope* (Berkeley, CA: University of California Press, 2000), 98.
4 Harvey, *Spaces of Hope*, 101.

Predecessors: The German Prehistory of the Berlin School

The filmmakers commonly associated with the Berlin School, despite their undeniable, numerous differences, share certain predilections, among which are an aesthetics of reduction and restraint, a penchant for image-focused rather than plot-driven constructions, a veristic resolve marked by an investment in the here and now, and a desire to negotiate the quotidian spaces as well as the less charted places of contemporary Germany and Europe where quite often transit sites become twilight zones. Theirs is a cinema of observation, not fabrication, more monstrative than narrative, a cinema that respects the weight of images and recognizes the substantial ethical responsibility of a medium that traffics in facsimiles of the real. This cinema of observation and nonintervention is, as Christoph Hochhäusler and others have emphasized, marked by Siegfried Kracauer's initiative to redeem physical reality. Like that of the late Kracauer, its understanding of realism is reflexive and highly self-conscious; for the exponents of the Berlin School, reality is produced, not given, shaped by the forces of nature but every bit as strongly determined by history and human agency.

In characterizations of the impulses that gave rise to this newer German cinema, certain filmmakers are regularly cited as essential precursors: Marco Abel mentions Robert Bresson, Michelangelo Antonioni, Michael Haneke, the Dardenne Brothers, Maurice Pialat, Jean Eustache, and Philippe Garrel; to this inventory Georg Seeßlen adds John Ford, Jean-Luc Godard, and John Cassavetes. One might also append to the collection of influences, Frederick Wiseman (particularly his trust in the viewer's power of judgment), James Benning (his acute sensitivity to both natural and built landscapes), and Apichatpong Weerasethakul (his stirring blend of acute realism and comic absurdism). It also would make sense to consider the See ECLECTIC AFFINITIES conspicuous impact of photographers like Walker Evans, Robert Frank, or the early Larry Clark as well as painters like Gerhard Richter and Edward Hopper.

For all its cosmopolitan sophistication, intellectual curiosity, and nuanced awareness of film history and contemporary world cinema, however, the Berlin School is an entity that came about in Germany under specific conditions and at a certain time. As such, various domestic forces and energies, even if they surely cannot be seen as fully defining its ultimate shape, figured crucially in the formation of the Berlin School. These include:

1. The Munich journal *Filmkritik* (1957–84), which, without question, remains to this day the most significant periodic film publication to have come from the FRG. What Olaf Möller describes as a '*Filmkritik*-style' was shared both by film critics like Peter Nau, Manfred Blank, and Helmut Färber (all of whom also taught film history at the dffb—the Berlin Film and Television Academy), and filmmakers like Hartmut Bitomsky and Harun Farocki (directors who attended and later assumed prominent functions at the dffb), as well as Wim Wenders, Rudolf Thome, and Gerhard Theuring (directors who were also writers). 'You wrote when you weren't filming,' argues Möller, 'you filmed when you weren't writing; writing and filming ultimately became a continuous stream in the flow of life.'[1] After a reconstitution of *Filmkritik*'s editorial board in the early 1970s, the prose in this journal privileged observation and description over analysis and evaluation. Single sequences from a film, as Möller elaborates, were often 'described for pages on end, very carefully, with each scrupulously weighed up against its implications, its resonance, its role in the logic and the poetry of the sentence and the text.' The director whom the editors of this journal most highly revered was himself a master of description and observation, namely Jean-Marie Straub, a filmmaker who had no ideological axe to grind and did not impose a vision on the viewer, whose images were precise, whose style was unadorned, and whose cinema pure. As a journal, *Filmkritik* provided a model for the Berlin School's house organ, *Revolver*. Like *Filmkritik*, *Revolver* would serve as a site for spirited cinephilia, a forum for talented young artists and critics to write about films that they appreciate and, in the journal's inimitable interviews, to talk at length with filmmakers whom they consider to be kindred spirits.

2. A German legacy of realist filmmaking that spans postwar German cinema and German film theory from the poetic realism of Helmut Käutner's *Unter den Brücken/Under the Bridges* (1945), a film particularly cherished by Christian Petzold (who extols its virtues at length in the recent homage to German film history, *Auge in Auge/Eye to Eye*, 2008), to Jürgen Böttcher's *Jahrgang 45/Born in 1945* (1966) and Roland Klick's *Bübchen*

(1968), both of which were screened in a *Revolver*-sponsored series curated by Christoph Hochhäusler in Paris during the spring of 2011, to the films of German sensibilism with their poetic empiricism (take, for instance, Wenders's 1971 *Summer in the City*). This tradition also includes the anti-Oberhausen Munich School of the late 1960s, especially the minimalism of Rudolf Thome's early features such as *Rote Sonne/Red Sun* (1969), a film that Wenders celebrated for its 'ability to display for ninety minutes without any sense of urgency nothing more than surface appearances.'[2] In addition, one might mention the *cinéma pur* of Straub/Huillet and the gritty urban sketches of Klaus Lemke.

Common to these endeavors is the impetus articulated in Siegfried Kracauer's *Theory of Film: The Redemption of Physical Reality* (1960), which (particularly in its epilogue) represents a master text in any approach to the Berlin School. What we need to do, claims Kracauer, is to regain touch with reality, to look at it more closely, to experience it more fully and concretely. Herein lies film's revelatory potential. What he desires is that we partake of and, at the same time, see through and look beyond a reality where everything has become abstract, functional, and determinate, where meaning is obvious and transparent. We need to restore to objects and the world their presence and poignance. Film's ultimate mission is to see and experience things in their concreteness: 'What we want,' maintains Kracauer, 'is to touch reality not with the fingertips but to seize it and shake hands with it.'[3]

Quite adamantly, the directors of the Berlin School assail what they consider to be the disregard for reality (*Realitätsferne*) in many contemporary German features, their absurd contrivances, implausible constructions, and spurious harmonies; especially the Nazi-Stasi retro films (e.g., *Der Untergang/Downfall* [Oliver Hirschbiegel, 2004] and *Das Leben der Anderen/The Lives of Others* [Florian Henckel von Donnersmarck, 2006]) come under harsh criticism. Very few productions, Petzold insists, reveal what the Federal Republic really looks like today and grant a more profound sense of what it feels like to be a denizen of postmillennial Europe. Germans fancy that they live in cities, says Petzold, but they really live in *Schlafstädte*, dreary places with 'those same shops, always Schlecker, Eiscafe San Marco, a french-fry stand, three or four hairdressers, a specialty store for electronics.'[4]

Berlin School features negotiate displaced places and interstices in a historical void; they emphasize sites off the beaten track (at times literally off the map), rarely traversed sectors of the country and the continent. Cameras

See ANTI-HAUPTSTADT

insistently fix on people in motion and offer the viewer a keen experience of physis; reality, seen in this way, means the province of physical things and human bodies, the empirical world apprehended in its diversity and complexity (rather than corseted within generic constraints and vitiated by the imperatives of narrative trajectories). These images allow viewers to probe the changed (and ever changing) terms of contemporary experience and to take sensual measure of the contradictions of supermodernity, be it for instance in the different existential spaces of the new bourgeoisie, the opaque workings and often dire consequences of global capitalism, or the dramatically transformed appearances of the buildings and streets that people on the continent today inhabit. The dreamscapes explored here often turn out to be nightmarish topographies. In the spectral images and dystopian prospects of this haunting cinema abides a reality that is doubly disturbing. These films show how *what is* is a function of *what was* while also offering presentiments or perhaps a hope of *what might be*. In this uncertain (and, for that reason, dynamic) mix of dread prospects and occasional (albeit subdued) glimmers of hope abides a unique realism whose equal measures of curiosity and critique alternate between being acerbic and redemptive.

See FAMILIAR PLACES

3. The legacy of the dffb: this impetus embraces the film academy's teachers as well as its students and their common culture of cinephilia (which included regular group screenings of a quite electic variety of films and which carries on, as noted, in the pages of *Revolver*). One can clearly see the impact of the 'technological lyricism'[5] of films by Harun Farocki and Hartmut Bitomsky (with whom Thomas Arslan, Angela Schanelec, and Christian Petzold studied) in the continuities between *Der VW Komplex* (Bitomsky, 1990) and *Wolfsburg* (2003) or, even more directly, in the direct influence of *Nicht ohne Risiko/Nothing Ventured* (Farocki, 2004) on *Yella*, endeavors that probe the eerie shapes of postindustrial modernity and the alienating aspects of commercial spaces. (Hochhäusler's *The City Below*, with its chilling views of Manhattan's temples of high capital, surely shares this impetus.) Petzold readily acknowledges how he learned from Farocki the art of making images that dissect the uncanny workings of modern capitalism.

Another lesson that Petzold learned from Farocki has to do with the importance of body language. In German film, argues Petzold (and, in the process, he also brings to mind the insights of Michael Klier's astute critique of New German Cinema, *Gesten und Gesichter/Gestures and Faces* [2001]), there has always been too much 'facial expression, eyebrow play, and theatrical language.' He elaborates about how, while working on his final film at the dffb (*Pilotinnen/Pilots*, 1995), Farocki was making *Der Ausdruck der Hände/The Expression of Hands* (1997), a documentary about the expressive capacity of hands; as a result Petzold found himself very interested in the play of hands and its creative potential. In the process he became particularly sensitive to how much physicality is lost in most German films, where the dialogue and the human face dominate so strongly. One need not send German actors to New York for lessons in method acting, Farocki had told dffb students; rather, they should go to Switzerland so that they might have their face muscles surgically severed. Olaf Möller calls Farocki's films 'Gespensterbilder,' or 'images of things that are not visible and yet are nonetheless present,' an appellation that also applies to Petzold's haunted cinema (especially his so-called 'Ghost Trilogy'). One might in fact say that the Berlin School as a whole does not put its faith in the self-evident immediacy of images, but rather lets things become visible above all in the spaces between images, so that, in Hochhäusler's words, 'Films are completed during the process of viewing them.' See GHOSTS

4. Subterranean currents in West German film culture of the 1980s and early 1990s: within a subterranean history of German cinema abides a prehistory of the Berlin School, works that cling to reality, that eschew the conventional politics of identification, that explore reality's lesser-known quadrants, that present characters whose lives are sketchy or (in the case of Behrens's *Berliner Stadtbahnbilder/Images from the Berlin S-Bahn* [1982] and Michael Klier's *Der Riese/The Giant* [1984]) show us no characters at all, features that meander through streets and cities. See PREDECESSORS

In the German prehistory of the Berlin School (which involves a much more elaborate chronicle and, for that reason, surely warrants more detailed study), one film is of particular significance. Speaking in an interview published in *Kinomagazin*, Christoph Petzold described the lasting impression that Michael Klier's 81-minute video film of 1984, *Der Riese*, had made on him and his fellow dffb students. It consists of surveillance camera footage shot in various West German cities over the course of three years: streets, traffic intersections, airports, banks, department stores, villas, and doctors' offices. The images include ambient sound as well as the musical accompaniment of Khachaturian, Rachmaninoff, and Wagner. It is called *Der Riese*, elaborates Petzold, because the cameras 'gaze at the world from on high and because the Giant is large and looks on people from above. At the same time the Giant is a little dumb.'[6] These camera eyes are ubiquitous See AMBIENT SOUND and unrelenting; they stare without cease and provide a painstaking record of current events. And yet, for all their omnipresence, they are undiscerning and indiscriminant. Marked by 'distance, abstraction, and a certain placid ambiguity,'[7] they do not make choices or provide emphases; rather, while taking in everything, they sort out nothing. Klier discerns an uncanny dimension in the workings of the Giant's affectless omniscient eyes; surveillance images, he claims, 'have the effect of documents about another planet, horrible scenes like those from a science fiction nightmare.' At a certain juncture the banality and ordinariness of these mechanical reproductions become fantastic and uncanny, even 'obscene in a way, because they attack people and rob them of their dignity.' For this reason, one might say, the film shows cinema's potential endpoint. Indeed, one might call this composite of German urban centers a symphony of bleak cities.

Despite the dystopic dimensions ascribed by Klier and Petzold to surveillance cameras, they do not only remain an object of critique and dystopia. Indeed, observation, which is an act of faith for the Berlin School, is an essential part of surveillance, 'a certain detached alertness, the act of carefully watching, listening, and registering events and their context without intervening in them.'[8] Throughout Berlin School features, surveillance functions as an undeniably suggestive point of reference. Repeatedly these films inscribe surveillance cameras and, in so doing, let the ambiguity and undecidabilty of surveillance serve a critical and constructive purpose, for instance in *Ghosts*, where surveillance footage documents the two female shoplifters as they exit from H&M in the Potsdamer Platz arcades; a few minutes later, we hear how the troubled mother in fact watched a surveillance video of a man abducting her daughter; this harrowing image will reappear as a mindscreen, an extension of the mourning mother's memory, a locus of traumatic loss in which the daughter is pulled off-screen and vanishes from sight **[Fig. 96]**. Similarly, in *Sleeper*, where the film's opening shots have the feel and texture of surveillance camera footage; a discussion between two characters about observation is captured from a perspective that itself both resembles—and operates like—a surveillance camera. Finally, the *Dreileben* trilogy is in fact framed by surveillance camera images. *One Minute of Darkness*, Hochhäusler's contribution and the film's final feature, refers to a missing slice of surveillance camera footage. And, to heighten the enigma and add a twist of irony, the film ends with its own act of withholding. We see a surveillance camera's record of a decidedly climactic moment, but the film freezes and, in a touch that consciously plays on the film's title, fades into darkness before we can determine what has actually happened **[Fig. 97]**.

See SURVEILLANCE

FIG. 96: *Ghosts.*

The quarry created by the surveillance apparatus needs to be processed, which is what viewers of *Der Riese* must do as they sift through the film's 80-some minutes, reviewing this profusion of sights and sounds, sorting it out and transforming it into audiovisual evidence. To rescan surveillance footage, subsequent Berlin School exercises in this vein suggest, the viewer must proceed like a detective, for only the reconstructive mind can assemble the discrete pieces and determine what they actually disclose. In that regard the surveillance camera, which is the ultimate cinema of

FIG. 97: *One Minute of Darkness.*

attractions, provides the raw material for *Denkbilder*, that is, thought images that process otherwise seemingly random signifiers and reclaim them as signs of time and signs with meanings. Such thought images are very much the point in the Berlin School's endeavor to make films that redeem reality.[9]

In the late 1980s Klier (especially after his breakthrough narrative feature, *Überall ist es besser wo wir nicht sind/The Grass Is Greener* [1989]) was often grouped together with well-regarded rising filmmakers such as Jan Schütte (*Drachenfutter/Dragon Chow* [1987]) and Uwe Schrader (*Kanakerbraut/White Trash* [1984] and *Sierra Leone* [1987]) and touted as a miniature realist or an exponent of a so-called New German Realism. Despite occasional festival successes and critical laudations, the films of these directors never registered (much less endured) as strongly as the products of the New German Cinema (which had gone out of style by the mid-1980s) because they had no compelling sense of context or belonging, which is to say that were not viewed as part of something more substantial. There existed no 'New Wave' or national movement or Berlin School in which one might have inserted these New German realists and which might have afforded them increased visibility and stronger resonance. As a consequence these efforts became orphan films, marginalized because they did not function within a particular context (*Zusammenhang*), forsaken and forgotten because they did not find a larger place in time. For all the confusions and misapprehensions it has engendered, the term 'Berlin School' has served quite effectively as a point of reference and a site of coherence and (for all the differences between individual directors) common cause, as well as a source of product recognition, an appellation that enables films to accrue meaning within significant creative and constructive constellations.

ER

Notes

1 Olaf Möller, 'Passage along the Shadow-Line: Farocki and Others—Approaching a Certain *Filmkritik*-style,' trans. Roger Hillman and Timothy Mathieson, *Senses of Cinema* 21, July 19, 2002, http://sensesofcinema.com/2002/21/farocki_moller/.

2 Wim Wenders, 'Rote Sonne. Zu Rudolf Thomes Film *Rote Sonne*,' *Emotion Pictures. Essays und Filmkritiken 1968–1984* (Frankfurt a. M: Verlag der Autoren, 1986), 54. Wenders' critique was originally published in 1970.

3 Siegfried Kracauer, *Theory of Film: The Redemption of Physical Reality* (Princeton: Princeton University Press, 1997), 297.

4 See Sven von Reden and Reinhard Wulf, 'Interview mit Christian Petzold. Auszug aus dem Kinomagazin,' *3Sat.de*, October 17, 2005, http://www.3sat.de/page/?source=/ard/kinomagazin/84498/index.html.

5 This is Christoph Hochhäusler's phrase. See Marco Abel, 'Tender Speaking: An Interview with Christoph Hochhäusler,' *Senses of Cinema* 42, February 13, 2007, http://sensesofcinema.com/2007/42/christoph-hochhausler/.

6 See von Reden and Wulf, 'Interview mit Christian Petzold.'

7 Sandra S. Phillips, 'Witnessing Violence,' *Exposed: Voyeurism, Surveillance, and the Camera since 1870*, ed. Sandra S. Phillips (San Francisco: San Francisco Museum of Modern Art in association with Yale University Press, 2010), 112.

8 Marta Gili, 'From Observation to Surveillance,' *Exposed: Voyeurism, Surveillance, and the Camera since 1870*, 241.

9 Shorts and features made at the dffb figure in this prehistory as well, films like Christoph Willem's *Der Mann aus dem Osten* (*The Man from the East*, 1990), Wolfgang Schmidt's *Navy Cut* (1993), and, above all, Michael Freerix's *Chronik des Regens* (*Chronicle of Rain*, 1992). Freerix's film manifests numerous attributes characteristic of the Berlin School. The film's protracted opening sequence, for example, offers a long take of a young man in an apartment eating breakfast and then clearing away things and doing the dishes with no sense of urgency whatsoever. The scene unfolds in full duration; during its course we will hear a scream in the distance and watch the unharried hero walk to the window and ask for quiet before he, undeterred, resumes his kitchen chores. The extended passage sets a tone and establishes a tempo; this is a film that is not in a rush, one that measures *temps morts* and takes time seriously.

Renovation

Fifteen minutes into Christoph Hochhäusler's haunting *This Very Moment*, we get our first glimpse of the house at the center of this contemporary 'Hansel and Gretel' story. The scene opens with a long shot of a quintessential suburban home—white, boxy, and generic, with only a small young evergreen and a stack of lumber to distinguish it **[Fig. 98]**. The camera remains static as a car pulls up the drive, and from a distance we recognize the figure of Sylvia emerging. Cut to a medium shot as she opens the trunk and stashes the two backpacks belonging to her stepchildren, Lea and Konstantin, whom she has just abandoned along a rural roadside across the Polish border. Looking pensive, but still quite as inscrutable as her actions, Sylvia enters the house. The film cuts to an interior shot of the family home, which is strikingly sterile: white, utterly lacking in adornment, and as the loose wiring and plastic-wrapped doorways indicate, unfinished **[Fig. 99]**.

The plastic sheeting that encases the doorframes and interior stairs will appear repeatedly in subsequent interior shots. Taken together with the

FIG. 98: *This Very Moment.*

FIG. 99: *This Very Moment.*

antiseptic white walls and rational grids of square tile, the end effect is of a domestic morgue—as though the home itself, if not perhaps itself a corpse, were ready to receive one. This impression is only heightened when, a short while later, Sylvia stands in the garage and watches as its door slides shut, leaving her in near-total darkness and the viewer with the impression of a tomb-like interior **[Fig. 99]**. It is a contemporary twist on the haunted spaces of traditional fairy tales: in *This Very Moment*, the home itself is stripped down and utterly inhospitable, seeming to expel life, even if the figure of Sylvia must bear the principal blame for her stepchildren's disappearance. The disturbingly blank space seems to have registered or even prefigured their absence: it is almost impossible to imagine the home echoing with the sounds of family life or the mess of children's toys and schoolwork. While the setting proves an ideal match for Hochhäusler's rendition of the classic fairy tale, giving plastic form to the underlying nightmare that is about to unfold, it also offers an emblematic example of the domestic spaces in the films of the Berlin School. These spaces are, by and large, lifeless, anonymous, unfinished, and quite often, in some state of renovation.

See INTERIORITY

The question of renovation is an important one for the Berlin School: the interiors featured in these films share a bland newness that corresponds to the school's more general embrace of the present. Renovation inevitably brings with it questions of futurity: it is, as the term itself suggests, the process of making 'new.' That the renovation projects in these films are often underway (rather than complete) speaks to the spirit of uncertainty that dominates the works. For if, in the words of Marco Abel, the Berlin School is deliberately 'presentist' in its focus, it is by no means certain what the future holds for the narrative worlds portrayed, so that virtually every example of this cinema ends without resolution or even a clear sense of direction.[1] At the same time, *re*novation (in the German, *Renovierung*)

See ENDINGS

inevitably implies a repetition of sorts—it represents a making new *again* that inevitably presupposes a past. Indeed, while the Berlin School does not explicitly engage with the overt questions of history that defined West German art cinema from the 1960s onward (such as the imperative to come to terms with the National Socialist past, and such attendant matters as guilt, complicity, and generational responsibility), it is through its exploration of the anodyne modern spaces and landscapes of the postwar, post-Wall nation, and in particular its attention to spaces undergoing renovation or abandonment, that questions of history re-emerge. The relentless focus on the present in these films, the historical depths they choose *not* to explore, lend them an uncanny quality—what we might think of as their 'un-history.' For these reasons, the motif of renovation provides a powerful lens through which to examine how the Berlin School figures the relationship of the contemporary moment to an absent, unrepresented past, as well as the very possibility of renewal at all. For if renovation brings with it a restoration of surfaces in these films, it does not breathe new life into them. It foregrounds a society *in progress*, but not necessarily moving forward. The result is a series of small-scale portraits of life in post-unification Germany that countermands any grand triumphalist narratives about the state of the Berlin Republic, national unification, or the process of 'normalization.'

See LANDSCAPE

In *This Very Moment*, the hostile qualities of the domestic sphere become evident in the shots that unfold immediately after Sylvia's entrance into the house. Just as she has lit a cigarette (under the kitchen exhaust fan, as though all traces human activity are literally to be sucked out of the house), her husband, Josef, returns. Fending off his question, 'The children aren't back yet?' Sylvia declares: 'I want to sleep with you.' The two share an awkward grapple in one of the sealed doorways—yet another instance of the bad sex that features so prominently in films of the Berlin School. When we next see them, they are upstairs and entangled in a postcoital embrace beneath the unfinished dormer walls of their bedroom. The scene is rendered legible through the narrative conventions of the fairy tale: the 'new' wife, having disposed, at least for a time, of her husband's preexisting offspring, seeks to create their own, replacement child, as if to close the loop between herself and her mate (as if to 'renovate' the very family itself, through the cycle of regeneration). That this effort seems unlikely to succeed in this barren setting is suggested at the film's midpoint: from a medium shot capturing the gentle, poetic flutter of the stairwell's plastic hull, Hochhäusler cuts to a close-up of Sylvia's abdomen, her hands thrown

See BAD SEX

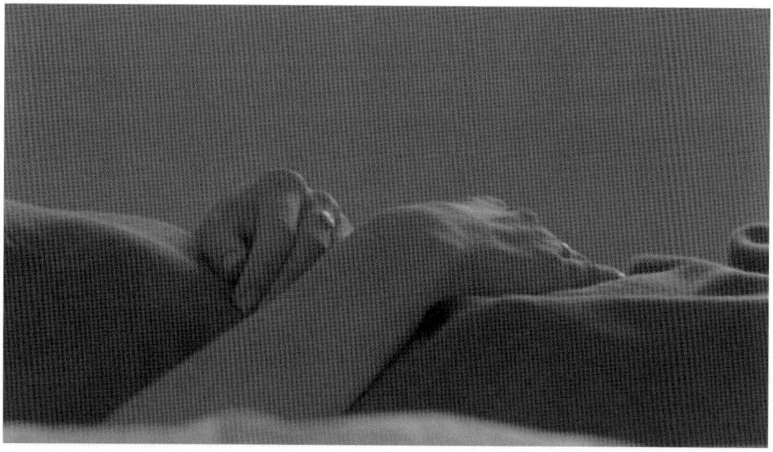

FIG. 100: *This Very Moment*.

across it, slowly rising and falling, the slow rhythm of her breath matching the deliberate pace of the sequence while the framing accentuates the flatness of her belly **[Fig. 100]**. There is an uncanny timbre to the brief sequence, not only signaling the film's deep-seated suspicion that rebirth is unachievable, but also insinuating that any life able to take hold here would be monstrous, always already haunted by the circumstances of its genesis.

The flat and bare modern spaces of Berlin School films recall the imagery of Rainer Maria Rilke's turn-of-the-(last)-century artist novel, *Die Aufzeichnungen des Malte Laurids Brigge/The Notebooks of Malte Laurids Brigge* (1910). Malte's exploration of Paris yields a sense of cloying but revelatory closeness: outside, the sights and scents of the metropolis overwhelm his senses; inside, the sounds of the city penetrate the walls of his room and literally infiltrate his body, an experience that the character links to a new capacity to see—as though achieving sight were a process of gazing as much inward as out at the world. This sense of estranged closeness is best embodied in the novel by the figure of the neighbor, whose simultaneous presence and distance (positioned right next door to Malte, and yet infinitely set apart by the walls of their shared building) seems emblematic of the fraught state of interpersonal relations in the modern metropolis.

Rilke's Malte strolls past a partially demolished row house and perceives a larger trajectory of human history in the bared layers of its structure. Like the renovation projects underway in the Berlin School's films, here the processes of demolition and reconstruction hold out the promise of revealing generational history in spatial terms. As Rilke's artist muses: 'The stubborn life of these rooms had not let itself be trampled out.'[2] Life adheres to the architectural strata, and their uncovering melds past and present—the layers of the building's former existence ironically brought to life, to coexistence with the present, as they are brought to light through the process of their destruction. As much as Rilke's novel portrays a world of new physical and emotional detachment, it is also characterized by a deep feeling of historicity, a sense that bygone eras still give form to the present, if only at the level of the substrate.

The architectural spaces that occupy the terrain of Berlin School films are different, though: their spaces afford no depths one might penetrate, and hence any promise held out by their seemingly multilayered surfaces goes deliberately unfulfilled. With apologies to Gertrude Stein, it is as though 'there is no there there.' For all the semblance of renovation that characterizes Berlin School cinema, the houses themselves are remarkably layerless. There appears literally no way to get behind the exterior of the anonymous homes and hotels in these films—as though peeling away the surface would reveal only more surface. The result is a form of architectural disaffection, a literalized expression of the opacity and impenetrability that characterize the human figures who inhabit these spaces, whose interior lives we as viewers are unable and even disinclined to access. It is no coincidence that many of the homes featured in Berlin School films are noticeably neighborless (or at least lack the next-door variety). If Rilke represents a voice and an age grappling with the new anonymity of an urbanite society and characterized by a spirit of mournful longing for a bygone era of wholeness, the films of the Berlin School seem to have dispensed altogether with dreams of connection and contact. Instead, they remain deliberately cool and superficial—confounding a viewer's effort to see into the psychology or the history of the characters and the spaces they inhabit. Their provocation to audiences resides precisely in their talent for drawing us into narratives to which they then deny us easy entrance (for without depth, we cannot possibly enter their psyches or their spaces, after all). At the same time, these films represent a significant thematic departure from the films of the New German Cinema with which they have so frequently been compared: these newer works seem to suggest that plumbing the national past for clues to the present may be as misguided or empty a gesture as any naïve faith in the future. In this sense, the Berlin School casts renovation as a doubly failed enterprise—not only calling

See HOTELS

See DISENGAGEMENT

See PREDECESSORS

into question the possibility of renewal (consider not only all the aborted home improvement projects in these films, but also their preoccupation with missing children and barren relationships), but also interrogating the logic of an earlier generation of art cinema that insisted upon the centrality of history for contemporary German self-understanding. For the Berlin School, the past appears a terrain every bit as unattainable and infertile as the future.

Windows on Monday embodies the Berlin School's preoccupation with stagnancy in a contemporary era purportedly characterized by progressive national transformation. *Windows on Monday*—the title of which references the home rehabbing project underway—centers on Nina, a physician grown tired of the humdrum nature of her professional and domestic life. Midway through an evening of stripping wallpaper with her partner, Frieder, she leaves with the declared intention of picking up their daughter **[see Fig. 4—AMBIENT SOUND]**. But in a sly enactment of her desire for a more substantive 'Tapetenwechsel' (figuratively meaning a 'change of scenery,' although the German term literally translates as a 'change in wallpaper') Nina only stops to watch her child through the window of her in-laws' home, and then without a word gets back into her car and keeps driving. The rest of the film pursues Nina and Frieder as they negotiate the terms of this spontaneous separation, infidelity, and Nina's worry that she may be pregnant with a second, seemingly unwanted child. A parallel narrative focuses on Nina's hapless younger brother, Christoph, a serial philanderer who utters what must be deemed the film's unfulfilled challenge: reflecting on his own struggling relationship, he declares: 'I've got to change something.' His words again echo strangely (and almost certainly unintentionally) those of Rilke, in this case, the closing line of the author's 1908 poem 'Archaic Torso of Apollo,' which exhorts the reader: 'You must change your life.' If Köhler's film shares a certain sense of urgency with Rilke's line from a century earlier, it does not share its hopeful energy. Indeed, as his film demonstrates amply, the search for change, for life rather than stultification, proves easy to declare and essentially impossible to accomplish. Like Christoph's empty resolution, the wallpaper that Nina and Frieder assiduously strip only succeeds in revealing another layer of blank surface, and both gestures fail entirely to bring renewal. It is as though the architecture around Nina prefigures her fate: neither her work to renovate the family home or her eventual flight to the alternate locations of her family weekend cabin and the neighboring hotel prove able to generate any substantive change in her life, and her character fails to achieve any insight into, much less a way out of, her dull reality.

From the outset, *Windows on Monday* presents us with spaces of antisepsis and illness, as if to underscore the moribund nature of Nina and Frieder's existence. The opening shot shows Frieder and daughter Charlotte donning scrubs and slowly making their way through the halls of Nina's hospital ward. As they pass by rooms full of bedridden patients, Charlotte whispers: 'They're dead.' When Frieder reassures her that they are merely asleep, she insists: 'I think they're dead.' The bluish pallor of the walls, the proliferation of plastic and other material safeguards against contamination, and the measured movement of the actors, camerawork, and spare editing, coupled with the uncanny sense of haunting introduced by Charlotte's reading of the hospital, echo the cold spaces of *This Very Moment*. And while the interior of Nina and Frieder's house evinces a bit more of the normal disorder and detritus of everyday life than that in *This Very Moment*, theirs is anything but lively. This missing warmth of Nina and Frieder's home is, as in the earlier film, closely linked to its unfinished state **[Fig. 101]**. Sealed in a state of waiting, the domestic space evokes a family and a larger cultural moment in a condition of suspension—of waiting for movement that may never come. If the half-renovated house represents the locus of this feeling in the film, a sense of malaise and stagnation seems to have permeated all of the spaces in Köhler's film. In a scene set at the cabin—where Nina has fled after leaving Frieder, only to barge in on the attempted reconciliation between Christoph and his girlfriend (Natalie, played by Elisa Seydel)— the younger couple argues about politics. Christoph insists that nothing changes; Natalie, who works in government, cites as a mark of progress the quantity of legislation passed in recent years. Nina does not chime in, but the film subtly sides with Christoph's pessimistic view of national progress.

See DISENGAGEMENT

FIG. 101: *Windows on Monday.*

Indeed, as if to counteract any notion of forward movement whether at the level of the individual or society, the film is bookended by death. In the closing scenes, Nina and Frieder come together to attend the funeral of a neighbor who has died in part as a result of an anticlotting drug Nina prescribed: the medicine prevented an embolism as intended, but triggered uncontrolled bleeding after the young man had a bicycle accident. Nina and Frieder cannot consummate their reunion, however: skipping the funeral, they half-heartedly try to have sex **[see Fig. 12—BAD SEX]** in the back of their car, but like every other gesture in the film that might lead to new life, their attempt misfires, with little satisfaction for either party or the audience. The film concludes with no clear sense of the direction of their relationship, their home renovation project, or Nina's probable pregnancy. The conclusion is typical of the skepticism that the Berlin School displays generally toward any logic of renewal; the universe of their films is characterized by a renovation that only ever seems to generate more of the same.

See BAD SEX

JMK

Notes

1 Marco Abel, 'Intensifying Life: The Cinema of the "Berlin School,"' *Cineaste* 33.4 (2008), http://www.*cineaste*.com/articles/the-berlin-school.htm.

2 Rainer Maria Rilke, *The Notebooks of Malte Laurids Brigge*, trans. M. D. Herter Norton (New York: Norton, 1992), 47.

Seeing and Saying

In an interview, German director Dominik Graf observes that one of the most significant connective textures holding together the films of the Berlin School is 'how characters talk in [them].' The protagonists in these films, Graf explains, 'talk all the time, but from this permanent communicating emerges a tremendous sense of their inability to come together,' which gives viewers the impression of a 'strong sense of oppression—oppression through language!'[1] Graf's diagnostic insight seems to apply to many Berlin School films, but perhaps to none more than those directed by Angela Schanelec. Her films confront head-on the incommensurability between seeing and saying and explore what happens to cinema's ability to communicate with viewers when films embrace this incommensurability between images and language as the condition of possibility for storytelling rather than (willfully) ignoring it. In Schanelec's films—but also in other Berlin School films, including most notably Henner Winckler's *School Trip* and Christoph Hochhäusler's *This Very Moment*—this incommensurability diegetically reveals itself when the protagonists suffer communicative breakdowns. Crucially, however, Schanelec and her colleagues are not merely interested in showing viewers how their characters struggle to express themselves. Time and again, these diegetic communicative breakdowns manifest themselves extradiegetically in *our* sense of (seemingly) being oppressed by how these films deploy language. While this potentially oppressive sense of language permeates many Berlin School films, Schanelec mobilizes the incommensurability between seeing and saying (and its consequences for communication) as *axiomatic.*

Schanelec pursued this strategy as early as in her 1994 dffb (Berlin Film and Television Academy) graduation film, *I Spent the Summer in Berlin*, and as recently as in her 2010 film *Orly*. In the former, Schanelec has one of her protagonists ask another whether he can hear her without his glasses on, thus playfully calling attention to the problematic epistemological relation between the visible and the audible. This moment sets the stage for the film's penultimate scene that explicitly thematizes the desire to be 'understood.'

Schanelec manages here to sever the concept of 'understanding' from its common(sense) attribution. Refusing to reduce 'understanding' to a matter of signification, Nadine (played by Schanelec) instead asserts that she wants to be understood in the way that one understands music, that is, through its asignifying, affective quality. The film thus acknowledges that its viewers are bound to struggle with understanding the film's events, not least because what is said and what is shown are difficult to reconcile. At the same time, the affective response to the film's performative staging of the incommensurability of its images and language leads to an alternative mode of participating in these events.

In *Orly*, Schanelec leaves her viewers with an image of a young girl who refuses to speak at the end of what is otherwise a film in which characters permanently talk **[Fig. 102]**, but, as in all of her films, they often use language at cross-purposes to one another. We also find variations of such a refusal to communicate in the work of Ulrich Köhler. There it tends to deprive us of the possibility of understanding the films' characters. Similar to Sabine, whose question the girl refuses to answer at the end of *Orly*, Max's efforts to impose a prefabricated identity onto his younger brother in *Bungalow* are steadfastly refused by the latter. In such cases, we are unable to ascribe a sense of identity to the protagonists, which, in turn, troubles our ability to make sense of them. At such moments, when the cinematic conventions enabling viewers to make sense are suspended, we find ourselves affectively confronted with the very sense of 'understanding' that Schanelec's films seek to contest. Schanelec refuses to facilitate the viewer's ability to understand by mobilizing the normativized rules of narrative filmmaking, which are explicitly predicated on a logic of commensurability, indeed, redundancy, between images and language, seeing and saying, the visual and the sonic.

See SIBLINGS

FIG. 102: *Orly*.

In so doing, her films end up instilling in us the affectively felt need to reframe, to resense, the very idea of 'understanding' as something that is in fact the effect of a process of presubjective sensations impinging upon our bodies. See INTERIORITY

It is, however, 'First Day (Erster Tag),' her short-film contribution to the omnibus film *Germany 09: 13 Short Films About the State of the Nation*, that offers her most concise filmic statement to date with regard to the incommensurability of images and language. This brilliant opening salvo to what is otherwise an uneven collective attempt to reflect on the state of Germany at the beginning of the third millennium pushes the logic of Schanelec's narrative work to its limit. Beyond this point, one enters the territory of experimental filmmaking that rejects narrative *tout court* in ways that Schanelec does not. 'First Day' consists of two handfuls of static images that are linked to each other mostly by an associative logic and that are marked by the presence of original sound; the measured, palpable distance the camera keeps to its ostensible points of interest; the precise framing of the images that are designed to render sensible the presence of off-screen space; and the often barely existing linkages between individual shots. These are cinematic aspects that dominate all of Schanelec's films. See THE CUT While it is possible for viewers to ascribe to these images—or, better, *in*scribe into them—a narrative, each of these images primarily confronts us in its own right, extracted out of a larger narrative that seeks to communicate a discernible meaning. The images *image* but do not speak; that is, they refuse to cater to habituated spectatorial desires for them to speak, to signify.

And yet, even in this minimalist short film, we cannot entirely deny the existence of a hint of narrative. Each shot is temporally linked through the lighting (the darkness inside the apartment; the colors of dawn in the landscape shots; the bright neon light of the hospital juxtaposed with the barely visible morning light shimmering through at the end of a hallway, far away from the camera) to suggest the beginning of *a* day. It is neither a special nor a common day, but *a* day, depicted in all the singularity that also marks its utter normality. Thus, it seems that at the beginning of this day—a 'first day,' which suggests there will be a second day, but of what?—a young girl gets up while we see her mother already at work. We also see cleaning women who make sure the students, including possibly the girl, begin their school day in an orderly, clean environment **[Fig. 103]**. Because the film neither identifies nor psychologizes them, we are left wondering who the girl, the nurse and the cleaning women are. We only observe them as they attend to the normal duties of their daily routine according to a

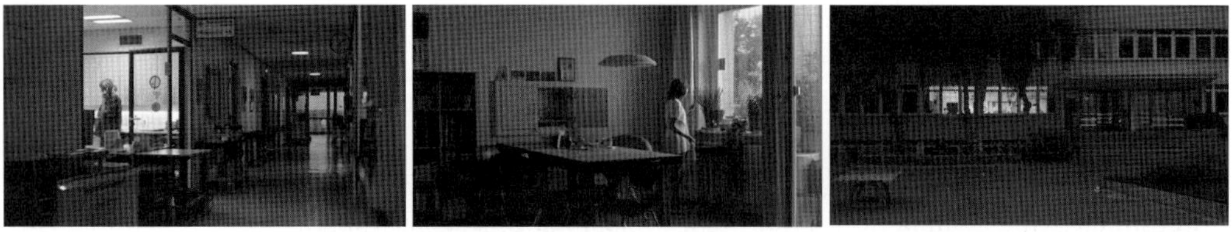

FIG. 103: *Germany 09: 13 Short Films About the State of the Nation.*

schedule, just as the ICE that traverses the frame undoubtedly crosses the field punctually every morning at the same time, and just as farmers begin their workday in the stable following a routine that is equally familiar to them—as well as to the donkey that appears in one of the film's images **[Fig. 104]**. Still, what do we gain by recounting the film in this basic narrative manner? What do we know, now that a story has emerged in embryonic form? Does our ability to understand 'First Day' depend on this implied or suggested narrative?

Crucially, the film's sparse dialogue does not help us at all as we try to make sense of the images. Indeed, the girl's answers to questions she is apparently asked are as minimal as Schanelec's terse response when asked about the story in *Marseille*: 'The Story?'[2] In fact, had Schanelec decided not to present us with any dialogue, we would not know any less about either the girl and her interlocutor or the story. And yet, the language the film does contain plays an important role, not because it *signifies* anything, but rather because, in its very reductive quality, it renders sensible the banality of everyday communication.

The girl's monosyllabic answers, however, are juxtaposed with both the richness of the film's final 'proper' image (of a lake landscape) and the *poetic* rhythm of the accompanying quotation from the late German author

FIG. 104: *Germany 09: 13 Short Films About the State of the Nation.*

Rolf Dieter Brinkmann: 'I'm not hungry at the moment, though I know hunger will continue, the moment will continue, the Earth will continue, social situations will continue, and the dog, which is locked in the apartment next door and has been barking all morning, will continue.'[3] The parallel constructions of its syntax induce a sense of repetition, continuation, and interminability, matching form to content to express the sense that things will keep on keeping on, like yesterday and the day before, like today and like tomorrow and the day after. The unwillingness of the girl to talk more, and thus the essential superfluousness of the dialogue in 'First Day,' is reframed by the poetic stringing together of mundane observations in Brinkman's poem. As a result, Schanelec 'melodically' emphasizes precisely that which seems to be maddeningly absent or, at most, present only in the least helpful way in her short film: the German language. In the hands of Schanelec's cinematic deployment, language is rendered sensible in ways that cut against the grain of our everyday perceptions, affecting us with its sheer asignifying force.

See LANGUAGE

Woven into this string of isolated moments taken from the everyday in Brinkman's poem is the assertion that 'social situations' (*soziale Lage*) will continue as well. This irruption of the political in abstract form into the sequence of singular images breaks up the sense of interminability. When the viewer is returned to these images, it is with a reframed social vision. What in other hands might have easily resulted in a film *about* the *soziale Lage*, denouncing this or that social ill, say, in the form of kitchen sink realism, becomes in Schanelec's hands a narrative experiment. 'First Day' seeks to discover whether it is possible to affect the viewer's sense of reality without narrating a story as such. To this end, the concreteness of the images, which is enhanced through the use of original sound that infuses a degree of autonomous reality into these heavily constructed images, is suddenly transformed through the sudden appearance of a *malerisch* or painterly image—one that formally is very much opposed to photo-realism. The disruptive force of this painterly image is intensified by the simultaneous eruption of a moment of extradiegetic classical music, thus undermining any sense that the images might possibly add up to a realistic story (in its conventional, normative sense).

Lest we think Schanelec's pointed use of this cinematic strategy is merely an isolated moment in the genealogy of Berlin School filmmaking, it is worth noting that one of the group's most celebrated films, Valeska Grisebach's *Longing*, deploys this same strategy, albeit in considerably more elaborate, even structural, fashion. Early on in the film, for example,

FIG. 105: *Longing*.

Grisebach cuts from a fire station to a very long shot of Markus standing by a lake at dusk, with his wife Ella gradually approaching. The camera is perfectly still and holds the shot for 40 seconds **[Fig. 105]**. With the diegetic sound emphasizing the rural setting, we observe the couple from a considerable distance in a perfectly framed shot as they eventually embrace each other. The shot's astonishing length and its well-balanced composition cannot help but call attention to itself. Unlike prior shots that were firmly anchored in a documentary-realist aesthetic due to both the improvised, 'real' dialogue spoken by the nonprofessional actors and the shots' seemingly less composed cinematic quality, this shot appears akin to a *tableau vivant*. It is as if we were beholding a painting, as if, that is, we were now looking at mediated rather than 'real' reality. In other words, at this moment the film affectively induces us to shift our perception of its aesthetic program from one firmly rooted in a documentary-realist tradition, as it was established *in medias res* by its opening moments, to one suddenly bordering on the melodramatic. Such abruptly occurring shifts in aesthetic register from the immediacy of the documentary-realist to the mediacy of the painterly melodramatic, which Grisebach iteratively intersperses throughout the film, allow *Longing* to act directly upon viewers' nervous systems, thus triggering in us a perceptive readjustment—a redistribution—of what we are sensing.

See AMBIENT SOUND

See LONG TAKES

See BEGINNINGS

These moments, whether in *Longing* or 'First Day,' force viewers to *reframe* the very (realist) narrative information, that we were cinematically encouraged to invest with our longing, with a form of understanding that is predicated on our conventional assumptions about—and expectations for—the relation between language and images in narrative filmmaking. And, in the end, it seems that the way in which Schanelec in particular, but also the Berlin School at large, including Grisebach, affects our sensation of the German language might not so much 'oppress' us as in fact enhance our capacity for action. For, by reconfiguring the realm of the sensible in a way that enacts the very incommensurability of language and images, their films confront processes of communication in post-unification capitalism that delimit our ability to imagine what is 'realistic.' To be sure, other Berlin School films, such as Petzold's *Yella*, Hochhäusler's *The City Below* and Benjamin Heisenberg's *Sleeper*, foreground these processes more explicitly. Yet, by affecting us with a different sensation of the relation between language and images, Schanelec and Grisebach's films aim, we might say, at countering the realism of capitalism with the reality of its manufactured realism.

MA

Notes

1 See '"I Build a Jigsaw Puzzle of a Dream-Germany": An Interview with German Filmmaker Dominik Graf,' interview with Marco Abel, *Senses of Cinema* 55 (2010), http://www.sensesofcinema.com/2010/feature-articles/"'i-build-a-jigsaw-puzzle-of-a-dream-germany'-an-interview-with-german-filmmaker-dominik-graf"-2.

2 See *Marseille* DVD, insert.

3 Rolf Dieter Brinkmann, *Westwärts 1 & 2: Gedichte* (Reinbek bei Hamburg: Rowohlt, 1975), 6. My translation.

Siblings

'Papa's film is dead' ('Papas Kino ist tot'), the title of the press conference at which the Oberhausen Manifesto was released in 1962, became the motto of New German Cinema. The attitude of the Berlin School toward both family relations and the anxiety of influence can be summed up more effectively by the words of a professor to his advisee, Valerie, in Angela Schanelec's *Passing Summer*, 'It's time you detached yourself from any kind of father figure.' New German Cinema defined itself against what it saw as a strong and limiting cinematic father. Although Berlin School films depart as radically from contemporary norms, their innovation is quieter. It is notable that the narrative trajectory of many Berlin School films entails characters returning, or trying to return, to their families of origin, even while often failing. The doomed hotel clerk in Jessica Hausner's haunted *Hotel* looks forward to a visit home as a salvation; the army deserter in Ulrich Köhler's *Bungalow* returns to his parents' house; the unhappy Laura in Thomas Arslan's *Vacation* brings her husband and children to her mother's house for vacation; while the lost children in Christoph Hochhäusler's *This Very Moment* attempt to find their way home. The familial spaces in these films, however, are empty of strong parental figures and often in a state of physical dissolution or incompleteness. The abdication of parental power is reflected in dying or prematurely aging parents and in the unfinished or incomplete houses they inhabit. Indeed, Schanelec's Valerie has just come from her father's deathbed when she receives her professor's advice. Parental death and dissolution in Berlin School films resonate with a vague sense that what is lost was never really there to begin with. Valerie muses after the funeral, 'I had the impression, he'd already been gone a long time.' The relationship between the generations is thus characterized less by an adversarial generation gap, than by an aura of disengagement and misunderstanding. Within the family, however, another relationship emerges as more intensely relevant, namely the sibling relationship; its logic in fact deeply permeates the Berlin School aesthetic and its narrative meanderings.

See RENOVATION

Thomas Arslan's *Geschwister—Kardeşler*, whose title repeats the word 'siblings' in both German and Turkish, may seem the most obvious place to seek an exploration of sibling relations among the Berlin School films. And yet, Angela Schanelec's *Passing Summer* and *Afternoon*; Ulrich Köhler's *Bungalow*, Christoph Hochhäusler's *This Very Moment*, and Thomas Arslan's *Vacation* could all just as easily have carried the title 'Siblings,' and siblings play a slightly less dominant, but still significant role in Köhler's *Windows on Monday*, and Hochhäusler's *I Am Guilty*, as well as a small but notable role in Elke Hauk's *Karger*. The advice of Laura's grandmother in Arslan's *Vacation* proves just as relevant to understanding Berlin School preoccupations as that of Valerie's professor; Laura's grandmother chides her for her lapsed contact with her sister 'But you mustn't let [your relationship] tear apart. You two were so inseparable.' In a repetition or illustration of the point, Laura's own young children appear on screen nearly exclusively as a pair, involved in joint activities. The single exception enacts the urgency of the grandmother's injunction: while Leyla reads, Aaron plays soccer with his father, who injures him in the course of the game through an overly aggressive move. The injury is minor, but the incident highlights the potential for dramatic competitiveness between parents and children that animates so much cinematic and literary work, only to resist the pull of such drama, competitiveness, and any hint of resolution to be found in a cycle by which children eventually grow up to replace their parents.

Identifying the significance for the Berlin School of the kind of relation that ties siblings to each other provides a strategy for moving beyond the naive form–content dichotomy that has sometimes characterized responses to the notable lethargy of plot and character in these films. See DISENGAGMENT While the films resist traditional symptomatic readings that 'uncover' latent content, they encourage another mode of producing meaning. Rather than relying on metaphor and symbol, the films favor suggestion and evocation to elicit associations in the viewers. Ostensible departures into the realm of symbols, such as the appearance of a stork in *This Very Moment* or the frequently encountered forest, actually resist the simple assignation of a referent. See FORESTS It never becomes clear whether Sylvia, who sees the stork, is pregnant; meanwhile the forest, whether in *This Very Moment*, *Hotel*, or *Yella*, never disgorges a secret kernel that would explain or legitimate its aura of uncanny danger. Attempts to 'get to the bottom' of these films, what one might call *vertical* interpretations, are thus less productive than *horizontal* readings. The methodological shift allows the viewer to follow the flow of relationships, events, and surface detail that replace traditional narrative arcs. The focus on associative interplay also flattens time; neither within the narrative nor in its interpretive reception is there a teleological trajectory that will deliver a final meaning. This pattern mimics the structure of sibling relations. It is not a coincidence that Laura's grandmother chooses the word for 'rip' or 'tear' to describe the rending of the sibling bond. Unlike the substitution logic of parent–child relations, sibling logic generates expanding networks or fabrics of association. The actual sibling relationships between the characters are neither idealized nor demonized, but they emerge through a combination of narrative and camerawork as a foundation for the characters' activity and connection to the world.

A closer look at three films will illuminate this function. *This Very Moment*, Hochhäusler's retelling of 'Hansel and Gretel,' enacts a somewhat ambiguous abandonment of two children by their stepmother. Sylvia orders Lea and Konstantin out of the car and drives away, while they choose to walk away from the road in an oblique direction before she returns several minutes later and is unable to find them. A combination of narrative and visual framing elicits a sense of bonds between the children that while not invulnerable—are both firmer and more elastic than those between parent and child. Both the first and last scenes of the film depict the children walking together along roads in spectacular long takes. In the first scene, as they walk toward the camera, the young boy Konstantin stops to tie his shoe. The long shot remains static while Lea approaches the viewer and then breaks the frame **[see Fig. 18—BEGINNINGS]**. A moment later, however, she reenters the still static shot in response to Konstantin's call that their stepmother has arrived to pick them up. Cinematographically, Lea's continued movement and return establishes a repeated pattern that locates the film's center of gravity between the two children, and that contrasts with their subsequent abandonment by Sylvia, which is never reversed. Significantly, Lea will tie Konstantin's shoes for him once they are on their own, as if to repudiate the original act of distancing. When they do become separated at a crowded bus station the following day, it is because Konstantin has again decided to tie his own shoe, and loses sight of Lea in the process. Each sibling's reaction to their separation emphasizes the difference between their relationship and that to their stepmother, as they search for each other with increasing desperation. Although they are reunited the following day, the separation, with the hint that Konstantin may have been abused during it, is depicted as traumatic for both in ways that the original distance from their parents

See BEGINNINGS

is not. In the film's final scene, the siblings' trauma is reflected in the loss of their shoes, which renders them still more vulnerable as they walk down the country road. The long take reverses the trajectory of the opening shot, as the children recede away from the viewer in the static frame that allows the world to slowly swallow them up, enacting the final line of dialogue, 'Verschwindet!' ('Get lost!' or more literally, 'Disappear!'). The credits do not roll until the small figures have entirely vanished, not out of the frame, but down the middle of it into the distance **[see Fig. 49—FAMILIAR PLACES]**.

See LONG TAKES

In one provocative moment before the irritating behavior of Lea, primarily, provokes Sylvia to abandon the children, Sylvia succeeds in getting the younger child Konstantin to join her in a round of 'Bruder Jakob' ('Are you sleeping?'). In German, the eponymous character in the song is Jacob rather than John. The biblical Jacob quarreled with his brother Esau over their birthright, but the strife was instigated by the divergent favoritism of their parents. Later in life, the siblings reconcile. The scene in the car in *This Very Moment* entails a struggle over Konstantin's affections, which Sylvia hopes to gain, and Lea hopes to prevent her from gaining, keeping his loyalty herself. The relative depth of Konstantin's trust and affection is reflected by his anger at Lea when they are reunited after losing each other. He displays an anger at her that he never showed over the original abandonment by their stepmother.

Passing Summer similarly constitutes the sibling relationship through two long takes in which siblings break and then reenter the frame elastically. In the first, Valerie dances with her brother at a nightclub during a visit to their hometown **[see Fig. 37—DORFDISKOS]** occasioned by their father's illness, and in the second, concluding scene of the film, the siblings Marie and Thomas walk in the park while they discuss both Marie's abortion and her husband's affair **[see Fig. 84—LANDSCAPES]**.The contexts of these scenes—the death of a parent and the betrayal of a spouse—are relevant. Siblings are often more present for each other in these films than are other relatives. Such being-present cannot be equated with a uniform or mutual supportiveness, however, as the sisters in *Vacation* and the brother–sister pair in *Afternoon* demonstrate. The key is not that the relationship is a 'good' one, but that, truly existing for better and worse, it serves as a vehicle to knit the characters into the world. Thomas, for example, meets his girlfriend Valerie through his sister, Marie, while Valerie connects to her father and catches up with an old love interest through her brother. More pointedly, a friend Thomas randomly encounters responds to the question 'How are you doing?' with a long complaint about her sister's marriage to an African

See DORFDISKOS

See INTERPELLATION

man and her own negative reaction to their extended stay in her apartment, before ending with her frustrated desire to have children. The tangential scene exemplifies the way that siblings mediate self-reflection, desire, and action. Without the presence of siblings, the characters threaten to dissolve or to become ciphers altogether. The sibling provides a scaffolding for interaction, emotion, narrative, and movement in film, while minimizing drama. Moreover, the sibling relationship accords with the sense of timing favored by Berlin School directors, and helps to instantiate it. Siblings connect the present to both the past and the future, thus taking over part of the function of plot. Unlike tales of progressive generations, however, which connect the past to the future through replacement, and gesture toward the existential moments of birth and death, siblings move together through time, leveling it.

To give a final example, a very different kind of long shot in *Geschwister—Kardeşler* also provides a visual representation of siblinghood as spatially horizontal and temporally aligned. Near the end of the film, the three siblings ride in the back of their father's cab as they deliver the oldest sibling to the airport because he has chosen to fulfill his military service in Turkey, the land of his citizenship. The three siblings sit silently; they neither look at each other nor do their gazes cross, but all three heads occupy the same horizontal plane as the car moves forward **[Fig. 106]**. The scene encapsulates the film's attitude toward the

FIG. 106: *Geschwister.*

siblings, the centrality of whose interactions could be overlooked if not for the title and this complex scene. A closer look at the film, however, reveals not only how the siblings process their somewhat minimal self-reflection through each other, but also how the film uses their interaction as a touchstone for an exploration of identity that proceeds less through self-analysis than through connections, collisions, and contrasts with peers. In the absence of plot, the sibling constellation carries the burden of cohesiveness.

The abundant presence of siblings in Berlin School films is still more notable given the current demographics. Fertility in Germany is the lowest in Europe, having fallen to an astounding 7.88 births per 1000 inhabitants, or 1.38 children per mother, in 2010.[1] Most of the siblings depicted in the films would have been born sometime between 1970 and 2000, so the focus on siblings may represent nostalgia for a moment when they were a relatively more likely phenomenon, although the average number of live births per woman has been under 2.0 across all of current Germany since 1970.[2] On the other hand, in a contemporary world whose self-definition depends on the experience of unprecedented and accelerating change, it might seem natural that siblings, however scarce in reality, would step in to provide a structural function that parents can no longer fulfill. Indeed, *Bungalow* seems to offer a complete Oedipal scenario displaced from the character Paul's absent parents onto his older brother and his girlfriend, with whom Paul eventually sleeps. In a Freudian vein, one could interpret Paul's observation of his brother and desire for his brother's girlfriend as a manifestation of a wish to become the more responsible member of society that his older brother, in lieu of a father figure, represents. And yet, the Freudian reading remains hollow. Paul's motives for deserting from the army, for selecting his parents' bungalow as a refuge, and for seducing his brother's girlfriend are all severely underdetermined. The ending of the film has Paul disappear from the audience's view in a scene that renders it impossible to establish whether he has returned to the army (that is, resumed the normal course of maturation toward responsible citizenship) or caught a ride down the highway from a stranger in an arbitrary direction **[see Fig. 91—LONG TAKES]**. This lack of closure nullifies rather than derailing or conforming to the educative teleology of a healthy Freudian resolution to the Oedipal complex.

See ENDINGS

Rather than replicate the parent–child relation on an accelerated timescale, siblings in Berlin School films create a distinct mode of inhabiting time and structuring interpersonal interaction. Against the teleological weight of expectations for the future that structure both parent–child and spousal or romantic relations, the sibling connection forms an elastic background fabric that exists in a permanent moment. The sibling relationship is thus allied with the reframing of narrative performed by the Berlin School in general. The nature of the siblings' connections to each other across so many of these films consists not in a shared perspective, but in a set of related experiences and shared moments, a sense of familiarity and attention without beginning or end. Recognizing the importance of the sibling to the Berlin School aesthetic allows us to readmit character and narrative to the realm of interpretation of Berlin School films, but also forces us to confront revised notions of both, and to redirect the interpretive imperative onto surface, detail, association, and the slow rhythm of time without goal.

SE

Notes

1 'European Birth Rates Data: What's Happening to Germany?' *Guardian datablog*, May 19, 2010, http://www.guardian.co.uk/news/datablog/2010/may/19/european-birth-rates-data-germany; 'Baby Gap: Germany's Birth Rate Hits Historic Low,' *Time*, May 23, 2010, http://www.time.com/time/world/article/0,8599,1991216,00.html.

2 Geburten in Deutschland; Statistisches Bundesamt, 2007; http://www.destatis.de/jetspeed/portal/cms/Sites/destatis/Internet/DE/Content/Publikationen/Fachveroeffentlichungen/Bevoelkerung/BroschuereGeburtenDeutschland,property=file.pdf.

Striesow, Devid

As a window salesman in Ulrich Köhler's *Windows on Monday*, Devid Striesow takes on, in some respects, the film's title role. Nina and Frieder, the couple at the center of the story, wait for their new windows to arrive. Nina has temporarily separated herself from Frieder, yet the unending project of house reconstruction marches onward, and the new windows appear at the appointed time. Frieder receives the windows about one hour into the film, and he is disheartened. Striesow, whose character has no name in the credits, apart from 'window builder' (*Fenstermacher*), is the consummate businessman. He is trying to hand over the wrong merchandise—the frames are constructed differently than was promised—yet he keeps focused on his customer and knows he has to make the sale. He is so single-minded that he neither turns nor flinches when a venetian blind in the background comes crashing down. Frieder exits the cinematic frame unsure and fatigued, but Köhler knows to let the camera linger on Striesow, who calmly calls out to his customer. His voice is simultaneously the sound of inevitable progress and the call of a dogged capitalist. Attempting to draw the deal to a close, Striesow's character asks an insistent question that could also be the epigraphic heart of the film: 'So, what do we do now?'

See RENOVATION

See AMBIENT SOUND

The son of an electrician and a nurse, Striesow grew up in the GDR city of Rostock. He moved to Berlin as an apprentice goldsmith, but, after the fall of the Berlin Wall, he started studying acting at the Ernst Busch Academy for Dramatic Arts and attended classes at the same time as Nina Hoss, with whom he stars in *Yella*. Striesow has accepted dozens of roles both major and minor, and he is now ubiquitous on German film and television screens. Many of his most notable and award-winning performances have been as Nazi functionaries. He played the craven SS officer Friedrich Herzog in *Die Fälscher/The Counterfeiters* (Stefan Ruzowitzky, 2007), a well-meaning nationalist boxing coach in *Napola—Elite für den Führer/Before the Fall* (Dennis Gansel, 2004) and Hitler's veterinarian, Fritz Tornow, in *Der Untergang/Downfall* (Oliver Hirschbiegel, 2004). The austere modernism and ostensibly extrahistorical milieu of the Berlin School possibly seemed to him like an opportunity to avoid, once again, having to wear the German uniform.

Functionality, however, is a term that bespeaks characteristics common to Striesow's performances. In Berlin School films, his particularly clear-cut style of elocution and his body language approximate clockwork. He is not machine-like, yet his characters are generally guided by their preference for order and rationality. The fact that he, in his small part in *Windows on Monday*, represents the inexorable forward movement of the couple's renovation project is expressed in his almost automatous comportment. In Angela Schanelec's *Passing Summer*, which centers on Valerie, a woman whiling away the summer in Berlin, Striesow plays the part of the protagonist's younger brother, Ben, who lives in southern Germany, near where they grew up. The film, which depicts a supposedly uneventful period in Valerie's life, takes a difficult turn when she receives a letter from Ben explaining that their father has had a stroke and is ailing. Striesow's role is once again peripheral but also central; he delivers to the film's main character bad news and brutal truths.

Following Valerie's visit with her father in the hospital, she meets her brother outside. With a sudden cut and no establishing shot, Schanelec See THE CUT depicts Striesow's lanky form moving headlong toward a tearful Valerie. His first words to her are unkind, but they fall perhaps within the purview See SIBLINGS of a petulant younger brother. He asks her, 'Did you cry in there too?' His subsequent observations are cruel in their matter-of-factness. Irrespective of her feelings, he is prepared to state realities such as 'He's an old man now' and 'He's doing badly.' The two face forward rather than toward one another, and the flies that have taken to buzzing around Valerie compound her unhappiness and frustration. They pay no attention to Ben, and it is as though he were, in contrast with his sister, composed of inorganic matter. She slaps at the air, batting the flies with broad swings, but as in *Windows on Monday*, when the venetian blinds clattered, Striesow scarcely reacts. Later, in the car, he continues to be unsympathetic to Valerie, agreeing that their father's condition is unlikely to change. If that is the case, he explains, then yes, he will die ('Dann wird er sterben'). The words are pronounced mechanistically, and it is the type of line that Striesow's Berlin School characters delight in delivering: harsh, clipped and clear.

The siblings later appear to understand one another better, and Ben's iciness briefly becomes affability as the two pass time in their small town See DORFDISKOS disco. He and his sister hit the dance floor and are wildly artificial in their movements **[see Fig. 37—DORFDISKOS]**. Akin to a puppet on strings,

FIG. 107: *Passing Summer.*

Striesow effectively disjoins his head and shoulders. His body language is simultaneously a reflection on the artificiality of disco dancing and on Ben's general inability to give himself completely over to the rhythm. The two dance distinctly, yet are in tandem with one another, perhaps because no cumbersome words need pass between them. When the night is over, however, Ben's cold clarity has returned. Working by daylight on one of the sails he builds and sells, he keeps his responses to Valerie terse **[Fig. 107]**. She talks about not wanting her father to live on in this way after the stroke, and without missing a beat in his work—hardly glancing up—Ben dutifully and hurtfully reports to her the sad truth: 'what you want makes no difference.' She asks him if he understands her feelings, and he responds, 'yes, I understand.' His every gesture, however, communicates that where Valerie's feelings are concerned—which are the subject of Schanelec's film insofar as it details the small dramas that take place during her seemingly ordinary summer—he remains indifferent.

Frequently playing the brother in these films, it is as though Striesow is the one against whom the protagonist is contrarily defined. In that he is a relentless and reliable foil, his performances are central to Berlin School films. He acts the part of Paul's brother, Max, in Ulrich Köhler's *Bungalow*, and initially the character seems quite ordinary, especially with respect to Paul, who is an unusually distanced protagonist. Max is affectionate with his girlfriend, Lene, and is also sympathetic to his absent parents, who have been concerned about their younger son. In his controlled normality, however, Max is his brother's obstacle; he is so comfortably adjusted that he becomes Paul's negative ego ideal. He represents not only the parents,

FIG. 108: *Bungalow*.

but also the law of the state insofar as he passes along messages between the Armed Forces and his AWOL brother, and later attempts to deliver Paul to the train station so that he can return to his post **[Fig. 108]**.

Striesow's Max is, for the most part, levelheaded, and his character's politics appear to follow suit. When it comes to an explosion that is widely perceived to have been the work of terrorists but later turns out to have been the consequence of a gas leak, Max calmly observes that capitalism has no more natural enemies and admits that he has no intention to think further about the incident **[see Fig. 117—VIOLENCE]**. Max comes across as irritating, especially insofar as, where the apparently accidental explosion is concerned, his bullish overconfidence may have proven correct. He also keeps cool when Paul deliberately fires a blowtorch at him, and even later, when Paul announces that he is in love with Lene. Max's response to his younger brother's declaration exhibits few indications of rage or jealously, and he instead offers the sensible-sounding observation, 'That's no reason to desert.' It is thus foreseeable that Paul would pursue Lene; he is privately and provocatively testing the limits of Max's control. Köhler offers little insight into Paul's emotions apart from making clear that he is bored, and falling for Lene reads more as a game-player's decision to antagonize his brother rather than as a response to a heartfelt imperative. In the absence of their apparently understanding parents, Max represents power to Paul, and from that perspective, Striesow, in a calm and collected performance, becomes the protagonist's principal rival.

See INTERIORITY

Although Max is casually dressed in *Bungalow*, his part could be linked to the industrious character he plays in Christoph Hochhäusler's

I Am Guilty. In that film Striesow repeats his role as the well-adjusted older brother of a diffident and inscrutable protagonist. Armin, akin to Paul in *Bungalow*, avoids assimilating and has to contend with Striesow's superior attitude. Armin agrees to a mock job interview with his successful brother, who here embodies the rationality of the job application process. Striesow is again the parents' deputy and here, as Martin Steeb Jr., he even bears his father's name. Martin coaches his brother on how to perform, pose and carry oneself at an interview. Weary of so much nonsense, Armin wryly accuses his brother: 'not everyone can be a stallion like you.' In Christian Petzold's *Yella*, however, Striesow is a sterling capitalist exemplar. As Philipp he represents the business world in the new post-Wall Germany, and his first words to Yella are not romantic, but are instead the sexist and sardonic rhetorical question, 'Are you interested in balance sheets?' Striesow's Philipp is mannered, and, in his measured way, he is the opposite of Ben, the emotional husband Yella left behind in Wittenberge. Ben is panicked; he has no hope of being an entrepreneur and is sure Yella will permanently abandon him. Conditions conspire to make Philipp look heroic. Yella is depressed and she imagines Philipp to have come along at exactly the right time. He is comfortable in the business world and has an arsenal of techniques for bluffing those with whom he negotiates. His 'broker posing' is a performance within a performance **[Fig. 109]**, but this masquerade only accentuates the degree to which he is, even in this world, a fraud. Striesow's Philipp likes playing games, is always negotiating, and he snickers precisely enough to convince us—and Yella—that he is no machine.

See INTERPELLATION

FIG. 109: *Yella*.

Perhaps the most central of Striesow's Berlin School roles, however, is that of Ivan in Angela Schanelec's *Marseille*. When we first see Striesow in that film he is loading camera equipment into a car preparing for his job as a photographer. He and Hanna, his wife, act as though the cleaning woman, who moves industriously around them, is not there. Ivan is mainly business minded, and the abrupt delivery of his lines as he responds to Hanna's statements about whether her mysterious physical pain can be treated—'I understand'—recalls the indifferent attitude Ben displayed toward his sister Valerie when she expressed grief about their father's suffering in *Passing Summer*. In both cases Striesow speaks the line similarly, professing to understand what he clearly does not. The two roles are similar; here too he is cool and reserved. Speaking about her pain, Hanna expresses nostalgia for the age of Chekhov, when families could rely on a country doctor who saw to the whole patient, not just to the symptoms. As she reflects on what has changed since the nineteenth century, Ivan makes an unrelated call on his cell phone. The two of them exit together and the camera lingers on the room where, in their absence, the maid's work continues.

In the subsequent sequence, Striesow's Ivan prepares for work on a factory floor where washing machines are being assembled. In the background of the wide and high angle shot, which makes clear that Ivan's activities are being absorbed into an industrial process, Striesow lowers the screen in front of which he will be photographing the company's employees **[Fig. 110]**. His photography is for corporate purposes and is thus juxtaposed to the type of photography practiced by the film's protagonist, Sophie. Once again Striesow

FIG. 110: *Marseille.*

is central: his work is the polar opposite of Sophie's self-conscious attempt to aesthetically enframe the world. For his Ivan, photography is only a job. He makes obliging yet minimal conversation with his subjects and the chitchat dissolves into the ambient noise that signals ongoing factory production. Beyond questions such as 'have you worked here long' Ivan's banter goes no farther. He seems to encourage discussion but then, in his distinctively clipped and clear style, willfully cuts it short. Schanelec's script evinces a sense of humor when, in this negligibly communicative scenario, one of the employees explains that they wear their nametags 'for purposes of communication.'

See AMBIENT SOUND

In a pivotal scene toward the end of the film, Sophie looks after Ivan and Anton. With an excited swing of his arm, Anton sends a drinking glass crashing to the floor, and Ivan goes directly into motion, mechanistically circumventing a stooped-over Sophie. When Anton exclaims to her, 'you're bleeding,' Striesow does not bat an eyelash. Again he is unflinching; this absence of physical reaction is his trademark. His response also foreshadows a coming conversation in which Sophie announces that she is returning to Marseille. Ivan asks whether she has informed Hanna, and Sophie's response is to ask him whether he loves Hanna. It cannot be concluded with certainty, but she may be asking because she wants their conversation to concern the two of them. She may have feelings for Ivan, yet it is essential for Schanelec's script that this remains unresolved. Striesow's face is inscrutable. Schanelec first films Ivan behind a large, frosted interior window, which may be meant to evoke his emotional opacity. She then cuts to a medium close-up in which he is decentered in the frame **[Fig. 111]**. His expression suggests calculation,

See ENDINGS

See FRAMINGS

FIG. 111: *Marseille.*

but it also intimates something more. His feelings may also not be known to him. This portrait parallels the medium close-up of Sophie that follows shortly thereafter in the French police station. Despite the incident in Marseille, Sophie is still in an inner conversation with Ivan. Even after she has left Berlin, his reaction to her is among the film's most significant unanswered questions.

At an intimate family gathering shortly before the end of *I Am Guilty*, Striesow's Martin listens to a guest explain about the paint store that has been caught paying kids to paint graffiti on walls so that they can then be given city contracts to repaint those same walls. The name of the paint store is 'Striesow.' Striesow's Martin of course, participates in the conversation without even the hint of a knowing wink. Composure is, after all, his stock-in-trade. Naming the duplicitous store after the actor could, however, constitute a knowing wink from Hochhäusler. It can be seen as an acknowledgment of the calculated role Striesow plays, and it is, of course, no coincidence that the story concerns a fraudulent capitalist. His characters are always well adjusted, and his performances express the opposite of the alienation that is taken for the source of most modern art. In this way, Striesow is always the fraud that the film exposes.

BP

Surveillance

Surveillance is a prominent theme, both literally and figuratively, in Berlin School cinema. The most obvious examples are in films by Christian Petzold, who frequently includes what appears to be actual surveillance footage in his movies. In *The State I Am In*, for example, we witness Jeanne's first visit to the bank and the fatal robbery through the eye of the bank's automatic security cameras. Similarly, *Ghosts* includes two brief video recordings of Nina stealing clothes and of the abduction of Françoise's daughter in front of the supermarket, while *Yella* features yet another security recording inside a bank, which shows Yella depositing the money in Philipp's name. Surveillance footage more or less bookends Petzold's *Beats Being Dead*, and it also makes a brief appearance in Benjamin Heisenberg's *The Robber*.

It is far from obvious how to assess the narrative function or aesthetic effect of these scenes. As far as the story is concerned, there is no apparent reason why Hans and Clara's bank robbery in *The State I Am In* or Nina's theft in *Ghosts* should *not* be shown in the same style as other scenes. In fact, Petzold's sudden cuts to surveillance footage usually serve little or no diegetic function. Although the surveillance footage introduces an ostensibly 'objective' dimension into the fictional narrative, it usually serves to authenticate either what we, the audience, already know or what we could have come to know just as well without the help of this footage. Michael Haneke's *Caché/Hidden* (2005) provides a counterexample that clarifies the point. *Caché* begins with what appears to be a traditional establishing shot: a static frame showing a city street and houses in the background, overlaid with the film's opening credits. Two minutes into the film, the image suddenly begins to blur, while two off-screen voices anxiously comment on what now appears as fast-forwarded footage rushing past our eyes. It takes a few moments to realize that the images screened thus far were not recorded by the extradiegetic film-camera—whose presence we, the viewers, necessarily take for granted and are supposed to forget—but are, instead, meant to be seen intradiegetically as part of the film's fictional narrative. What at first sight appeared to be a traditional (nondiegetic) establishing shot suddenly turns out to be—or rather, has been all along—a video recording taken by a hidden camera stationed in front of the protagonists' house. We, the viewers of Haneke's film, are watching this tape at precisely the same time as they do—a fact we do not realize until the couple fast-forwards the image on their home VCR. It is only when we see the protagonists in their living room watching the video that the audience's gaze is finally severed from theirs, at which moment the diegetic and nondiegetic worlds separate—and we, the viewers, are safely back in control of the cinematic gaze.

The contrast between this scene and Petzold's use of surveillance footage is striking. Haneke's film not only thematizes surveillance within the narrative, but literally uses it as a lens to observe and examine cinematic spectatorship in general. Unlike Petzold, Haneke deliberately plays with the verbal and the visual, the subjective and the objective dimensions of film in order to explore the constitutive tension between the different layers of signs and reality that sustain the art of cinema. This play leads to what might be called 'scopic paranoia'—not only for the protagonists in the film, but for the audience as well. Just as Georges and Anne, the protagonists of *Caché*, cannot exclude the possibility of being under constant surveillance, the audience cannot exclude the possibility that the images shown on screen are not what they seem. This scopic paranoia undermines the viewers' belief in the sovereignty of their cinematic gaze, which, at any moment, they might be forced to share with the fictional characters on the screen. In Christian Metz's terminology, Haneke undermines the spectators' primary cinematic identification with the camera: 'Who, besides me, is watching this, and why?'

By contrast, Petzold's sudden cuts from regular film stock to a grainy, black-and-white video-image yields the exact opposite effect: it accentuates—rather than dissimulates—the gap between the diegetic and the extradiegetic world. It seems reasonable to conclude that this aesthetics ultimately serves a political function—a visual reminder about the increasing omnipresence of state surveillance and automated control in daily life. It is well known that Petzold shares this critical perspective with his friend and collaborator Harun Farocki, with whom he coauthored *Ghosts*. Farocki's frequent use of surveillance footage in his films and installations likewise exposes the increasingly sophisticated control mechanisms of Western society.

This reading also makes sense in the context of Petzold's most overtly political film, *The State I Am In*, which depicts the German police and the state's entire security apparatus as some anonymous, yet well-informed force ready to strike, literally, out of the blue sky. At times, the mysterious borders the grotesque, for example, when Hans suddenly and inexplicably finds himself cornered by what appears to be a well-organized group of secret agents in black caravans—but who then, just as suddenly and inexplicably, drive off only seconds later. Reminiscent of a scene from the *X-Files*, this encounter remains as mysterious as the entire surveillance system that, presumably, was able to orchestrate it. Although the police are not omniscient and cannot prevent the bank robbery itself, the surveillance apparatus works well enough for the state's agents to pursue and detonate an explosion in the family's car at the film's end. Surveillance, this scene reminds us, is real, and the reason why security videos are ubiquitous in Petzold's films seems due to the simple fact that surveillance has become omnipresent in everyday life as well.

Yet this reading, valid as far as it goes, is too restrictive nonetheless. Nothing, in principle, prevents Petzold's audience from assigning diegetic meaning to the surveillance tapes it encounters in his films. For regardless of whatever intentions, if any, the director might or might not have had, we are free to interpret the surveillance footage as potentially meaningful within the narrative proper. The surveillance images of Yella making her bank deposit, for example, seem to 'represent' or 'symbolize' or 'signal' her feeling of being watched by Philipp **[Fig. 112]**—who has, in fact, been observing her all along (otherwise, the viewer would have to presume that Philipp just accidentally happened to arrive at precisely the right moment

FIG. 112: *Yella.*

to prevent Yella from depositing the 25,000 Euros into the mailbox). Another, more complex example is the footage of Nina stealing clothes in the department store, which might 'represent' both her guilty conscience and her worst fear at that very moment—'Somebody is watching!'

And, indeed, it does seem as though someone is watching Nina. At one point the automatic camera that surveys the floor suddenly readjusts its focus and begins tracking her on her way to the escalator. Yet with the stolen merchandize desensitized and tucked away under her clothes, there is nothing that could have possibly triggered a fully automated response of the surveillance camera. Instead, its sudden movement stipulates some kind of intentionality; it signals the presence of a conscious observer able to manipulate the camera. But who is watching this scene—besides us, the audience? For if Nina were indeed being observed by suspicious security guards, they would most likely have tried to apprehend her—but nobody does. At the same time, we should note that Petzold deliberately plays with the audience's expectation of this happening. Like Nina, we initially suspect that the anonymous hand reaching out and touching her shoulder outside the store belongs to a guard, when, in fact, it belongs to Françoise who has been waiting there for Nina to appear **[Fig. 113]**. This brings up an intriguing idea, namely that the secret observer is none other than her, Françoise, and that the camera's tracking of Nina inside the store figuratively represents Françoise's sudden hope that she has found her missing daughter. The store's surveillance apparatus, in other words, not only mimics, but mysteriously operates in lieu of Françoise's psychic apparatus, sharing her obsessive focus on Nina.

This reading receives additional support in a later scene showing a close-up of Françoise driving through Berlin and looking for Nina. After about a minute, the film suddenly cuts to the surveillance

FIG. 113: *Ghosts.*

footage of a toddler being abducted in front of a supermarket **[see Fig. 96—PREDECESSORS]**—a traumatic memory, we presume, literally burned into Françoise's mind from having studied the videotape again and again for clues that might help locate her daughter (Françoise, in fact, explicitly refers to the footage early on during her first conversation with Nina). This scene, too, correlates video images and mental images, which provides further evidence for the intimate connection between (automated) camera and (human) consciousness in Petzold's film.

But this is about as far as this reading will take us before it encounters insurmountable obstacles. The abduction video, much like the surveillance footage of Nina, implies intentionality; the automated camera clearly moves left in an effort to track the stolen cart until it eventually crosses the security system's spatial parameters and moves out of sight. As before, it is crucial to realize that there simply is no technological device, no matter how sophisticated, that could possibly recognize the significance of this action and 'choose' to follow the cart without being told to do so by a human observer. As in the previous surveillance scene, it remains unclear who actually manipulated the camera. Yet there is also an important difference between these two scenes regarding the potential meaning of the footage. The previous scene insinuates a close relation between the automated camera and Françoise's gaze, which allows us to interpret the footage 'symbolically' with reference to her obsessive state of mind 'zooming' in on Nina. The current scene, by contrast, forecloses this possibility, because we cannot interpret the camera's deliberate movements as a figurative representation of Françoise's (or anybody else's) mental processes. It is clear that Françoise keeps milling over this footage in her mind, but there is no indication in the film to suggest that she was involved in its original recording years ago. Both literally and figuratively, the very existence of this video thus remains inexplicable in narrative terms.

This deliberate inexplicability raises a host of other questions about Petzold's use of surveillance footage, particularly when it shows no criminal activity or when such activity could not possibly have been detected by any of the fictional characters. Since the footage of Nina stealing clothes literally goes unnoticed, it will likely be taped over and thus cease to exist a mere 24 or 72 hours after it had originally been recorded. Its diegetic (non)existence and its probable erasure, however, have no consequence in narrative terms, because it literally does not matter whether or not this scene was ever recorded to begin with. The same is true of the aforementioned sequences in *Yella*. Who, besides the audience, is actually watching Yella depositing the money? And in *The State I Am In*, who observes Jeanne exit the bank through the back door?

If anything, the provocations produced by these questions seem to underscore what we already know: any method based on psychologizing fictional characters ('do they feel as though they are being watched?') quickly reaches a dead end, finding itself entangled in a hermeneutic web of speculative answers to unanswerable questions. In many Berlin School films the protagonists remain opaque and do not easily lend themselves to psychological analyses. Instead, the viewer remains merely a distant observer as the camera follows the protagonists' physical movement through space, which corresponds to the figurative use of surveillance in Berlin School cinema. Heisenberg's *Sleeper*, to take one example, begins with an open, deep-focus shot of people leisurely spending a nice summer day in the park. Taken from behind a row of trees, this static view gets periodically interrupted by a series of stark, black-and-white intertitles announcing the film's credits. After the third interruption, the frame moves slightly to the right, but due to the visual density of the scene and the many objects moving in and out of the frame, it remains unclear which of them, if any, the camera is tracking **[Fig. 114]**: is it the child playing ball in the foreground, or the woman in the far background walking leftward? Or is it the couple in the right background slowing moving toward the camera? Although it clearly looks like somebody is watching, we, the audience, are given no clue as to who that might be, nor do we know what exactly we are supposed to look at. Although we hear bits and pieces of conversation, the scene's muffled sound and ambient noise likewise disables a positive identification of the speakers.

See PREDECESSORS

See LANGUAGE

See AMBIENT SOUND

FIG. 114: *Sleeper.*

It is not until the final credit has passed and the couple comes to a halt in the center of the shot, framed by a pole on the left and a tree on the right, that we can finally be sure about the camera's target—and, at this moment, we also overhear the object of the couple's conversation: surveillance. 'Why are you watching him?' (*Warum beobachten Sie ihn*?) the man asks—a diegetic question that clearly resonates on the extradiegetic level as well: whom, indeed, are we watching, and why? Heisenberg's opening shot, in other words, appropriates the aesthetics of surveillance not only to introduce the film's central topic, but also to expose film viewing as little more than the dubious act of spying on others. Overall, the scene functions much like the establishing shot in *Caché*: both films explicitly thematize surveillance on the level of the plot, except that Haneke, like Petzold, incorporates 'real' surveillance footage into the narrative, which implies that a diegetic observer is (or might be) watching. Heisenberg, foregoing this option, entices the audience to play its part and fill the void. Thus, we become the spy that Johannes, Heisenberg's protagonist, refuses to be.

See FRAMINGS

Numerous other Berlin School features deliberately cast the audience in this role of secret observer. Yet unlike the previous examples, most of them do not reflect or comment upon surveillance on the plot level, meaning that we, the audience, have no reason to assume that anybody else besides us is watching these images. And yet, remarkably, the aesthetic of surveillance nonetheless characterizes these films as well. Schanelec's *Passing Summer* features a scene in the park whose cinematic aesthetics, similar to Heisenberg's opening shot, mimics the act of spying by showing the protagonists only from afar—as if the person holding the camera dared not come any closer for fear of being discovered **[see Fig. 84 –LANDSCAPE]**. At the same time, however, there is no reason to assume that anybody else is watching this scene. So why does the camera remain so distant and allow the characters to walk in and out of the frame? And why is our view constantly blocked by the row of trees standing between us and them? If the main purpose of the scene is to make the audience aware of its voyeurism by frustrating our desire to get closer, then what, if anything, distinguishes this aesthetics of surveillance from the generic postmodern obsession with irony and medial self-reflexivity?

More is at stake here. Although, at times, the aesthetics of surveillance serves to expose the 'suspension of disbelief' that characterizes cinematic spectatorship, its overall purpose seems less 'critical' and more 'constructive' in nature. The goal is not just to make the viewers aware of their complicity with the camera, but instead to presuppose this complicity in order to mobilize its productive potential as it entices the audience to look for something that remains to be seen. In most cases, the figurative use of surveillance remains decisively nonvoyeuristic: neither the protagonist's nor the filmmaker's gaze seems primarily driven by the forbidden desire and perverse pleasure of looking behind the scenes—a desire explored in classical cinema and exemplified in Hitchcock's *Rear Window* (1954) or the famous opening shot of his *Psycho* (1960). On the contrary, the cinematic realism—in fact, the aesthetics of surveillance—in these films usually helps to ensure that See LONG TAKES everything remains in plain sight, out in the open, and there for us to see. Yet it is precisely this openness that causes bewilderment, because, all too often, there is nothing particular to see, no secret to expose, no meaning to reveal. Like the couple in *Caché*, whose anxious frustration about the anonymous tape is largely due to their complete lack of understanding of its meaning, we keep looking for something significant as we follow Sophie's meandering walk through the city of Marseille in Schanelec's *Marseille* or Nina's illicit See HOTELS exploration of the hotel in Köhler's *Windows on Monday*.

Thus, a different set of questions emerges as our analytic focus shifts from the literal to the figurative use of surveillance in Berlin School cinema. '*Who* is watching?' seems less crucial a question in this context than 'Why am *I* watching this?' or 'What do I see *now*?' A critical look at these films yields more than just the usual pleasure of exposing (once again) the ideological apparatus of cinematic spectatorship. Important as it is, this critique has little to say about the potential reconstruction of the art of cinema that might entice us to see things differently—whatever this reconstruction might entail (including inventing new venues for individual and communal film viewing, improving existing technologies of film production such as 3D, or developing bio-engineered devices to enhance human perception). The Berlin School's aesthetics of surveillance, for its part, actively invites—or better: gently coerces—the viewers to shoulder the burden of looking. The viewers' task, in other words, is to make sense of what they see, and the overall goal of these films remains, quite simply, what Christoph Hochhäusler would call 'attentiveness.' Although this might not be enough to change the nature of cinematic spectatorship, it does, at least, give the viewers both something new to *look at* as well as something to *look forward to*. If today's world is controlled by the automatized and impersonal gaze of the surveillance camera, as Petzold suggests, the Berlin School challenges its audience to live up to what Walter Benjamin claimed it already was some 80 years ago: a critical examiner and active interpreter of the world around us.

CS

Urban Miniatures: New Berlin Films of the 1980s

Out of a past in which nearly everyone, from serious cineastes to conservative politicians, considered New German Cinema to be dead and buried, productions from West Berlin from the mid-1980s provide a number of surprises for us today. Although the national cinema seemed back then in most people's minds to be moribund and unexciting, annual visits to the city's film festival still made the visitor aware of a thriving film community, a vast network of video and documentary collectives, low-budget endeavors, alternative activists, high-profile feature-filmmakers, as well as a host of distributors and archives, a distinguished film academy (the dffb celebrated its twentieth anniversary in 1985), a planned *Filmhaus*, more than 40 repertory cinemas (so-called *Programmkinos*), and continuing public forums on film in places like the *Akademie der Künste* or the *Filmbühne am Steinplatz*. A remarkable municipal film subsidy (hailed as the *Berlin-Effekt*), a public television station (*Sender Freies Berlin*), and a growing cable network; the city was a crucial site of production, an impressive image factory with a wide range of modalities and voices, both official and subversive, of films for the mainstream as well as ones off the beaten track.

The New Berlin Film arose out of the 1980s and, looked at retrospectively, confirms that the state of things in West German cinema was neither as dire nor as depleted as many critics claimed at the time. Journalistic coroners, assessing an ostensibly expired New German Film, spoke of a national cinema that had, following a shift of leadership as the new CDU/CSU government introduced dramatic changes in the arrangements that governed film subsidy and television support, lost its stylistic élan and formal flair. And this, to a great extent, was the case. The most visible and highly touted films like Doris Dörrie's *Männer/Men* (1985) and a profusion of new German comedies eschewed the authorial willfulness of the New German Cinema and privileged more generic approaches. New Berlin films, made for the most part by independent artists on very limited budgets, had no interest in mass audiences or accepted

See PREDECESSORS

patterns of recognition. Looking back, we find in fact a veritable profusion of films produced in West Berlin marked by a similar impetus and a consonant *Zeitgeist*, emanations ranging from the austere and subdued to the brash and outré, films by Peter Fratzscher (*Asphaltnacht/Asphalt Night* [1980]), Clemens Klopfenstein (*Das Schlesische Tor* [1982]), Cynthia Beatt (*Böse zu sein ist auch ein Beweis von Gefühl/Being Mean is Also a Sign of Emotion* [1983]), Dieter Köster and Hannelore Conradsen (*Berliner am Sonntag/Berliners on Sunday* [1983]), Uwe Schrader (*Kanakerbraut* [1983]), Klaus Tuschen (*Frontstadt/Front City* [1983]), Uwe Friessner (*Baby* [1984]), Knut Hoffmeister (*Der Goldene Oktober/Golden October* [1984]), Verena Rudolph (*Lucy* [1984]), Marcel Gisler (*Tagediebe/Hangin' Around,* [1985]), Wieland Speck (*Westler,* [1985]), Lienhard Wawrzyn (*German Dreams* [1985]), Michael Bartlett (*Konzert für die rechte Hand/Concert for the Right Hand* [1986]), Lilly Grote (*Oranisches Tor* [1986]), Dani Levi and Helmut Berger (*Du mich auch/You Can Kiss Mine Too* [1986]), Martin Theo Krieger (*Zischke* [1986]), and Thorsten Näter (*Zeit der Stille/Time of Stillness* [1986]), among many others. These works, virtually lost in time and next to never mentioned by film historians, coexisted next to endeavors by more recognized artists, New German filmmakers like Rudolf Thome, Helma Sanders-Brahms, Helke Sander, Ulrike Ottinger, Lothar Lambert, Rosa von Praunheim, Dagmar Beiersdorf, Christian Ziewer, Jutta Brückner, Ula Stöckl, Jeanine Meerapfel, Harun Farocki, Frank Ripploh, to list just a few of the established directors who lived and worked in West Berlin during the epoch.

See FAMILIAR PLACES, LONG TAKES

As we consider the contemporary Berlin School with its different regard for temporality, its preference for observation over narration, and its more patient negotiation of spaces and places, we can in fact return to these all but forgotten West German films of the 1980s with a fresh regard and make some intriguing discoveries. Indeed, these films offer a prehistory for the Berlin School; as lost bodies, they surely come to life and resonate more strongly when we bear the Berlin School in mind; as orphan films, their striking anticipations of Berlin School endeavors suggest a sense of kinship and belonging that they might not otherwise possess. Made after the death of New German Cinema and at a time when the Federal Republic's once highly visible national film culture had lost its international presence, these subterranean productions address themselves to a place and a time, Berlin in the 1980s, fully mindful of previous efforts to survey this space, equally aware of how overdetermined any utterance about the city is. How to circumvent official rhetoric, to avoid leftist clichés, to go past a long line of images and words about Berlin, to do more than simply recycle or quote after all the representations and accounts devoted to this space over the years? How to make room for imagination, freshness, and novelty in a place so cognizant of its significance and special status, in a setting where literally thousands of people on an ongoing basis transmitted images of the city, be they cultural bureaucrats, mainstream intellectuals, media employees, or alternative artists? The writer Bodo Morshäuser outlined the predicament in his book, *Die Berliner Simulation* (1983): 'Someone says, all we have now are quotations and then starts reciting several quotations himself. "Repressed imaginations remain limited to their own experience" (Nicolas Born).' The writer makes his point about borrowed experience using a further quotation, replicating and at the same time commenting on the dilemma. Repeatedly in the New Berlin films of the mid-1980s, we will confront a quest for immediacy, an unmediated authenticity, and a less encumbered way of seeing in the streets and structures of present-day Berlin.

See ANTI-HAUPTSTADT

What is initially striking about the New Berlin Film is its decidedly understated tone and its undramatic disposition. A blend of reserve and patience operates here, a will to explore, discover, and collect. The Berlin we enter in Alfred Behrens's *Walkman Blues* (1985) and Thomas Brasch's *Domino* (1982) is an iced over expanse, cold and uninviting at first glance, but a place that, upon closer observation, transfixes and transports the onlooker. Behrens's and Brasch's approaches to the metropolis have a surface similarity: in minimal narratives that only suggest the contours of a story, we follow a solitary individual through a number of days in the winter. The films organize themselves as dated chronicles with random starts and sudden stops. Both *Walkman Blues* and *Domino* feature protagonists dwelling in austere and hermetic digs, cubbyholes from which they constantly flee onto the street. If any sensibility prevails here, it is a radical exteriority merging anticipation, curiosity, and appetite, a yearning for an undefined something else. The governing mood is what Michael Rutschky (drawing on an early essay by Siegfried Kracauer) terms 'Wartezeit' ('time spent waiting'), the feeling of the traveler sitting in a station prior to departure. The New Berlin Film is, above all, about watching and waiting.

Walkman Blues is Alfred Behrens's first feature film; its original title was 'The Deserter.' In an early scenario, the director imagined a work governed by spaces and colors set in a Berlin that would serve as a 'filmic site.' Behrens wanted 'to make a feature film in which the real world where it takes place—houses, streets, buses and subways, factories, cinemas, rehearsal rooms where music is being produced—is every bit as important as the plot itself.' For some people, the 90-minute film will seem slow-paced, monochromatic, and monotonous, short on action and story. Behrens firmly believes that narratives, for all the fascination gripping tales can offer, tend to divest individual images of their potential richness. A story imposes a hierarchy of value upon frames, rendering certain sectors of the image as more meaningful, prompting the spectator to privilege the signs containing story information and to overlook everything else. Like Wim Wenders, Behrens is fond of quoting Siegfried Kracauer's *Theory of Film* (1960) and the writings of Béla Balázs. His film work aims to capture 'things in their concreteness,' to expose the everyday world which our deadened senses, pressured by the pragmatics and priorities of daily routines, tend to obscure and ignore. The interest of his camera is phenomenological rather than psychological.

A young musician, a recent arrival from Hamburg, lives in a West Berlin attic, works in a slaughterhouse, and spends his time wandering through the streets and expanses of the new city, taping sounds and collecting impressions. One night he listens to the British group, the Blurt, at the Loft on Nollendorfplatz and meets a photographer from London with whom he spends some time before she returns to England. As with other New Berlin films, the attempt to summarize events at best touches the surface of things and in no way accords to the actual richness and texture of the viewing experience. The opening sequence, prior to the credits, uncompromisingly intimates the film's project: we are in a train yard, the camera tracks left across boxcars to a figure whose back is turned to us. The musician (played with a sympathetic directness by Heikko Deutschmann) gathers industrial sounds, noises of rocks being processed by a mighty machine, of braking trains and roaring tractors. The excursion does not mean anything more than what we see and hear. It is an act of discovering and retrieval, soundseeing in a location deserted and forlorn, a foray into the remnants of a city's industrial past, a recycling of fragments one might otherwise pass off as acoustic terror. As it surveys a no-man's-land and a frozen terrain, Claus Deubel's camera finds poetry in the seemingly unextraordinary, solemn beauty in the abandoned buildings and forsaken stretches of Wedding and Moabit.

See AMBIENT SOUND

The city, its objects and locales, never become symbols for something else. At night we see the youth and his friends break into a yard. Someone mutters something about getting the 'Kohle' (which in German can mean either coal, or figuratively, money) so that we might assume a robbery is in progress. The impression is confirmed by subsequent shots of the boy dragging the plunder into his garret. But this booty is no more than what the word promised: coal. (Who needs metaphors when it's so cold?) Extended takes detailing his labors in the slaughterhouse, shots stressing repetition and tedium, counter any temptation to impose metaphorical significance of the kind we might see in similar settings from Döblin's *Berlin Alexanderplatz*. What we are witnessing is, plain and simple, *temps morts*, wasted portions of a life spent making the money one needs to do the things that are really important to one's well-being.

The camera attends to the youth's search for wonder. A visit to a cinema to watch Chris Petit's *Radio On* receives the same undramatic treatment as a bus ride down the street: unbroken shots focus on people in transit, looking out of windows. The female interlocutor (one could hardly call her a romantic interest) is likewise a foreigner possessed by a desire for the undefined, a photographer and sightseer, but definitely not a tourist. Changing back and forth between English and German, as if the boundaries of different languages did not obtain here, she talks of a hunger for appetite: 'I didn't find the Berlin I was looking for. But looking for it I found something stronger. Something closer to me . . . I just walked in the streets with no definite direction, for hours and hours on end. I walked through the streets and took pictures . . . taking in everything you can see. Berlin's a winter town, I think. *Ein* [*sic*] *Winterstadt*. I can't imagine what it's like in the summer.' In Behrens's film Berlin is indeed a winter city (*Winterstadt*), but this is no metaphorical contrivance. It is rather a seasonal backdrop allowing us pristine perspectives onto otherwise ignored sectors of reality, stark and frozen images that refuse to congeal into a narrative flow.

See SEEING AND SAYING

Thomas Brasch's *Domino* opens with scenes of Christmas bustle and glimpses of the Kurfürstendamm shrouded in snow. Lisa, a successful actress at the Schiller Theatre, drops off her daughter at the Bahnhof Zoo and faces the presentiment of spending the holidays alone. In the week to come, her life will come unraveled and her taken-for-granted security called into question. An undercurrent of the inexplicable and the unexpected will grip the *artiste* and ultimately sweep her into oblivion. *Domino* focuses on a woman living in abeyance, who sits in her apartment feeling a vague discontent, finding herself literally locked into the confines of this space at one point and forced to exit through a window. Repeatedly she stares out into the wintry void with an empty gaze. Everywhere she turns, the past seems to be on her trail: she confronts visions of her deceased mother (also an actress) while thinking of her own daughter. She learns that the director Lehrter, who wants her to star in his comeback production of Goethe's *Stella*, may very well be her father. Lehrter (played by Bernhard Wicki with a mixture of churlishness and melancholy) is a walking memory bank. In his office he screens footage from the summer of 1941, shots of German tanks on the Russian front. From a fledgling dramatist, Lisa learns of Lehrter's wartime internment in a concentration camp. Encounters on the street irritate and befuddle her. Passersby speak of mass unemployment, worry about the prospect of war, and wander about sobbing, disoriented and confused. Flights away from responsibility (she walks out during a performance of *Macbeth*) and into the night bring no cathartic release. In a surrealistic conclusion, we watch Lisa disappear in the snow and witness a final hallucination in which she joins the masses of the unemployed who are being shipped off to work camps in the South Seas.

Possessed by a present that has not yet arrived, occupied by a past that intervenes at unexpected moments, *Domino*'s protagonist tumbles into a historical vortex. Brasch, in contrast to Behrens, allows sites and spaces to become ciphers, symbolic representations of a lurking disquiet and an inexorable paralysis. Berlin appears as a collective storehouse of memories and traumas, a city whose past has been put on ice, a place where the black hole of history engulfs the unwary. Time stands still and, once again, we have *temps morts*, the feeling of sitting in a waiting room, anticipating relief and succor. Brasch uses a quotation from Robert Musil (whose *Die Verwirrungen des Zöglings Törleß/The Confusions of Young Törless* [1906] was the object of an extended study by the East German emigrant writer/director) as a motto for the script: 'There are moments in life where things slow down noticeably, as if life were hesitating to go on or was wanting to change its direction. It may well be that at such times one is more susceptible to mishaps.' To slow things down, to find a way of intensifying the immediate, to gain access to the mystery and magic in everyday objects and occurrences: Brasch's film in the snow alternates between impasse and epiphany. Like other New Berlin films, it involves people with time on their hands who search for an authentic, different existence.

In Behrens's feature, different voices chant the phrase, 'Going for a ride, going for a ride' on the young musician's walkman. The variations bring strange nuances, rhythms, and inflections to the words, and they assume a hallucinatory strangeness. In the director's nonfiction film, *Berliner Stadtbahnbilder* (*Images from the Berlin S-Bahn*, 1982), we go for a ride in time and space, an outing in a phantom vehicle through forsaken train stations haunted by the past. Long traveling shots out of train windows allow the spectator views of passing places, some of which are idyllic and others ravaged. Behrens has called the pictures of stations, tracks, and landscapes, shot over the course of three seasons, 'an extreme film, a pure film, a film of images, a film of noises. A film for the eye of the explorer.' An amalgam of trance and transit, *Images from the*

Berlin S-Bahn conveys a tactile and concrete feeling for the history of a city and the senses of a place. It might be described as an eccentric detective film, an investigation into the secrets and mysteries tucked away in abandoned train platforms, ticket halls, and underground corridors. The film alternates between short takes of details (billboards, window latches, doorways, parts of machines) and protracted scenes of movement. There is not a single image or sound in the film which intervenes in Behrens's presentation of 'a self-evident-everyday understanding of history.'

The specular resolve behind this film is unrelenting. Behrens had to be convinced to add the short voice-over passages in which he talks of the history of the *S-Bahn*, its planning and development, its controversial status after World War II, its implications for East–West confrontations, the manner in which one all but did without this important means of transportation in West Berlin due to disagreements with East German transit officials. The *Stadtbahn* was built in an undivided Berlin; operating it in a city with a wall between sectors has posed extreme problems. Behrens's film seeks to rescue its object and to restore it. He sees in the *Stadtbahn* a remarkable historical museum, a space where time has stood still in a city often so eager to tear down or bury over its past. These train stations and tracks bring us back to the rise of an industrial age. Riding on the *S-Bahn* is an archaeological excursion, a peregrination through spaces whose surfaces bear the inscriptions and traces of long past epochs.

A single shot essentializes the film's formal will: we partake of worn billboards from various stations and then cut to a blank white surface on a platform, a *tabula rasa* that piques our curiosity and fills us with expectation. A woman whose face we cannot see dashes across the platform, from left to right, into and out of the frame, her shoes clacking all the while in the station hum. A train pulls in, moving from left to right, the interiors illuminated, the rims of the windows sharply outlined. We hear the screeching of brakes and linger for many seconds as the car waits. A voice issues from a loudspeaker. No one enters the compartments. The train starts up and pulls out. Then, running this time from right to left, the same woman scrambles across the frame, leaving in her wake the empty screen with which the long take commenced. Once asked whether, contrary to his radical phenomenology, Behrens had, just this once, let a formative urge get the better of him, he insisted: no. The waiting camera simply happened to be there at a serendipitous moment. What it captured was an eloquent ballet of motion, a scene whose choreographer was reality itself, a dancing flux more sensual than significant. Behrens believes in the integrity of locations (what he calls 'die Moral der Motive'). His definition of space is an architectural one rather than a psychological one, a further instance of agreement with Kracauer. We could not be further from the permeation of mind into physical objects characteristic of German Expressionism. If anything, *Berliner Stadtbahnbilder* is a minimalistic urban *Heimatfilm*, an exploration of modernity and its roots in the former capital of an empire.

Short on drama and spectacle, New Berlin films of the mid-1980s like those of Behrens and Brasch skirt generic fixities and discursive boundaries in an attempt to apprehend the surfaces and substances of a city and a situation. Commingling narrative wisps and imagistic fragments, New Berlin films gravitate around objects, places, and sounds rather than interpersonal contacts. The denizens of these features are neither hip nor chic. They are solitary spirits, subdued and uncertain, but remarkably curious. Inveterate flaneurs, these modern incarnations of Walter Benjamin's botanizer on the blacktop and Franz Hessel's city stroller want to see and worry little about being seen; in their lives, input takes precedence over output. Dialogues are See LANGUAGE clipped, gestures spare, looks lingering. These specular figures stand at the threshold between past and present, seeking to fathom the signs of time which abide in 'the estranging distance between that which no longer is and that which does not yet exist.'[1] This cinema has a unique and unmistakable repertoire: makeshift and ascetic living spaces, fascinating albeit ugly streets, a multicultural and heteroglossic community, a remarkably nuanced sense of sound and music, an alertness to the rhythms and resonances of buildings and landscapes, an obsessive concern with *objèts trouvés*, frequent shots of elevated railways and speeding *S-Bahns*, scenes of departure in train stations. Anything but grandiose big city symphonies, these films are urban miniatures, both improvisational and spontaneous. In *Walkman Blues* we see rock musicians rehearsing in an abandoned warehouse; we will never see them perform publicly. The New Berlin Film comes to us today as a provisory entity as well as a rehearsal for the Berlin School, a cinema in transit and in the state See BORDERS of becoming, the work of fugitives and outsiders living in a borderline city.

ER

Note

1 Inka Mülder-Bach, *Siegfried Kracauer—Grenzgänger zwischen Theorie und Literatur: Seine frühen Schriften, 1913–1933* (Stuttgart: J.B. Metzler, 1985), 78.

Violence

Contrary to what the name of the group's representative journal *Revolver* might imply, the films of the Berlin School present an aesthetic of violence that rejects the images and narrational strategies of Hollywood film violence, including the latter's emphasis on guns, guts, and fast-paced sequences. Unlike these more conventional forms of cinematic representation, violence in films by Petzold, Schanelec, and others is not contained within any coherent sequence but rather marked by gaps, delays, and detours. It is unmotivated, undramatic, and coincidental, and, once it appears to emerge, it frequently fizzles out as it is absorbed into the banal events of everyday life. Essentially, the violence in these films is anticinematic: not only does it abandon its traditional role of titillating viewers in energetic, kinetically charged sequences, but it also typically fails to match up to any particular cause or fit neatly within the logic of the films' narratives. In this way the films deny viewers the pleasure of knowing exactly how, why, or when an act of violence occurs, something audiences of more generically conservative crime films and other thrillers take for granted. Though varied in their representations of violence, all of the films tend to dedramatize and displace violence, shifting it to places where it is less visible and neatly packaged. This aesthetic of violence upsets viewers' conventional viewing practices, consistently frustrating expectations and thereby bringing these very conditioned expectations and desires into relief. To this extent, the Berlin School, very much in the same vein as the New German Cinema, is a cinema about cinema, pointing to the limits of Hollywood mainstream strategies and to lesser-explored potentials of the medium in ways that speak to a global film audience.

See BOREDOM

The Berlin School films conspicuously leave out scenes of violence, denying viewers the sensory gratification that such scenes typically bring. Given that today's audiences are accustomed to and now expect violence in the cinema, its obvious absence when the narrative implies its occurrence is provocative. Moreover this absence does not serve to build suspense as in many contemporary thrillers and horror films. Instead, films such as *This Very*

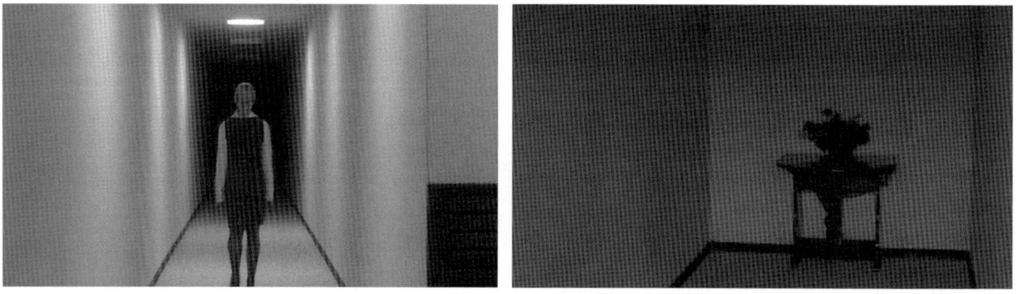

FIG. 115: *Hotel.*

Moment, *Hotel*, *The State I Am In*, and *Marseille* withhold violence when it is most anticipated and replace it with scenes that are languid and undramatic, through which they teasingly direct attention to our desire to experience film violence. Both *This Very Moment* and *Hotel*, for example, employ cinematic strategies that traditionally accompany or announce upcoming scenes of violence, particularly in horror films, only to disappoint their viewers. These strategies include the crescendo of violins that recalls Alfred Hitchcock's *Psycho* (1960) as well as handheld camera footage, settings in dark hallways, gloomy woods and hotel pools at night, young women who bathe or shower alone, and unsettling, eerie music. None of these traditional cues for violence fulfills its standard function, as the anticipated acts of bloodshed rarely happen. In fact, instead of leading to violence, many of these cues are followed by images that self-reflexively foreground the triviality and mundaneness of everyday life. In *Hotel*, when Irene finally musters up enough courage to walk into the pitch-dark hallway, the camera lingers on the hallway's entrance before jumping to its opposite end, revealing a dainty little table with a vase of flowers on top **[Fig. 115]**. While evoking the ominous neon-lit hallways of the hotel in Stanley Kubrick's *The Shining* (1980), the image here seems to play a joke on us as it starkly contradicts our expectations: violence is replaced by domestic kitsch, the shocking and spectacular by the banal.

In Christian Petzold's *The State I Am In*, we are led away from the scene of violence just as it threatens to erupt and instead redirected into Jeanne's normal everyday experiences. The film thus almost appears to be a response to Christopher Roth's violent and action-packed *Baader* (2002), another German film dealing with terrorism that was released around the same time. In one instance in Petzold's film, the camera follows Jeanne as she leaves the room where the tension between her parents and Achim, an old friend, quickly escalates after he refuses to give them money. The camera then meets Jeanne upstairs where she joins Paulina, another teenage girl, to listen to music, smoke cigarettes, and chat about the song. When her mother calls her back downstairs, she sees that Achim has a bloody nose and her father a bloody knuckle, presented in a close-up shot with his hand on the steering wheel as he drives off. One can therefore assume that the two men were involved in a fight, but instead of portraying it, the film offers Jeanne's perspective in the room upstairs. In stark contrast to the typical fight sequence of a Hollywood action film, the scene with Jeanne and Paulina is undramatic, smooth, and, like the electronic song that is playing, subdued and relaxed. The viewer is exposed only to the before-and-after of the scene of violence, its sensational dramatization omitted and replaced by quotidian, normal events in the life of a teenage girl. Contrary to what one might expect from a film on terrorism, this film focuses on the subjective perspectives and desires of Jeanne rather than on the more titillating and suspenseful acts of violence.

Only at the end of the slow-paced and apparently uneventful *Marseille* do we discover that Schanelec's protagonist Sophie had experienced a dramatically violent attack within the duration of the film's narrative, one that had been concealed from us. The film consists primarily of long takes and long shots of the city of Marseille, and here, little that is remarkable seems to 'happen.' The final moments thus come as a surprise: Sophie sits in a police interrogation room in Marseille, explaining how a man forced her to swap clothes with him while holding her at gunpoint **[see Fig. 22—BORDERS]**. She mentions in particular that she had tried to hide in a building as the man chased her but that the glass entrance-door was locked. Although the viewer does not see Sophie's attack, he or she might recall images in which Sophie unsuccessfully tries to open a glass door and then goes home to change her clothes before going out to a bar. The viewer attempts to piece together Sophie's narrative by recalling earlier images that might point to signs or traces of the violent act. In a sense, then, the images become significant and engaging for the viewer only once he or she realizes that they might reveal some remarkable event or traces thereof. It is at this point that the viewer actively reads, registers, and organizes the previous images that he or she had let pass by, images whose purpose had seemed, above all, to evoke the atmosphere of the French coastal city rather than narrate an event See BORDERS. Prevented from participating in the excitement that the act of violence could have offered in an otherwise undramatic film, we are tempted to ask ourselves the following questions: Was I not looking closely enough? Had I simply stopped paying attention at that point? Or was I not reading these images properly? *Marseille* critically illustrates how film violence, or more generally drama, renders images visible to the action-craving viewer in the first place. At the same time, it demonstrates that film violence need not be restricted to corporeally stimulating, immediately visible representations. Indeed, it is precisely such fascinating images that distract us from other aspects of violence, including the pain experienced by the victim. Despite the fact that the long-term experience of pain is often more debilitating for the victim than the act of violence itself, it is underrepresented in mainstream Hollywood cinema at the expense of more visually arousing images of blood and brutality. *Marseille* directs our attention to this experience of pain when Sophie, who had been emotionally resilient throughout the film in spite of her problematic relationship with Hanna and Ivan, unexpectedly breaks into tears when she tries, without success, to recount what happened to her. Because we do not know any more than she does about what happened, we are placed alongside her in a similar position as the confused, and shocked, victim. Like Sophie, we are urged to prompt our memory in attempting to reconstruct the events, a task that forces us to engage actively and critically with the film's images rather than simply let them work on us.

By contrast, the violence in Jessica Hausner's *Lovely Rita* is visible and direct. It does not avoid portraying violence like *The State I Am In* or *Marseille*, yet akin to *Bungalow* and *I Am Guilty*, it dedramatizes violence by flattening it out and dissolving it into the banal routineness of everyday life. Rita can no longer tolerate her monotonous and oppressive life in her lower-middle-class family and so she shoots her parents on a whim. While the murders certainly come as a surprise, they occur in a relatively banal and unexciting context. Not only does Rita use an everyday, immediately accessible object, namely the gun her father uses for his routine shooting practice, but she also shoots him as he stands at the target board, framing him quite unambiguously as the target of See FRAMINGS her shot in a manner that appears tongue-in-cheek **[Fig. 116]**. With its body outline and various marked scores, the target board in this scene is both ironic and redundant. After she proceeds to shoot her mother in the kitchen, Rita washes the gun in the kitchen sink and sets it on the countertop as though it were a normal kitchen utensil, a scene that somewhat cynically frames her acts of violence as quotidian and banal rather than exceptional and exciting. Even after the murders, she remains preoccupied with her petty everyday habits and activities as though nothing had happened. In the hotel she stays in, for example, she tilts a painting in her room to make it hang more evenly, one of her quirks that surfaces earlier in the film when she realigns a painting in her house. Before she gets out of bed to fix it, she stares directly ahead at the camera in a medium close-up shot. As we meet her gaze with contempt and

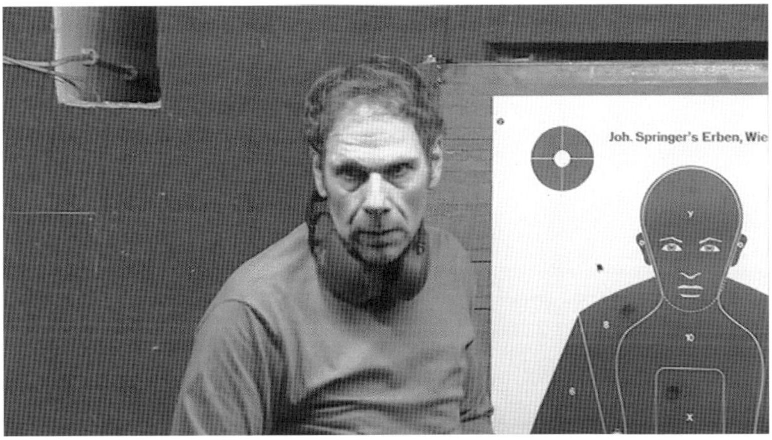

FIG. 116: *Lovely Rita.*

horror at her apparent apathy, she scoots herself up to lean against the wall, giving us the impression that she suddenly feels vulnerable and afraid after contemplating what she had done and the potential consequences. Instead, however, the countershot takes us to the painting hanging across her bed that she then nonchalantly tilts back into place. Here, Rita's everyday habits replace what could have been the continuation of the narrative of violence, where Rita decides, for example, to dispose of the bodies or flee. Finally, she returns home to eat some bread and listen to the news on the couch, casually brushing a fly away that morbidly reminds us of the decomposing bodies in the house. Yet the film refuses to show us these bodies, or to catapult the murders into a riveting crime narrative. Rather, it redirects our view to the more mundane aspects of everyday life that absorb the potential for more stimulating forms of film violence. It is precisely this leveling-out of violence onto the surface of everyday life, however, that makes this film so unsettling. Given the ubiquity of Hollywood-style film violence today, *Lovely Rita* seems to suggest that cinematic violence must take on new forms and appear in new contexts if it is to preserve its ability to move audiences.

Violence forfeits its function as spectacle in Köhler's *Bungalow*, where it is diluted into mere small talk. Deprived of action and excitement in their humdrum bourgeois lives, the film's protagonists, particularly Max's ex-girlfriend Dunja, inflate undramatic, coincidental, or accidental events into exciting conspiracies in their conversations. One of these events is depicted in the film in a flat, panoramic long shot that, in establishing distance to the potentially exciting event, appropriately corresponds to the

FIG. 117: *Bungalow*.

mundaneness of the dialogue. In this shot and after hearing a loud boom, Max and Paul look out into the landscape at a rising puff of smoke with their backs toward the camera **[Fig. 117]**. The sequence is antithetical to conventional sequences portraying catastrophe and violence in that it is still, silent, and presented in one take rather than in a series of quick cuts, resembling a sort of one-dimensional tableau. As they look on, Max suggests that they drive by and take a closer look, arousing our anticipation despite his flat observation that they ought to go grocery shopping in that area anyway. Once they arrive, Max runs into Dunja who makes small talk about the explosion, speculating that it was probably caused by terrorists aiming to blow up the prison. As in the earlier long shot, the site of the accident is disappointingly withheld from view in this sequence, as the camera is located inside the car where Paul is waiting for his brother. Dunja raises the topic once more at Max's cookout, but her speculations are proven false in the next scene when Lene and Max hear on the radio that the explosion was caused by a broken gas pipe. The potential drama of what might have been a deliberate, politically motivated attack is tempered down to an unmotivated, unexciting accident with no particular consequences, disappointing both Dunja and the viewer, whose desire for tension and action remains unfulfilled. Such disappointments occur from the beginning of the film. In contrast to many Hollywood films that deal with war and the lives of soldiers, *Bungalow* begins not with hypervigilant troops fighting a loud and bloody battle but with a still, quiet shot of Paul as he dozes in and out of sleep on a bus with other young, sleepy soldiers **[Fig. 118]**. Far from

FIG. 118: *Bungalow.*

appearing dangerous or rebellious, Paul deserts the army without effort, as he simply neglects to get back on the bus after the soldiers stop at Burger King, his motives based on laziness and disinterest rather than on any political or moral principles. Later Lene playfully jokes with him for being 'on the run' with a hint of sarcasm, as his actions, which consist primarily of lounging in and around the bungalow, hardly match up to the danger and suspense that the expression implies. *Bungalow* is not a war film nor exactly an antiwar film but rather an 'anti-warfilm,' presenting the potential for violence simply to extinguish it with subdued, languid images and quotidian events.

See DISENGAGEMENT

I Am Guilty falls in the same category as *Bungalow* in terms of its approach to violence, emphasizing Armin's desire to experience violence in his tedious bourgeois life rather than dramatic depictions of violence itself. Throughout the film, Armin fantasizes that he is the perpetrator of various accidents that occur in his hometown, sending anonymous letters to the police in which he claims responsibility for the acts. The film's violence is not contained within any coherent sequence nor is it immediately visible; instead, Armin's violent fantasies are brief, sporadic, and overwhelmingly dark, preventing the viewer from understanding exactly what happens and how the images fit within the film's larger narrative. Indeed, it is unclear whether Armin is fantasizing his involvement in the accidents or whether the images are flashbacks. Like *Marseille*, this film denies viewers the gratification of knowing the details surrounding the violent events. Armin begins to confuse his reality with his fantasies. For example, after he fantasizes about altering his friend Ulrich's motorcycle in such a way that causes him to crash, Armin goes to visit him

See INTERPELLATION

FIG. 119: *Hotel*.

in the hospital only to find another person named Ulrich Wendt. In another instance, Armin, so bent on incorporating violence into his everyday life, tells his mother that she is bleeding even though she and the viewer know that the red liquid on her forehead is the red hair dye she was using in the previous scene. In a sense, the bored, action-craving Armin is a mirror reflection of the viewer who also tends to pin narratives of motivated violence onto events. Just as Armin transforms coincidences and accidents into acts of motivated violence, we also find ourselves desiring and anticipating film violence or even perceiving it when it is not actually there.

Like Armin, we transform the events we see in film into suspenseful and stimulating moments for our own pleasure and entertainment, a viewing habit that *I Am Guilty* and other Berlin School films challenge. For the sake of drama and action, we want to believe that Armin is indeed arrested at the end of the film for the crimes he really committed, and that it is not just a fantasy in which he impresses his love interest. In spite of signs that point to the contrary, we want to believe that Rita's troubled look in the final zoom-in is caused by her recognition of the police at her door that will arrest her for her crimes, just like we want to believe that the cry at the end of *Hotel* **[Fig. 119]**, though we have heard it before, belongs to Irene as she disappears in the darkness of the woods **[see Fig. 55—FORESTS]**. And yet, as these films show, these very desires and expectations may change as filmmakers continue to experiment with other forms of cinematic expression.

LH

Wind

The films of the Berlin School have, above all, been praised by film critics for advancing the art of filmmaking in Germany. In Christian Petzold's *Ghosts*, for example, Georg Seeßlen sees a film that (re)presents a reality that one sees everyday yet has never actually seen before.[1] Similarly, Marco Abel views such films as 'instilling in the viewer a sense of being exposed to visualization of a world that is simultaneously familiar and mysterious,'[2] and thus providing a sharper regard for the fabric of the everyday. But as much as these films want us to look again, they also want us to listen again as part of this strategy. Speaking of Berlin's Tiergarten, one of the focal spaces in *Ghosts*, Petzold says that, 'instead of incorporating artificial wind sounds we have recorded many original sounds. We have attempted to hear the location.'[3] This entry considers the poetic use of diegetic sound, in particular the motif of wind, in two of Petzold's films—*The State I Am In* and *Yella*—and in Valeska Grisebach's *Longing*.

See AMBIENT SOUND

In *The State I Am In* an opportunistic burglary compels a former terrorist couple to return to Germany after years spent on the run in Europe. For their 15-year-old daughter, Jeanne, this return marks a first encounter with what is actually a foreign land; although she might have been born in Germany, she has never lived there. In a shot that is as precisely framed as it long, the small yet unmistakable figure of Jeanne emerges from the family car at the border region Germany shares with France. There is no dialogue. Instead, ambient diegetic noise recorded on location dominates the shot; we hear the rushing of the wind as it races through the trees and whips across the water on this gray, rain-soaked autumn day. The film then cuts to an extreme close-up of the cold Jeanne, arms folded and shoulders hunched as she casts her gaze upwards to what becomes another lingering close-up, now of the German national flag [**Fig. 120**]. In this moment the viewer assumes Jeanne's position and thus continues her interrogation of the flag, which violently contorts and cracks against itself in the fierce gusts. The sound of the wind—which seemingly gives voice to the flag as interlocutor in an otherwise silent conversation with Jeanne—works in conjunction

FIG. 120: *The State I Am In.*

with the long take to represent what should be *the* most familiar symbol of national identity to a German audience as somehow unfamiliar. Such moments of visual and acoustic congruence epitomize the way films of the Berlin School, according to Abel, afford 'viewers an intensified encounter with their own social reality, as they find themselves confronted with the necessity to rethink the very relation between what and *how* they see'[4].

See LONG TAKES

See SEEING AND SAYING

The recurring motif of wind also compliments Petzold's visual preoccupation with in-between spaces (which feature heavily in the films of the Berlin School more broadly), and not least with border regions. The peripatetic lifestyle of this family-on-the-run is stressed by their constant inhabitation of transitory spaces such as the villa on the edge of the town and the numerous motorways they travel along. Viewed through Jeanne's eyes, the transient, torrid 'talk' of the windswept flag becomes foreboding, and foreshadows the turmoil that is to come. It sharpens the viewer's regard for her sense of alienation in the here and now of the reunified Germany, a space that does not represent an end point but just another brief stop in the seemingly endless flight to which the teenager is subjected. Indeed, throughout the film, wind serves as a metaphor for the unwilling drift that has Jeanne caught in a liminal, ghost-like state of existence.

See BORDERS

See DISENGAGEMENT

Talk of ghosts resonates strongly within the cinema of Petzold, who, in his own words, 'makes films in the cemetery of genre cinema.'[5] In particular, *The State I Am In* and *Ghosts* belong to the director's so-called 'Ghost Trilogy,' a cycle of films that also includes his internationally best-known feature *Yella* and refunctions the tropes of the horror genre. In so doing, Petzold makes particular use of ambient wind on the sound tracks of these films. In *The State I Am In*, the family of terrorists on the run is coded in terms of the supernatural; Hans and Clara are presented as living anachronisms, as apparitions from a failed utopia with their reluctant daughter in tow.

Desperately seeking the normality that her extraordinary family circumstances otherwise preclude, Jeanne steals a night with her secret boyfriend, Heinrich, in a scene that brings the ending of F. W. Murnau's *Nosferatu* (1921) to mind. The lure of young love distracts Jeanne from the approaching dawn, which threatens to expose her illicit absence from the family's temporary home, and so, with Heinrich out of the room, she leaps through the bedroom window and races home through the woodland. The only sounds to be heard are those of Jeanne's bare feet on the damp ground, the morning chorus of birdsong and the soft breeze in the trees (again, recorded on location). In a medium-long shot we see Jeanne momentarily pause for breath and put on her trainers. This action is continued in a brief close-up before the camera offers a refrain of the previous shot, only now Jeanne's mother occupies the left of the frame. She instinctively knows the cause of her daughter's mysterious absence, the details of which seem to have been carried on the all-pervading breeze that conjured her out of thin air. More than once in the film, the ambient sound of wind characterizes the omniscient reach of Jeanne's parents and the hold they possess over their daughter even when they are not physically present. Like the wind they are an absent presence: an unseen yet powerful force that is keenly felt by their indentured daughter

Wind is also used to characterize Jeanne's loss of identity. On the eve of the family's final flight from Germany she plans to remain behind with Heinrich, but her bid for autonomy and stability is short-lived. Unwilling to abandon her parents, Jeanne once more flees through the bedroom window when her boyfriend's back is turned. This time, however, we do not witness the act of Jeanne's departure. Rather, we are shown the now empty bed and half-open window. A stormy gust pushes the window open further and causes the curtain to flutter. The lack of bodily presence here signifies Jeanne's loss of identity: by making the decision to commit to her parents and their fleeting, ghost-like daily existence she gives up on the opportunity for stability, and on the chance to forge her own narrative. Carried on the wind, she disappears into the night like a phantom **[Fig. 121]**.

Perhaps the most frequently cited use of wind in the Berlin School again belongs to a film by Petzold. *Yella* is, in certain respects, best known for its twist-ending. At the start of the film the eponymous heroine's estranged husband Ben drives them off a bridge in what appears to be an attempted suicide/murder, but Yella escapes the sinking Range Rover and continues her journey to the former West Germany to look for work. Or at least we think she does, for in the closing moments of the film we are taken back to the river bank that Yella had pulled herself on to, where she is pronounced dead by the emergency team

FIG. 121: *The State I Am In.*

that has arrived at the scene. We discover that most of the plot is a product of Yella's imagination, conjured by her in the final moments before she dies. Here wind becomes an uncanny motif, or a set of clues to Yella's demise that runs throughout the film. When Yella first 'wakes' on the riverbank it is to the off-screen cawing of a crow. As she opens her eyes the camera changes to her point-of-view, holding its gaze on a tree swaying in the audible wind whilst water laps against the bank's edge **[see Fig. 5—AMBIENT SOUNDS]**. At several key points in the film the sound of the crow, the rustling water and wind are heard again. When Yella knocks over a glass of water during a boardroom meeting she is almost deafened by the sound of rushing water and wind racing through the

FIG. 122: *Yella.*

trees outside [**Fig. 122**]. This use of diegetic sounds, which, as Abel notes, 'evoke the otherworldly atmosphere of Japanese horror films,' brings 'unbelievable, mysterious, dream- or ghost-like levels' to what are otherwise 'seemingly realistic situations'; here, the cutthroat world of venture capitalism.[6]

See GHOSTS

The motif of wind often serves another function in the films of the Berlin School, where the sparse use of dialogue points to mistrust of the spoken word. Speaking of her film *Longing*, for example, Valeska Grisebach notes that 'Markus says things like "I'd do anything for you." Statements of this kind frequently appear in books and songs—in the whole of pop culture in fact—and also in everyday life. They are important and sincere but fraudulent at the same time because such things can't be fixed to mere words.'[7] Indeed, Markus, who is consumed and driven by an itinerant drive toward romantic (be)longing, breaks the ardent promises made to his wife by entering into an affair with a waitress. On numerous occasions characters are either unable to find words to express themselves or, as Grisebach suggests, the words they use prove ultimately fraudulent no matter how well intended. But where words fail, ambient diegetic sound, in conjunction with images, can take over. Markus's turmoil might not be articulated by the spoken word but it does have an acoustic.

When Markus takes a moment of contemplation on the lakeshore he is presented in a long shot with his back turned, thereby becoming a *Rückenfigur* ('back figure') who sees and is seen by us. He is an experiencing self whose plaintive regard for the landscape is both foregrounded and concealed by the film's precise framing, which keeps him at an emotional distance from the viewer. His presence draws us into the scene, but although the mise-en-scène of the windswept lake in the fading light is suggestive of the loneliness and isolation that Markus feels, the camera does not take us to him, thus denying us a close-up, and with it the clearest visible representation of his psychological state [**Fig. 123**]. Slowly, Markus's wife enters the frame and puts an arm around his shoulder. He reciprocates and rests his head on her shoulder but there is no dialogue between the two, only the sound of the brisk breeze traversing the water and tugging at the tree canopies on the lakeshore. As William Whittington notes, 'In typical Hollywood films, ambiences provide the equivalent of a sonic long shot (wind through trees or waves crashing on a beach) then recede in relation to the dialogue, only to return in their original intensity when words are exhausted.'[8] In *Longing*, however, such ambiences often take the place of words, which, more often than not, appear to have been exhausted before they have been uttered. The cold mise-en-scène and the harsh 'chatter' of the wind belie the apparent

See FRAMINGS

See LANGUAGE

FIG. 123: *Longing*.

warmth of the couple's embrace. Markus's verbal declarations of devoted belonging to his wife, which achieve verbal expression elsewhere, prove false, whereas the wind articulates the transient desire that will pull him back and forth throughout the film.

Ambient wind noises throughout these films become representations of outer and inner landscapes. Such diegetic sounds (in conjunction with the images) intensify the materiality of the everyday, thus rendering it 'affectively sensible' to the viewer.[9] The acoustics of wind, therefore, has the power to communicate greater 'truths' than the characters' spoken words. In the cinema of the Berlin School, the story is carried more on the wind than by the characters themselves.

CH

Notes

1 Georg Seeßlen, 'Gespenster: Gegen die Verhältnisse,' *Die Tageszeitung*, September 14, 2006: 15.
2 Marco Abel, 'Imaging Germany: The (Political) Cinema of Christian Petzold,' in *The Collapse of the Conventional: German Film and Politics at the Turn of the Twenty-First Century*, eds Jaimey Fisher and Brad Prager (Detroit: Wayne State University Press, 2010), 258–84; here 262–63.

3 Christina Nord, 'Notizen zur Berliner Schule,' *new filmkritik*, July 7, 2007, http://newfilmkritik.de/archiv/2007-07/notizen-zur-berliner-schule.
4 Marco Abel, 'Intensifying Life: The Cinema of the "Berlin School,"' *Cineaste* 33.4 (2008), http://cineaste.com/articles/the-berlin-school.htm.
5 Marco Abel, 'The Cinema of Identification Gets on my Nerves: An Interview with Christian Petzold,' *Cineaste* 33.3 (2008), http://www.cineaste.com/articles/an-interview-with-christian-petzold.htm.
6 Abel, 'Imaging Germany,' 267.
7 Marjus Grundtner, 'Sehnsucht—Interview mit Regisseurin Valeska Grisebach,' *MovieGod.de*, October 19, 2006, http://www.moviegod.de/kino/interview/822/sehnsucht-interview-mit-regisseurin-valeska-grisebach/seite-3.
8 William Brian Whittington, *Sound Design and Science Fiction* (Austin: University of Texas Press, 2007), 137.
9 See Marco Abel, '"A sharpening of our regard": Realism, Affect and the Redistribution of the Sensible in Valeska Grisebach's *Longing* (2006),' *New Directions in German Cinema*, eds Paul Cooke and Chris Homewood (London and New York: I.B. Tauris, 2011), 204–22; here, 212.

Image Sources

Figs. 1, 2, 17, 19, 20, 21, 22, 23, 27, 28, 46, 50, 83, 110, and 111 from *Marseille* (directed by Angela Schanelec) © 2004 Schramm Film Koerner & Weber.

Figs. 3, 9, 10, 26, 33, 36, 37, 59, 60, 84, and 107 from *Passing Summer* (directed by Angela Schanelec) © 2001 Schramm Film Koerner & Weber.

Figs. 4, 12, 54, 63, 94, 95, and 101 from *Windows on Monday* (directed by Ulrich Köhler) © 2006 Ö-Filmproduktion.

Figs. 5, 6, 7, 8, 24, 25, 32, 68, 69, 74, 109, 112, and 122 from *Yella* (directed by Christian Petzold) © 2007 Schramm Film Koerner & Weber.

Figs. 11, 13, 18, 31, 48, 49, 53, 75, 86, 88, 98, 99, and 100 from *This Very Moment* (directed by Christoph Hochhäusler) © 2003 Cine Image.

Figs. 14, 15, 44, 45, 51, 52, 105, and 123 from *Longing* (directed by Valeska Grisebach) © 2006 Rommel Film e.K. and Home Run Pictures.

Figs. 16, 34, 41, 62, 87, 91, 93, 108, 117, and 118 from *Bungalow* (directed by Ulrich Köhler) © 2002 Peter Stockhaus Filmproduktion.

Figs. 29, 30, 43, 70, 71, 76b, 90, 96 and 113 from *Ghosts* (directed by Christian Petzold) © 2005 Schramm Film Koerner & Weber.

Fig. 35 from *The Forest for the Trees* (directed by Maren Ade) © 2003 Komplizen Film.

Figs. 38, and 39 from *Falling* (directed by Barbara Albert) © 2006 coop99 Filmproduktion.

Figs. 40, 55, 56, 57, 58, 72, 73, 77b, 85, 92, 115, and 119 from *Hotel* (directed by Jessica Hausner) © 2004 coop99 Filmproduktion.

Fig. 42 from *The Robber* (directed by Benjamin Heisenberg) © 2010 Nikolaus Geyrhalter Filmproduktion.

Fig. 47 from *Vacation* (directed by Thomas Arslan) © 2007 Pickpocket Filmproduktion.

Fig. 61 from *Afternoon* (directed by Angela Schanelec) © 2007 Nachmittagfilm.

Figs. 64, 89, and 114 from *Sleeper* (directed by Benjamin Heisenberg) © 2005 Juicy Film.

Figs. 65, 66, 67, 120, and 121 from *The State I Am In* (directed by Christian Petzold) © 2000 Schramm Film Koerner & Weber.

Fig. 76a from Candida Höfer, *Bank Oldenburg* (1997) © Candida Höfer.

Fig. 77a from Candida Höfer, *Bauhaus Dessau* (1995) © Candida Höfer.

Figs. 78, 79, and 116 from *Lovely Rita* (directed by Jessica Hausner) © 2001 coop99 Filmproduktion.

Figs. 80, 81, and 82 from *I Am Guilty* (directed by Christoph Hochhäusler) © 2005 Heimatfilm.

Fig. 97 from *One Minute of Darkness* (directed by Christoph Hochhäusler) © 2011 Heimatfilm.

Fig. 102 from *Orly* (directed by Angela Schanelec) © 2010 Nachmittagfilm and Ringel Filmproduktion.

Figs. 103, and 104 from *Germany 09: 13 Short Films About the State of the Nation* (directed by Angela Schanelec, et al.) © 2009 Herbstfilm Produktion.

Fig. 106 from *Geschwister* (directed by Thomas Arslan) © 1997 Zweites Deutsches Fernsehen and Trans-Film.

Index

Titles of Key Films Cross Referenced to Entries